Politics and Literature at the Dawn of World War II

Politics and Literature at the Dawn of World War II

James A. W. Heffernan
Dartmouth College, USA

BLOOMSBURY ACADEMIC
LONDON • NEW YORK • OXFORD • NEW DELHI • SYDNEY

BLOOMSBURY ACADEMIC
Bloomsbury Publishing Plc
50 Bedford Square, London, WC1B 3DP, UK
1385 Broadway, New York, NY 10018, USA
29 Earlsfort Terrace, Dublin 2, Ireland

BLOOMSBURY, BLOOMSBURY ACADEMIC and the Diana logo are trademarks
of Bloomsbury Publishing Plc

First published in Great Britain 2023
Paperback edition published 2025

Cover design: Rebecca Heselton
Cover image © Wystan Hugh Auden (1907-1973). English poet; photographed in 1936 ©
GRANGER - Historical Picture Archvie / Alamy Stock Photo. Map of Europe
shortly before World War 2, 1938 © Antiqua Print Gallery / Alamy Stock Photo

A catalogue record for this book is available from the British Library.

Library of Congress Cataloging-in-Publication Data
Names: Heffernan, James A. W., author.
Title: Politics and literature at the dawn of World War II / James A. W. Heffernan.
Description: London ; New York : Bloomsbury Academic, 2024. |
Includes bibliographical references and index.
Identifiers: LCCN 2024020492 (print) | LCCN 2024020493 (ebook) |
ISBN 9781350474802 (paperback) | ISBN 9781350324961 (pdf) |
ISBN 9781350324978 (ebook)
Subjects: LCSH: War in literature. | World War, 1939–1945–Literature and the war. |
American literature–20th century–History and criticism. | English literature–20th century–
History and criticism. | European literature–20th century–History and criticism. |
LCGFT: Literary criticism.
Classification: LCC PN56.W3 H44 2024 (print) | LCC PN56.W3 (ebook) |
DDC 809/.933581—dc23/eng/20240626
LC record available at https://lccn.loc.gov/2024020492
LC ebook record available at https://lccn.loc.gov/2024020493

ISBN: HB: 978-1-3503-2495-4
        PB: 978-1-3504-7480-2
        ePDF: 978-1-3503-2496-1
        eBook: 978-1-3503-2497-8

Typeset by RefineCatch Limited, Bungay, Suffolk

To find out more about our authors and books visit www.bloomsbury.com
and sign up for our newsletters.

For my grandchildren:

Kate Robin, Ben, Dylan, and Susannah

Contents

Abbreviations

A and P	Bertolt Brecht, *Brecht on Art and Politics*
AI	Edward Mendelson, "The Auden-Isherwood Collaboration"
BD	William F. Shirer, *Berlin Diary*
CP	Bertolt Brecht, *The Collected Poems*
D	Evelyn Waugh, *The Diaries of Evelyn Waugh*
EA	Edward Mendelson, *Early Auden*
ED	Marc Bloch, *Étrange Defaite* (French original)
EH:LS	Carlos Baker, *Ernest Hemingway: A Life Story*
EH:WA	Carlos Baker, *Ernest Hemingway: The Writer as Artist*
EW:NM	John Rossi, "Evelyn Waugh's Neglected Masterpiece"
EW:SS	John Rossi, "Evelyn Waugh: From Savage to Sober"
FA	Ernest Hemingway, *A Farewell to Arms*
FRUS	US State Department. *Foreign Relations of the United States*
FW	James Joyce, *Finnegans Wake*
FWBT	Ernest Hemingway. *For Whom the Bell Tolls*
FWBT_CH	Jeffrey Meyers, "*For Whom the Bell Tolls* as Contemporary History"
FYB	Avalon Project, "The French Yellow Book"
GBA	Brecht, Bertolt. *Werke*
GF	Olivia Manning, *The Great Fortune*
GW	Marcel Proust, *In Search of Lost Time, vol. III: The Guermantes Way*
H	Ian Kershaw, *Hitler 1936–45: Nemesis*
H:B	Jeffrey Meyers, *Hemingway: A Biography*
HPW	Jeffrey Meyers, "Hemingway and the Peninsular War"
IOM	International Organization for Migration
J	Bertolt Brecht. *Journals 1934–1955*

L	Evelyn Waugh, *The Letters of Evelyn Waugh*
LA	Edward Mendelson, *Later Auden*
LAT	*Los Angeles Times*
M	Haydon V. White, *Metahistory*
MC	Bertolt Brecht, *Mother Courage and Her Children*
MW	Ernest Hemingway, *Men at War*
NCDL 1	Robert Self, *The Neville Chamberlain Diary Letters*, vol. 1
NCDL 4	Self, Robert. *The Neville Chamberlain Diary Letters*, vol. 4
NTP	Avalon Project, "Nuremberg Trial Proceedings"
P2	W. H. Auden, *Prose*, vol. 2
POMF	Evelyn Waugh, *Put Out More Flags*
SD	Marc Bloch, *Strange Defeat,* trans. Gerard Hopkins
SF	Irène Némirovsky, *Suite Française* (French original)
SF_T	*Suite Française,* trans. Sandra Smith
SG	Bertolt Brecht. *Svendborger Gedichte* (German original)
SG/B	Bertolt Brecht. *Svendborger Gedichte* with commentary by Walter Benjamin
SL	Ernest Hemingway, *Selected Letters, 1917–1961*
SS	Jan Karski, *Story of a Secret State*
StF	Martha Gellhorn, *A Stricken Field*
SW	Walter Benjamin, *Selected Writings*
U	James Joyce, *Ulysses*

Acknowledgments

I must first thank Philip Pochoda for steering me away from my original conception of this book—a general history of the year 1939—into a study of how the outbreak of World War II shaped the literary history of the period surrounding that fateful year.

John Guare (a voracious reader as well as a prolific playwright) alerted me to Martha Gellhorn's novel about refugees in Czechoslovakia in the fall of 1938. Jerome McGann read an early draft of the Prologue and prompted me to clarify an important point about Thucydides. For reading and annotating my chapter on Bertolt Brecht's *Svendborg Poems*, I thank Ronald Speirs. I am also grateful to James Tatum for critiquing my chapters on both the *Svendborg Poems* and *Mother Courage*, and to Edward Bradley for advice on my treatment of Irène Némirovsky's *Suite Française* in Chapter 8.

The Leslie Humanities Center at Dartmouth College kindly helped me to pay the fees required for permission to quote from copyrighted material throughout the book.

For unfailingly helpful service I thank the staffs of the Baker-Berry Library at Dartmouth College and the University of Virginia Library.

I am also heavily indebted to Wikipedia, whose often underestimated services to the study of history I discuss in the Prologue. Though its entries are anonymous, they not only furnish basic facts about virtually any historical event that one might wish to investigate, but also carefully and thoroughly cite their sources.

Starting with Ben Doyle, who not only welcomed my proposal of this book but thoughtfully steered it through a major revision, the staff of Bloomsbury Academic has been indispensable to its publication. Laura Cope supervised the arduous process of obtaining permissions; Dave Cummings copyedited the manuscript; Rebecca Heselton designed the arresting cover; Nicola King compiled the index; and Merv Honeywood oversaw correction of the proofs.

Finally, I thank my wife, Nancy Coffey Heffernan, who read all of this book as she has also read all of its predecessors, and whose advice I always appreciate—even if I don't always take it.

Below is a list of credits for copyrighted material quoted in each chapter.

Chapter 1

Partisan Review issues of Spring and Summer 1939 by permission of the Howard Gotlieb Archival Research Center at Boston University.

"A Letter to Hitler" by James Laughlin, from *The Collected Poems of James Laughlin*. Copyright © 1945 by James Laughlin. Reprinted by permission of New Directions Publishing Corp.

Chapter 2

For Whom the Bell Tolls by Ernest Hemingway published by Jonathan Cape. Copyright © 1941 by Hemingway Foreign Rights Trust. Reprinted by permission of The Random House Group Limited.

For Whom The Bell Tolls by Ernest Hemingway. Copyright © 1940 by Ernest Hemingway. Copyright renewed © 1968 by Mary Hemingway.

Men at War by Ernest Hemingway. Copyright © Hemingway Foreign Rights Trust.

Ernest Hemingway, *Selected Letters 1917–1961*, edited by Carlos Baker. Copyright © 1981 by Carlos Baker and The Ernest Hemingway Foundation, Inc.

Chapter 3

Martha Gellhorn, *A Stricken Field*, quoted by kind permission of Dr. Alexander Matthews, literary executor of the Martha Gellhorn estate.

Chapter 4

The notebooks of W. H. Auden are quoted with the permission of the Estate of W. H. Auden.

W. H. Auden, "In Memory of W. B. Yeats," "September 1, 1939," and "Refugee Blues," copyright © 1940 and copyright renewed by W. H. Auden; from *Collected Poems* by W. H. Auden, edited by Edward Mendelson. Used by permission of Random House, an imprint and division of Penguin Random House LLC. All rights reserved.

E-Book: Copyright © 1939, 1940 by W. H. Auden, renewed. Reprinted by permission of Curtis Brown, Ltd. All rights reserved.

Chapter 5

John Heartfield, *Programm.* The Heartfield Community of Heirs / Artists Rights Society (ARS), New York, 2021.

Bertolt Brecht, *Svendborger Gedichte*, in *Werke. Grosse Kommentierte Berliner und Frankfurter Ausgabe. Band 12: Gedichte 2.* Copyright © Bertolt-Brecht-Erben / Suhrkamp Verlag 1988.

Chapter 6

"Children's Crusade 1939," originally published in German in 1942 as "Kinderkreuzzug 1939," translated by David Constantine. Copyright © 1942 by Bertolt-Brecht-Erben / Suhrkamp Verlag. Translation copyright © 2019, 2015 by Tom Kuhn and David Constantine, from *Collected Poems of Bertolt Brecht* by Bertolt Brecht, translated by Tom Kuhn and David Constantine. Used by permission of Liveright Publishing Corporation.

Bertolt Brecht's *Journals 1934–55,* trans. Hugh Rorrison and ed. John Willett (© Methuen Drama, 1993, New York: Routledge, 1993) by permission of Bloomsbury Publishing plc.

Bertolt Brecht's *Mother Courage and Her Children*, including "Texts by Brecht," trans. John Willett (© Eyre Methuen 1980, New York: Arcade Publishing 1994), Methuen Drama, an imprint of Bloomsbury Publishing plc, by permission of Bloomsbury Publishing plc.

Chapter 7

Between The Acts by Virginia Woolf. Copyright ©1941 by HarperCollins Publishers, renewed 1969 by Leonard Woolf. Reprinted by permission of Mariner Books, an imprint of HarperCollins Publishers.

Put Out More Flags by Evelyn Waugh, published by Penguin Classics. Copyright © Evelyn Waugh 1942. Reprinted by permission of Penguin Books.

Chapter 8

Marc Bloch, *Étrange Defait*, quoted from *Strange Defeat*, trans. Gerard Hopkins (1968/1999) by permission of W.W. Norton & Company.

Suite Française by Irène Némirovsky, translated by Sandra Smith, translation copyright © 2006 by Sandra Smith. Used by permission of Alfred A. Knopf, an imprint of the Knopf Doubleday Publishing Group, a division of Penguin Random House LLC. All rights reserved. French original © Éditions Denoël, 2004.

Chapter 9

Marc Bloch, *Étrange Defait*, quoted from *Strange Defeat*, trans. Gerard Hopkins (1968/1999) by permission of W.W. Norton & Company.

Caught by Henry Green published by Chatto & Windus. Copyright © Henry Green 1943. Reprinted by permission of The Random House Group Limited.

Prologue: History and Literature

This book aims to show how the imminence and outbreak of World War II ignited the imaginations of writers ranging from Ernest Hemingway and W. H. Auden to Bertolt Brecht and Evelyn Waugh. To those familiar with previous studies of war-themed literature in this period, my topic may seem hardly new. The numerous books on such literature in England alone, for instance, include Steve Ellis's *British Writers and the Approach of World War II* (2015), which examines the writing of what he calls the "long 1939" (Ellis 7)—the period stretching from the Munich Agreement of late September 1938 to the start of the Blitz in September 1940.[1] While the long 1939 largely overlaps the period examined by this book, my approach is different. Besides casting an international net that includes writing from America, Germany, and France as well as England, I aim to set this writing beside the historical facts of the period and as much as possible beside historical narratives of it. Obviously, literary creations differ from historical narratives in language, form, and perspective. But the works considered here can also rival such narratives in their power to re-create a momentous phase of the twentieth century.

Can such re-creations be true in any sense? All literature born of actual events sparks questions about its relation to what we normally consider a reliable record of them—namely history. Cameron Watt, for instance, has written an entire book—*How War Came* (1989)—about the origins of World War II, and along with many other studies of the first stages of this war, I have found it an indispensable resource. Yet while Watt lucidly recapitulates the political, military, and diplomatic events surrounding the outbreak of World War II, my own book ploughs a field that historians of such events normally avoid: literary history.

Since history aims above all to recover the truth of the past, we may well wonder how any such truth can be found in works of poetry, drama, and fiction, whose very name opposes it to fact. Yet the written *record* of things done (*historia rerum gestarum*, as Latinists say) is hardly the same as things done (*res gestae*), still less everything done in what a renowned master of European history—Charles Maier—has aptly called *The Unmasterable Past*. Like the "whole truth" that court witnesses routinely swear to tell, the whole truth of the past—including every thought that might have flickered through the brain of every participant in a given event—has never been told.

Of course the whole truth may simply be all facts *relevant* to the purpose of a particular investigation. If I had shoplifted a comb while buying a tube of toothpaste, I would be telling less than the whole truth if I testified only that I had bought the toothpaste while suffering a toothache. For purposes of legal inquiry, my toothache is irrelevant to the "whole truth," which includes only the purchase and the theft.

But how do we decide which facts are relevant about a past event of historical significance? Arguably, for instance, the most relevant facts about the battle of Iwo Jima in the winter of 1945 are that U.S. Marines defeated the Japanese on this small island in the Pacific after fighting for over a month and suffering more than 26,000 casualties, including 6,281 lives. Yet the most *memorable* fact about the battle was not the final victory but the marines' raising of the American flag on Mount Suribachi on February 23, 1945—just five days into a 35-day battle. Though the flag killed not one of the enemy, its visibility from the summit of the mountain raised the morale of U.S. troops all around the island. Also, since Joe Rosenthal's photograph of the flag raising was circulated to millions of newspaper readers around the world, it shortly became not only an iconic sign of American might but also the chief way of commemorating the battle—especially when re-created as a bronze-and-granite monument in the nation's capital. The picture of the flag raising thus became essential to all ways of commemorating the battle, including historical narrative.

In Western culture, aptly enough, historical narrative begins with the commemoration of war in two works of epic poetry: Homer's account of the Trojan War and its aftermath in *The Iliad* and *The Odyssey*. Though both of these epics are studded with divine interventions and fantastic episodes (especially in the latter), they also represent a war that actually occurred in the late thirteenth or early twelfth century BCE, some 400 years before Homer is thought to have written his epics. The ruins of Troy, whose location is now known as Hisarlik, can still be seen in northwest Turkey.

To be sure, nobody would call the epics of Homer "history" in the modern sense. The writing of history proper—sometimes called "scientific history"—is usually thought to have begun in the fifth century BCE with a later Greek named Thucydides.[2] In the introduction to his *History of the Peloponnesian War*, Thucydides pledges to tell no tales of divine intervention and instead to base his narrative (written not in Homeric hexameters but good sturdy prose) on the gathering of evidence and the analysis of cause and effect. Furthermore, while Homer's epics about the Trojan War were written hundreds of years after it, Thucydides recorded a war that not only occurred in his own time but ended well before his death.[3]

Nevertheless, he scarcely claims to be superseding Homer. On the contrary, writes Steven Lattimore, "the *Iliad* was at once his most formidable rival and his most inspiring model," and by focusing on "human motivation and experience," he aimed "to make the Peloponnesian War as unforgettable as the Trojan War."[4] His history of that war includes something that straddles the line between history and literature, or—more precisely—the hairline between judicious inference and informed conjecture. When Thucydides set out to narrate the war between Athens and Sparta, he had not heard or could not remember exactly what was said in all of the speeches that led up to it or punctuated its various stages. Guided by all he knew about the war, then, he conjectured its speeches. "[I]n the way I thought each would have said what was especially required in the given situation," he writes, "I have stated accordingly, with the greatest possible fidelity on my part to the overall sense of what was said" (Thucydides, Book 1, section 22). In *The Idea of History* (1946), R. G. Collingwood sternly rejects this claim.

"[H]istorically speaking," he asks, "[i]s it not … an outrage to make all these very different characters [of Thucydides' *History*] talk in one and the same fashion, and that a fashion in which no one can ever have spoken when addressing troops or when pleading for the lives of the conquered?" (Collingwood 30). But absent any other record of the speeches that Thucydides invents, can we or must we purge them altogether from the history of ancient Greece?

Whatever the answer, historians have long recognized the impossibility of recording any past event "as it actually was" (*wie es eigentlich gewesen ist*), in the 200-year-old words of Leopold von Ranke (Stern 57). Though Walter Benjamin scathingly called this formulation "the strongest narcotic" of the nineteenth century (qtd. Presner 359n4), several of the century's leading historians—including von Ranke himself—have been read as far more than mere recorders of the past. Fifty years ago, a major theorist of historiography argued that nineteenth-century historians were men of style. Implicitly invoking the ancient spirit of Homeric storytelling, Haydon White not only defined history as narrative but also closely aligned it with literature. The very subtitle of his most influential book— *Metahistory: The Historical Imagination in Nineteenth-Century Europe* (1973)—bound history to imagination, which is commonly thought to be both the lifeblood of literature and the antithesis of verifiable fact. Yet White treats historical narrative as itself a kind of literature that can be analyzed in terms of its linguistic or poetic style.

According to White, the narratives composed by the "master historians" of the nineteenth century—such as Michelet and von Ranke himself—are prefigured by one of four "linguistic protocols" defined as rhetorical figures: Metaphor, Metonymy, Synecdoche, and Irony. The linguistic protocol is said to "prefigure the historical field" before the historian brings to it "the various 'explanatory' strategies he used to fashion a 'story' out of the 'chronicle' of events contained in the historical record" (*M* 426). In turn, the explanatory strategies include argument, emplotment, and ideological implication, and the four strategies of emplotment (for instance) are based on Northrop Fyre's quartet of literary categories: Romance, Tragedy, Comedy, and Satire (*M* 427).

Without digging further into such technicalities, one might be inclined to reject this theory at once, for it seems to erase not just the line between history and literature but also the line between history and poetry, the domain of metaphor. Yet consider just one example of metaphor in modern historiography—the writing of history. For centuries, the word "holocaust" meant ritual sacrifice, "a whole burnt offering" (*OED*). But ever since the 1940s, historians have used it as a metaphor for the wholesale extermination of human beings, and in particular for the Nazis' mass murder of Jews. In giving its name to "holocaust studies," this metaphor illustrates a point that White made some years before *Metahistory* appeared:

> An explanation need not be assigned unilaterally to the category of the literally truthful on the one hand or the purely imaginary on the other, but can be judged solely in terms of the richness of the metaphors which govern its sequence of articulation. ("Burden" 130)

Consider two recent histories of American immigration, both published in 2020: Jin Lynn Young's *One Mighty and Irresistible Tide: The Epic Struggle Over American*

Immigration, 1924–1965 and Adam Goodman's *The Deportation Machine: America's Long History of Expelling Immigrants.* Young's book commemorates a metaphorical "tide." As David Nasaw observes, it charts "the victory of tolerant reformers over bigoted obstructionists" in the "epic struggle" to pass the Immigration Act of 1965. But as Nasaw also notes, Young's argument ignores the fact that even as the Immigration Act opened doors to Asian immigrants, its quota system largely closed them to Latin Americans, chiefly Mexicans, who remain to this day victims of what Goodman metaphorically calls "the deportation machine" (qtd. Nasaw 16). Each of these books, then, builds an historical argument by selecting and metaphorically marshalling the relevant facts about American immigration over the past hundred years.

Nevertheless, as John S. Nelson has incisively demonstrated, White's key terms are confusingly applied to his nineteenth-century historical texts. While White says that Michelet's work is prefigured by Metaphor, it turns out to have been even more deeply prefigured by Irony (Nelson 86). Likewise, Herder's allegiance to Metaphor did not keep him from forging "a Synecdochic integration of the field by the explanatory strategies of Organicism and the emplotting strategies of Comedy" (Nelson 85). In defense of his own explanatory strategy, which seems more like a recipe for self-entanglement, White claims that every "master historian" generates a "dialectical tension" between modes of emplotment and modes of argument (*M* 29). But how do we square such tension with White's insistence that great histories are "prefigured" by just *one* of four rhetorical figures?

A further problem is that no matter how well White's *Metahistory* explains the work of major nineteenth-century historians, it has nothing to say about what has happened to historical narrative since 1900—let alone since 2000. In the past two decades, the supremacy of plot in historical narrative has been challenged by the potency of virtual experience. As Ann Rigney explains,

> there has been a shift of emphasis from the structure of narrative to its effects, with "immersivity" and "experientiality" replacing plot as a central feature of storytelling: stories work as such because they allow readers and viewers to become imaginatively immersed in the lives of others and in worlds other than their own. (Rigney 108)

Insofar as it foregrounds imagination, this concept of historical narrative has a history of its own. Well before Haydon White began writing about "the historical imagination," Collingwood argued that imagination is "indispensable" to the historian: not just as an ornament "to make his narrative affecting and picturesque," as Macauley observed, but as the architect of its structure. By "imagination," however, he meant not the power to invent—to make things up—but the capacity to *infer* what happened between one recorded event and another. If, for instance, "our authorities tell us that on one day Caesar was in Rome and on a later day in Gaul," the historian cannot fill the gap with stories of the people he met and what he said to them, for that "would be the kind of construction which is done by *an historical novelist*" (emphasis added). But so long as the "construction involves nothing that is not necessitated by the evidence, it is a legitimate historical construction of a kind without which there can be no history at all" (Collingwood 240–41). In other words, the fact that Caesar was first in Rome and then in Gaul warrants the inference that he travelled from one place to the other.

But would that simple inference enable any reader to become "imaginatively immersed" in Caesar's life? How vivid is the picture evoked by the word "travelled"? And how many details imagined about a particular journey would be inferences "necessitated" by the evidence? These questions are not easily answered. At a Conversation on literary fact and fiction sponsored by PEN in 2000, Simon Schama strongly endorsed Collingwood's argument that historical narrative must be shaped by imagination, but he also declared that "[h]istorians use their imagination to tell the truth about the past." Likewise, while "flattered to hear" Charles McGrath say that his biography of Rembrandt—*Rembrandt's Eyes* (2015)—"reads like a novel," Schama insisted that it contains "absolutely nothing invented" (McGrath 116–17). But Schama has also written one book that he considers a novel: *Dead Certainties* (1992), subtitled *Unwarranted Speculations*, which fictively re-creates the deaths of two historically notable men. To Schama's astonishment, however, this book was reviewed as a work of *non*-fiction.[5] Generically, then, does the book that "reads like a novel" absolutely differ from what Schama calls his "novel"? Even granting that the visual evidence furnished by paintings differs radically from purely verbal records, I venture to wonder if every single detail so artfully woven into the novelistic tapestry of *Rembrandt's Eyes* was demonstrably "necessitated" by evidence. In other words, while Collingwood may justifiably claim that the speeches constructed by Thucydides far exceed the limits of judicious inference, the line between that and "unwarranted speculation" has at the very least been shrinking as historians strive to immerse us in lives and worlds quite different from our own. For this reason I will shortly consider the differences between historical narrative and historical literature—especially fiction—as a prelude to my analysis of specific literary works.

But first I must say something more about what has happened to historical narrative in our own time.

In her provocative study of this topic, Rigney shows that the supremacy of "the stand-alone monograph"—the work of a single historian guided (or not) by what White called a single linguistic protocol—is now being challenged by Wikipedia. Undirected by professional historians, its myriad entries on historical events do not even bear bylines, let alone the stamp of monographic authority. But for everything from typos to factual errors, new material is constantly screened by Wikipedia's editors, including robots who catch errors automatically.[6] As a result, the articles in this "perpetual work in progress" (as it calls itself) are thoroughly collaborative, assimilative, and always open to new information from a vast variety of visual as well as verbal sources that keep it up to date. In August 2009, for instance, Rigney found that its main article on the battle of Iwo Jima is a "fairly classic narrative" that systematically and chronologically explains everything from the background of the battle and "the famous flag-raising" to "the afterlife of the event." But also, besides including "metadata on the minor revisions of the article going back to its inception in 2002," the story of the battle is both richly illustrated and "dynamic," easily revised and studded with hyperlinks to related topics (Rigney 112).

As a further illustration of what might be called this editorial elasticity, consider Wikipedia's treatment of the execution of Saddam Hussein near Baghdad on December 30, 2006.[7] After explaining that the "official video of his execution" ended with the placement of a noose over Saddam's head, the article reports what a mobile phone recording of the execution revealed: a crowd of his jeering countrymen shouting the name of his arch-enemy, the Shiite cleric Muqtada al-Sadr. Furthermore, for its detailed account of everything said at the event by Saddam himself as well as his hecklers, the "Unidentified Videographer" is just one of fifteen carefully cited sources—including not just newspaper articles but also television broadcasts by the BBC, Sky News, and Al Jazeera.

What then can be said about historiography at present? Apart from all the never-ending sources and proliferating hyperlinks of Wikipedia, what generalizations can enable us to distinguish historical narrative or "storytelling"—as it so often called—from literature?

If even Wikipedia finds room for "classic narrative," as Rigney calls it, a historical narrative might not always have to be the work of a single historian. Generically, it might include a product of collaboration, a synthesis of contributions made by an unspecified number of unnamed writers. In fact, if the main Wikipedia account of the battle of Iwo Jima follows established conventions of history-writing, it seems to leave classic narrative largely intact even as it supplements that form with many other ways—especially visual—of representing the past. On the other hand, if historical narrative has begun to shift its emphasis from plot structure to immersion and experience, as Rigney suggests, can we still distinguish it from literature—from the imaginative re-creation of past events?

Let me offer some tentative generalizations.

Generically speaking, historical narrative is proleptic, keeping its eye on the end result of whatever event it reconstructs. Forestalling any suspense, Cameron Watt's history of the run-up to World War II is not *Would War Come?* but *How War Came.* Even the individual sentences of an historical narrative typically look well ahead, as in this sentence about Sir Isaac Newton composed by Arthur Danto:

> [T]he author of the Principia was born at Woolethorpe on Christmas Day, 1642. (Danto 160)

To see how this kind of sentence would sabotage the structure of a literary narrative, suppose Herman Melville had introduced the protagonist of *Moby Dick* like this:

> Captain Ahab, who would eventually be dragged to his death at the bottom of the sea by the great white whale he sought to kill, stood upon the deck.

A howling spoiler. For unlike historical narratives, literary narrative and dramatic plots are *suspenseful*—premonitory but not predetermined. In Chapter 117 of *Moby Dick*, Fedallah tells Ahab that "[t]hough it come to the last, I shall still go before thee thy pilot." But neither Ahab nor the reader can know what that means until the end of the novel. Likewise, though Chekhov famously decreed that a pistol hung on the wall in the first act of a play must be fired in the second, a hanging pistol leaves us hanging about who will fire it and who will get shot. Likewise again, the title of Bertolt Brecht's famous play about war is not *How All of Mother Courage's Children Died* but *Mother Courage and Her Children*. We have to see the play—above all the scene in which Mother Courage fatefully bargains for the life of her last surviving son—to know the end of her story.[8]

Secondly, while historical narrative is as explicit as it can be in light of verifiable facts and the laws of inference, literary narratives are *suggestive,* often ambiguous or misleading, and sometimes indeterminate right to the end.[9] In a short story called "An Occurrence at Owl Creek Bridge" (1899), Ambrose Bierce makes the reader think that a man dropped from a bridge with a noose around his neck has somehow managed to escape and return to his plantation; only at the end do we learn (spoiler alert!) that he never escaped at all, but only imagined doing so just before the noose broke his neck. In *Tess of the d'Urbervilles*, Thomas Hardy aimed—he wrote afterward—to show how Tess was victimized by "seduction . . . pure and simple," and at the end of Chapter 44 of the novel itself he explicitly calls the man who took her virginity "her seducer." But his account of this taking is so ambiguous that many critics insist she was raped (Heffernan, "'Cruel Persuasion'").

Besides telling stories ambiguously, novels can end indeterminately. By the end of Henry James's *Portrait of a Lady* (1881), the titular heroine has come to hate the man she chose to marry because his tyrannical egotism threatens to suffocate her. But in defiance of all sentiment, she spurns the love of the bold American businessman who has been all along yearning to rescue her and decides to return to her husband: a decision that superficially "saves" her marriage but also dooms her, it seems, to the marital equivalent of cold war. The novel thus ends at an impasse.

Thirdly, historical narratives differ from fictional or dramatic stories in their respective casts of characters. In recapitulating the past, historians highlight major events as well as the major figures who shaped them while treating just about everyone else in collective, anonymous terms. By contrast, literature names and particularizes just the kind of people who fly beneath the radar of historical inquiry. In Chapter 3 of this book, I cite a recent historical study of how Czechoslovakia treated refugees in 1938. Almost as if launching a novel, the author begins with a story about an Austrian journalist who felt "saved" from Nazism after crossing the Czech border—only to be promptly sent back to his Nazi-occupied homeland (Frankl 537–38). This poignantly particularized story, however, simply raises the curtain on a study of Czech refugee policy in 1938, especially its rejection of Jewish refugees (Frankl 539). No more stories of individual refugees are told.

On the other hand, those are exactly the kind of stories that Martha Gellhorn tells in *A Stricken Field* (1940), the novel she wrote just after *Colliers* magazine published her article on the plight of refugees in Czechoslovakia in the wake of Munich. Turning from reporting to fiction, she tells a story about a female journalist named Mary Douglas—a fictionalized version of herself—who comes to know several refugees intimately, including a man eventually and fatefully detained after her car accidentally knocks him down. So while the historian's story of the Austrian journalist simply launches his analysis of how the Czechs treated Jewish refugees in general,

Gellhorn's account of her narrator's encounter with the victim of her partner's careless driving—a prolonged study of a slow-motion disaster—is essential to her novel.

The dramatized narrator in Gellhorn's novel illustrates one more important difference between fiction and historical narrative. Except for historians who happen to have played a major role in the events they narrate, as Winston Churchill did before writing *The Second World War* (1948–1953), historians seldom use the pronoun "I," much less incorporate in their narratives any version of themselves. Historians know very well that every historical narrative makes a selection of facts about the past and surveys those facts from a given perspective.[10] Even so, historians typically strive for the kind of detachment that precludes any sign of subjectivity—any reference to the historian's personal involvement in what he or she narrates. By contrast, works of literature often feature some version of the author, as Gellhorn's novel does in the character of Mary Douglas, or Henry Green's *Caught* (1943) does in the character of Richard Roe. In drama, of course, which typically speaks with several different voices, the author seems to disappear. But poetry—above all modern poetry, including the poetry of Auden and Brecht that I examine in this book—typically speaks for the author, and even when a fictional narrative is "omniscient," with no narrator named or dramatized, the voice of the author can be fully audible. In Chapter 5 of James Joyce's first novel, *Portrait of the Artist as a Young Man* (1916), Stephen Dedalus speaks of "the artist," meaning the writer—the artist of words. "The artist," he says, "like the god of the creation, remains within or behind or beyond or above his handiwork, invisible, refined out of existence, indifferent, paring his fingernails" (Joyce, *Portrait* 215). Yet the formulator of this doctrine of Olympian detachment is a fictionalized version of Joyce himself, and Stephen re-appears throughout *Ulysses*, Joyce's second novel, which is at once omniscient in its multiplicity of perspectives, dramatic in its diversity of voices, and autobiographical in its portrayal of Stephen.

Besides displaying elements that are seldom if ever found in historical narratives—suspense, ambiguity, indeterminacy, minor characters, and often some version of the author him/herself—the works of fiction, poetry, and drama examined in this book exemplify what I call *punctual* literature: literature not only generated by the public events of a specific point in time but also written by someone who has lived through that moment. Punctual literature differs from both diaries and journalism. While a diary is a set of disconnected entries on a succession of days, journalism typically weaves the events of one or more days into a coherent report. But as its very name implies, this kind of writing foregrounds what is commonly called the news of the day, which the French call *jour*: it typically feeds publications eager to circulate such news as quickly as possible and unwilling to wait for anything more fully retrospective. No such deadline constrains punctual literature.

Nevertheless, it *is* constrained by a special kind of ignorance. Besides its freedom from the obligation to be wholly factual, punctual literature does not know just where the events that it re-creates will lead. It thus differs radically from history, which—in the words of C. V. Wedgewood—"is lived forwards but ... written in retrospect. We know the end before we consider the beginning and we can never wholly recapture what it was to know the beginning only" (Wedgewood 35). All of the literary works considered here were written by authors who did indeed "know the beginning only":

the coming of World War II, its outbreak in 1939, and one or at most two of the years that followed. Not even historians could foresee how the war would end. In the summer of 1940, Marc Bloch was a distinguished professor of history at the Sorbonne as well as a decorated veteran of both World Wars, but when he sat down to assess the catastrophe that had just befallen France, he felt bound to pose a question to which he had no ready answer: "What will become of us if, by some hideous mischance, Great Britain is in turn defeated?" (Bloch, *SD* 174). And of course he knew nothing of what the United States might do.

Is such ignorance an advantage? Is un-knowing a kind of knowing? William Wordsworth might well have said yes. In Book 9 of the long autobiographical poem that came to be titled *The Prelude*, the great English Romantic poet recalls his year-long sojourn in France in the early 1790s, during the first years of the French Revolution. Though he wrote this part of the poem in 1805, eleven years after the fall of Robespierre had ended the bloodiest phase of the Revolution within France and six years after Napoleon had come to power, he knew nothing of what would happen at Waterloo in 1815. Yet he defies history to capture what he and so many others *felt* at the very point of the Revolutionary spear or, to switch the metaphor, in the eye of a political hurricane:

> Oft said I then,
> And not then only, "What a mockery this
> Of history, the past and that to come!
> Now do I feel how I have been deceived,
> Reading of nations and their works in faith—
> Faith given to vanity and emptiness—
> Oh, laughter for the page that would reflect
> To future times the face of what now is!"
> The land all swarmed with passion. . . .
>
> (Wordsworth, 1805 *Prelude* 9, 170–77)

No one, of course, can ever capture everything about a phase of human history. But the uncertainty of being *in medias res*—in the middle of things—is precisely what punctual literature aims to represent. It springs from contemporary experience of the events it re-creates, which means either living through them personally, reading news of them, or hearing radio broadcasts—all of which figure, sometimes quite dramatically, in the punctual literature of 1939 to the early 1940s.

In England, two of the writers considered here brought firsthand experience to their novels about what the English did during the first year of the war. Before depicting the madcap antics of the so-called "joke war" in *Put Out More Flags*, Evelyn Waugh had served for well over a year in the Royal Marines, including several days of grueling combat in Crete. Henry Green remained in England, but by the time he finished re-creating in *Caught* both the run-up to the London Blitz and the blitz itself, he had served for over two years in the Auxiliary Fire Service and spent several months fighting incendiary bombs.

For all its focus on the relation between literature and history, however, this book is not a study of historical fiction in the normal sense of the term. As exemplified by novels such as Walter Scott's *Waverley* or, much more recently, Hilary Mantel's celebrated trilogy on the life of Thomas Cromwell, historical fiction typically builds a house of imagination on a foundation of archival research: extensive or even exhaustive study of a period remote from the author's own life.[11] By contrast, the works of literature considered here spring largely from that life. Brecht's *Mother Courage* re-imagines a set of wars fought in the early seventeenth century, but all six of the novels examined in this book originate from the author's personal experience of major events surrounding the outbreak of war, and most of the poetry treated here articulates a personal response to the news of such events.

A further complication springs from the simple fact that all of these literary works about the imminence or outbreak of World War II were written well before any formal history of this period could be composed. For this reason, none of these works is in any sense "based" on such a history in the way that—let us say—Shakespeare's *Julius Caesar*, originally performed in 1599, is based on Plutarch's *Lives of Noble Grecians and Romans*, translated by Thomas North in 1574.[12] Furthermore, I cannot systematically compare every one of these literary works with a professional history of the events that inspired it. While I approach Hemingway's *For Whom the Bell Tolls*, for instance, by way of Anthony Beevor's *The Battle for Spain* (2006), I can merely juxtapose what historians have written about the German invasion of Poland with W. H. Auden's "September 1, 1939," which is so intensely personal that it does not even mention Poland. Likewise, rather than narrating the history of Germany from 1933 to 1939, most of the poems that Bertolt Brecht wrote in those years—the *Svendborg Poems*—express his ongoing hatred of fascism and his sympathy for the ongoing "struggle" ("Kampf") that his countrymen are undergoing. And while *Mother Courage* was provoked by the Soviet invasion of Poland in mid-September 1939, as I argue, it cannot be systematically linked to any history of Poland in that time. Essentially, then, I aim to show how each of these writers re-created not so much a particular set of events as their own experience—their own reading—of those events.

Before investigating any particular work of literature, however, I raise the curtain by exploring what a group of New York intellectuals—leading poets, novelists, and critics based in and around the city—thought about the advent of World War II. When canvassed by the editors of the *Partisan Review* in the spring of 1939, not one of them cheered the prospect of a war against Germany even after Hitler's murderous acts and aggressive aims had been vividly set forth in the New Year's issue of *Time* magazine, which ironically named him Man of the Year just passed (1938). Yet while some of these writers absolutely refused to fight under any circumstances or dismissed the war as absolutely irrelevant to literature, several of them stated that in time of war, the writer's responsibility is to tell the truth: to "guard against the tendency to become a liar for propaganda's sake," wrote William Carlos Williams; "*not to find the 'good side' of war*," wrote Harold Rosenberg (original emphasis); and "to tell the truth, as he sees it," wrote Kenneth Fearing. That is exactly what Hemingway aimed to do in his novel about the Spanish Civil War (the grim prelude to World War II), and likewise what writers such as Auden, Brecht, Waugh, and Némirovsky sought to achieve. Eschewing propaganda in favor of truths refracted through the lens of literature, they set their imaginations to work on what must have seemed an appalling prospect. With all the horrors of the Great War still raw in memory, they were forced—as Auden wrote near the end of "September 1, 1939"—to "suffer them all again."

Percy Bysshe Shelley, Wordsworth's younger contemporary, once wrote that "poets" are not only "the creators" but also "the creations, of their age" (Shelley 135). All the writers examined in this book—not just its poets—were thus created: captivated and inspired by the greatest event of their time. While writers traditionally yearn to be timeless, virtually every word of the works I consider here was meant to be time*ly*: an all-but-immediate response to the onset or outbreak of a new world war. Yet precisely because we have suffered war many times "again" since World War II, albeit on a more limited scale, these works can still deliver shocks of recognition. In launching a wholly unprovoked invasion of Ukraine on February 24, 2022, Vladimir Putin re-enacted the equally unprovoked German invasion of Poland on September 1, 1939. With breathtaking hypocrisy, Putin announced that the aim of this "special military operation" was the "demilitarization and denazification of Ukraine" (Troianovski). But in charging the would-be "neo-Nazis" of Ukraine with committing "genocide" against "the millions" of ethnically Russian people living there (Fisher), Putin took his cue from the playbook of Adolf Hitler, who—as we will see in Chapter 3—justified his invasion of Czechoslovakia on October 1, 1938 by falsely accusing the Czechs of persecuting the "millions" of ethnic Germans living there. In relentlessly striking civilian targets as well as in echoing Hitler's baseless charge against the Czechs, Putin has proved himself just as ruthless as the god of Nazism.[13]

As of March 2022, when I write these words, it is far too soon for this new war to have spawned any works of literature. But a Ukrainian novelist based in Kyiv has just reported what a "beautiful" friend in Donetsk wrote to her on her birthday: "I'd like to give you Putin's balls on a skewer. But they're not done cooking" (Stiazhkina). Whether or not that piquant wish ever finds its way into a novel, the tide of refugees now pouring out of Ukraine lends fresh resonance to one of the novels I examine here: Irène Némirovsky's *Storm in June*—the first of the two novels of her *Suite Française. Storm in June* re-creates the tumultuous summer of 1940, when eight to ten million French people were driven from their homes by the invading German army. The Ukrainians have relived this disaster in our own time. By March 21, 2022, just under a month after Russian troops invaded Ukraine, more than 3.5 million of its people were driven out of their country by Russian forces, and almost 6.5 million were internally displaced (*IOM*, "Ukraine").

The present book does not pretend to examine all the literature precipitated by the outbreak of World War II. But it does highlight major works of literature from Europe and America as well as England. Since Bertolt Brecht was both a poet and a playwright, I have given him two chapters: one on his *Svendborg Poems* of the later 1930s and the other on *Mother Courage*, which he wrote in the fall of 1939. I have also considered both of Némirovsky's novels about the German invasion of France, setting each of them against histories of the events they fictionalize: the massive exodus of French people from the northern to the southern half of the country, and the ensuing occupation of the country by German forces.[14] But I have largely focused on works written and/or published in or around the year 1939, and except for *Mother Courage*, I have not considered any works of literature that are "historical" in the sense defined above: based on research rather than personal experience.[15] In any case, I have tried throughout these chapters to show how each of the works discussed emerged from the author's life at the time the war broke out. Probing the impact of politics on literature at the outset of a great war, I believe, is not just an adjunct to the study of history, but itself a way of reading the past.

Notes

1   Other books on this topic include Kristine Miller's *British Literature of the Blitz* (2009), which I consider in Chapter 9, and I have more to say about Ellis's book in Chapter 4.

2   According to R. G. Collingwood, scientific history was invented in the fifth century BCE by Thucydides and Herodotus, who both "recognized that history is, or can be, a science, and that it has to do with human actions." Scientific history, Collingwood writes, "asks questions about things done by men at determinate times in the past." It is also "rational," meaning based on evidence: a point made by Thucydides, who thereby "improves on Herodotus" (Collingwood 18–20).

3   The war ended in 404, and Thucydides may have lived to 393 (Lattimore xv).

4   Lattimore xvii, xix. Likewise, as we shall see in Chapter 8, Irène Némirovsky took Tolstoy's *War and Peace* as the model for her suite of novels about Germany's defeat and occupation of France in the early 1940s.

5   Though not in the published transcript of the Conversation, Schama makes this comment at about 11 minutes into the Soundcloud recording of it (https:// soundcloud.com/penamerican/the-real-story-literary-fact-and-fiction).

6   "Once material is added to Wikipedia, an army of volunteers organized under various departments check and recheck it to make sure it conforms to the high standards set forth in Wikipedia's policies and guidelines ... There are departments for everything from typos to factual errors ... And Wikipedia even has robots, automated users that monitor for errors and correct them automatically" (https://en.wikipedia.org/wiki/ Wikipedia:Quality_control).

7   https://en.wikipedia.org/wiki/Execution_of_Saddam_Hussein. Accessed April 15, 2021.

8   As a counter-example, the very title of Leo Tolstoy's novella, *The Death of Ivan Ilyich* (1886), foretells its ending, but does not foretell what Ivan discovers about life—his own in particular—just before he dies. Conversely, Steven Lattimore notes that the "digressions" in Thucydides' *History* "build suspense" (Introduction xvii). But Thucydides could hardly build suspense about the outcome of the war, which Athens lost, for unlike fiction and drama, historical narrative does not *feature* suspense as a defining element.

9   Schama says that historical narratives can sometimes be open-ended when the known facts do not clearly point to any one conclusion ("The Real Story"), but unlike works of literature, most historical narratives aim to reach determinate ends.

10   The "work of selection," Collingwood writes, is essential to "historical thought" (Collingwood 236).

11   A borderline case is the fiction of Patrick Modiano, born in 1945, whose novels about France in the early 1940s spring from no firsthand experience of France during the "années noires" of the Occupation. Yet as one critic has recently noted, "however vicarious Modiano's perception of those years, there is no denying its impact; the

spectre of the Occupation looms obsessively in the backdrop of his texts, an obstinate presence further echoed through the quasi-compulsive peregrinations of the internal narrator through the streets of Paris" (Grenaudier-Klijn 220–21).

12 According to Dana Jackson, "Shakespeare based his play almost exclusively on Plutarch's narrative of Roman characters."

13 As of March 13, 2022, Russian bombs and missiles had already killed at least 1582 civilians in the southeast Ukrainian city of Mariupol alone (Santora).

14 Just as this book was going to press, I learned that during the last weeks of 1938, right after the Nazi atrocities of *Kristallnacht* (November 9–10) and the shipment of 30,000 Jewish men to concentrations camps, a 23-year-old German novelist named Ulrich Alexander Boschwitz drafted *The Passenger*, a novel about a Jewish Berliner whose wealth allows him to take flight by taking endless train rides. After drafting the novel in England, he re-worked it in Australia, where he had been sent to an internment camp, but on returning to England in 1942, his ship was torpedoed by a German submarine, ending his life at the age of twenty-seven (Margalit).

15 For instance, Aharon Appelfeld's *Badenheim 1939* (first published in Hebrew in 1978) is a novel about middle-class Jews vacationing in an Austrian resort town just before the war begins—and with no idea of what lies ahead for them. Though Linda Grant has called this allegorical satire "the greatest novel of the Holocaust," it is based not on personal experience but on the author's study of the period.

1

Hitler, FDR, and the *Partisan Review* in 1939

Whether or not we are always in transition, as Ralph Waldo Emerson once declared, 1939 was a year of extraordinary transition for the United States. In the spring of 1938, after struggling to keep the New Deal alive in the face of massive labor strikes, the Recession of 1937, and a recalcitrant Supreme Court (whose size he tried in vain to increase), President Franklin Delano Roosevelt decided to stop worrying about balancing the budget and start attacking deflation with a five billion dollar spending program. The stubborn tenacity of the Depression, which in various ways persisted right through the 1930s, was perhaps nowhere better illustrated than by the top-selling novel of 1939: John Steinbeck's *Grapes of Wrath*, the story of a family of tenant farmers in the Oklahoma dust bowl who are forced off their land by predatory banks and who slowly make their way to California, where they earn barely enough to keep them alive.

By the opening months of 1939, however, Roosevelt had turned his attention elsewhere—from the plight of American farmers and workers to the rise of Adolf Hitler, whose ruthlessness was quite literally illustrated on the New Year's cover of *Time* magazine for January 2, 1939, which named him "Man of 1938."[1]

I

Time's cover was drawn by Baron Rudolph Charles von Ripper, a 33-year-old Austrian artist who had endured three and half months in a Nazi concentration camp during the winter of 1933–34, had been rescued by the Austrian government (then still independent), and had already depicted his ordeal in a series of Goyesque etchings called *Écraser l'Infâme*—"*Wipe out Infamy*."

For *Time* von Ripper drew Hitler as an "unholy organist" playing a "hymn of hate" in a desecrated cathedral whose cross appears at the top of the picture. Unlike every other New Year's cover in the history of *Time*, this one hides the face of its subject. Viewed from behind at the base of the picture and dressed in his Nazi uniform, he sits beneath the pipes of a gigantic organ supporting a medieval instrument of torture known as a St. Catherine wheel: a large wooden wheel to which victims were bound so that their limbs could be broken by repeated blows with a cudgel or club, after which the wheel was sometimes erected on a pole so that its victims could be left there to rot. This method of execution ended in Germany about a hundred years before Hitler's time. But the fate of the emaciated figures shown hanging from the wheel in this picture fittingly represents what Nazism had already done to thousands of its victims by the end of 1938.[2] Since then, in fact, pictures of hanged men and women have remained conspicuous in the iconography of Nazism, most recently in *Jo-Jo Rabbit* (2019), a satirical film about the Hitler Youth.

In *Time*'s cover picture, the pipes of the organ played by Hitler fittingly support a wheel of torture. More than any other dictator who came before or after him, Hitler gained and kept his power by means of his own vocal pipes: by a torrent of speeches whose manic stridency mesmerized his hearers even while appalling Bertolt Brecht, as we shall see in Chapter 5. His very voice inspired them with his virulent antisemitism, his hatred of anyone who opposed him, and his megalomaniacal lust for war. On the eve of the Nazi party rally held in Nuremberg in September 1934, the American journalist William F. Shirer was struck by the rapture on the faces of those gathered in thousands around Hitler's hotel. When he appeared on the balcony, wrote Shirer, "they looked up at him as if he were a Messiah." At the opening of the rally the next morning, Hitler showed himself a master of spectacle as well as sound: a god of pageantry. The first meeting of the day, Shirer wrote, "was more than a gorgeous show; it also had something of the mysticism and religious fervor of an Easter or Christmas Mass in a great Gothic cathedral" (Shirer, *BD* 17). No wonder von Ripper placed him in a desecrated cathedral rededicated to the religion of fascism, whose very name derives from the bundle of rods (*fasces*) so vividly evoked by the close-bound vertical pipes of the organ.

Given the record of atrocities that Hitler had compiled by the end of 1938, we should expect to find at least some reference to him in the New Year address ("State of the Union 1939") that FDR delivered to Congress on January 4. But this long speech is a masterpiece of evasion. Nowhere does it mention Hitler, the plight of German Jews (whom he had just privately proposed settling in "a part of Ethiopia and surrounding colonies" [Ciano, *TCD* 5]), or the vulnerability of a Czechoslovakia freshly shorn of the fortified frontier that had previously protected it from Germany. Nevertheless, Roosevelt had good reason for his reticence. Since the Neutrality Act of 1937 forbade U.S. ships to furnish any passengers or goods to belligerents, let alone send troops, the president could do little more to combat German belligerence than wring his hands.

In late September 1938, when Hitler's determination to seize the "Sudetenland" of Czechoslovakia had driven Europe to the brink of war, Roosevelt wrote twice to Hitler and Czech president Edvard Beneš, urging both to reach a "fair, peaceful, and constructive settlement of the questions at issue."[3] They reached a settlement only because England and France forced Beneš to swallow terms that were grossly unfair— and thus to reward Hitler's relentless campaign of intimidation. Since FDR's letters helped to midwife this brutal resolution, it is ironic to find him declaring in his New Year's address not only that "God-fearing democracies of the world … cannot forever let pass, without effective protest, acts of aggression against sister nations," but also that "at the very least, we can and should avoid any action, or lack of action, which will encourage, assist, or build up the aggressor." Could he himself make "effective protest" without even mentioning either Hitler or Czechoslovakia? And if, as he says, "we rightly decline to intervene with arms to prevent acts of aggression," could the U.S. "avoid any action. or lack of action" that might help the aggressor? FDR's only answer to this question is to challenge the wisdom of neutrality laws, which "may operate unevenly and unfairly—may actually give aid to an aggressor and deny it to the victim." Implicitly, then, in the face of all the voices raised for isolationism, he begins to make the case for intervention. But all he dares to say explicitly is that the United States must have "adequate defense": "armed forces and defenses strong enough to ward off sudden attack."

Behind the scenes, however, FDR was urgently planning for war. By the end of 1938, he had already made secret arrangements to furnish planes to the French and British, and in late January of 1939, just weeks after his non-committal New Year's address, he nearly blew his cover by allowing a French Air Force Captain to join an American pilot in test-flying a Douglas 7B, the secret prototype of an American warplane. When the flight ended in a flaming disaster that only the Frenchman survived (*LAT*, "Bomber Fall Kills Pilot"), FDR told a press conference not only that the French could order planes from private American companies but also—in what was surely one of his biggest whoppers—that the whole episode was just "a perfectly normal testing out of the plane" (Press Conference #521, 1–3).

By the spring of 1939, FDR was gradually steering the ship of state toward war. Isolationists still controlled both houses of Congress; his own Ambassador to the United Kingdom—Joseph P. Kennedy—resolutely opposed intervention; and in a Gallup Poll taken in late February, only 17% of its respondents thought the U.S. should send troops to Britain and France. But in the same poll, 52% thought that if war broke out in Europe, the U.S. should sell planes and other materials to Great Britain and France. Just as important, prominent writers such as Walter Lippmann and Dorothy Thompson began to make the case for war as well as to cast Roosevelt as their champion. In the long lead article of the Spring 1939 issue of the *Partisan Review*, Dwight McDonald claimed, "All sections of the intelligentsia are swinging in behind the New Deal in its drive toward a new world war to save democracy" (McDonald, "This Quarter" 3).

Given the outcome of World War II, we might well salute the prescience of the American intelligentsia, of writers who shared Roosevelt's conviction that America must eventually enter it. But McDonald's statement is actually the prelude to a long, ferocious argument against war, which he saw as essentially a project of bourgeois capitalism that would re-enact all the murderous atrocities of World War I. In 1939, many other writers for the *Partisan Review* shared what can only be called his militant pacifism even as they exemplified what has been called "the dilemma of the intellectual (the writer, the artist) in politics" (Laqueur). This is the phrase that Walter Laqueur applied to Thomas Mann's brief for German nationalism during World War I: *Reflections of a Nonpolitical Man*, published just one month before the armistice of November 1918. As a rising German novelist who would later win the Nobel Prize for Literature and become one of the most admired writers of his time, Mann argued in *Reflections* that war was both politically unifying and morally elevating, and that Germany was totally justified in taking arms against the decadence of Britain and France. By 1939, six years after the ascent of Hitler had driven him out of his native land and one year after he arrived in America, Mann had radically shifted, urging the Western allies to take on Germany.[4] But was this call to arms any wiser than the one he had made before, or than the bellicose words of the American intelligentsia cited by McDonald? Insofar as the *Partisan Review* of 1939 represents the views of the literary left in America, it shows them struggling to find a bloodless alternative to "anti-fascist hysteria" as well as to Stalinist totalitarianism, which had sorely tried their faith in the revolutionary promises of Marxism.

II

Historians have long recognized that in 1939, Roosevelt's determination to join the looming war against Nazi Germany was staunchly opposed by isolationists in Congress and the Senate. But during the same year, a much more complicated set of arguments against Roosevelt's goals was made by a band of contributors to the *Partisan Review*. Founded in 1934 in a Greenwich village loft by a brilliant pair of 26-year-olds, a bohemian of European stock named William Phillips and a Russian immigrant named Philip Rahv, the *PR* initially flaunted its support for the Communist Party—as manifested by its very name.[5] But while Rahv and Phillips launched the *Partisan Review* as a vehicle of socialist resistance to capitalism, they also—just as importantly--conceived it as a forum for free-wheeling intellectual discourse untethered to any particular political doctrine. In 1937, the Moscow trials of Stalin's opponents led the magazine to renounce the Stalinist line and endorse Leon Trotsky, his chief antagonist, who insisted that "[a]rt must be true to itself and free of Stalinist bureaucracy." Making this statement in *PR* itself in the late summer of 1938, Trotsky deplored the stifling constraints of "Socialist Realism" and saluted the vibrant frescoes of Diego Rivera for both exemplifying the power of art and expressing the force of social revolution (Trotsky, "Art and Politics").

For Trotsky, these two things were equally important. In 1938, he is generally thought to have collaborated with André Breton and Diego Rivera on a document signed by only the other two: *Manifesto for an Independent Revolutionary Art* (Breton). Expanding the argument made by the essay just cited, the manifesto decries the suffocation of art by "reactionary forces armed with the entire arsenal of modern technology." In particular, the manifesto charges, Hitler's Germany has driven out all artists who care at all for liberty and turned the rest into propagandists of the Nazi regime, and the Soviet Union has done the same. Yet instead of parroting "the currently fashionable catchword, 'Neither fascism nor communism,'" the manifesto reaffirms the original spirit of communism. Rejecting "the bureaucracy now in control of the Soviet Union," it proclaims that "true art" aspires only "to a complete and radical reconstruction of society," and that only "the social revolution can sweep the path clean for a new culture." Rather than fearing art, the manifesto contends, the Communist revolution takes the artist as its "natural ally" in a psychoanalytic struggle to emancipate the individual from "the unbearable present reality." Embodying "all those powers of the interior world … which are common to all men," the "id" is said to be an "individual spirit" following a "natural course" toward a "primeval necessity—the need for the emancipation of man."

Tellingly, however, the manifesto oscillates between individualism and whatever is "common to all men," between the id and the unnamed ego of self-regulation, between the necessity of building "a socialist regime with centralized control" and the need to found "an anarchist regime of individual liberty" with "no authority, no dictation, not the least trace of orders from above!" Can a *regime* be anarchist? Can anarchic individuals be centrally controlled? Like Walt Whitman, who freely admitted that he contradicted himself, the manifesto promises to liberate creative individuals by finding "a *common ground* on which *all* revolutionary writers and artists may be *reunited*, the better to *serve the revolution* by their art ..." (my emphases). The Communist International, which the authors of the manifesto rejected, was to be thus replaced by another bureaucracy: the International Federation of Independent Revolutionary Art. Its life, however, was short. Though Breton set up branches in Paris, London, and New York as well as Mexico, and though he won the support of some notable writers and artists, especially fellow Surrealists, he had lost heart by June of 1939, when he lamented in a letter to Trotsky the "enormous obstacles" he had faced (Polizzotti 472).

Chief among them was the imminence of war. While the manifesto mentions this topic in its opening paragraph, its argument largely assumes a world without war, a world of bloodless abstractions such as capitalism, fascism, and a "social revolution" spawned by art and literature rather than guns and bombs. By contrast, the *Partisan Review* treated the prospect of war as a topic that no writer of any kind could ignore or evade. For its summer 1939 issue, the editors invited about a dozen notable writers to answer a set of seven questions ending in this two-part query:

> *"Have you considered . . . your attitude toward the possible entry of the United States into the next world war?*
> *What do you think the responsibilities of writers in general are when and if war comes?"* ("Situation" 26)

The writers' answers ranged all the way from willingness to join the fight—if only morally—up to pacifism and airy abdication of all responsibility. John Dos Passos, who had written a trilogy of novels titled *U.S.A.* and published in the earlier 1930s, wrote that he would "probably try to get my old job back driving an ambulance" ("Situation" 27). William Carlos Williams, the New Jersey doctor who was also an Imagist poet, pledged to enter the fray. Though he was then fifty-six and busy with patients as well as poetry, he sounds ready to enlist. "If war comes," he writes,

> we've got to fight. Writing would be secondary. The one thing to guard against would be the tendency to become a liar for propaganda's sake. . . . If I had to be shot, I'd hope fervently that the guys on the other end would make an artistic job of it by shooting straight. The value always comes out, in one form or another, if we stick to our guns. ("Situation" 44)

To be sure, Williams hedges his pledge. Though he takes fighting as a simple duty ("we've got to fight"), he says nothing to justify it; on the contrary, he says, he will resist the temptation to lie for his country. He will also maintain his artistic integrity, even in assessing the artfulness of those who might shoot at him: the artistic value of literally sticking to one's guns. In a deliciously wry way, he turns fighting itself into an art.

Yet Williams aptly names what is probably the greatest temptation faced by a writer in time of war: the impulse to tell patriotic lies. The art critic Harold Rosenberg took one step further. In the single sentence with which he answered the *PR*'s second question, he wrote, "In time of war, the writer has at least the obligation *not to find the 'good side' of it*" ("Situation" 49, original emphasis). Less explicitly but no less cogently, Wallace Stevens declared that, "[t]he role of the writer in war remains the fundamental role of the writer intensified and concentrated" ("Situation" 40). In other words, more than usually vigilant on behalf of the writer's creative freedom.

In place of such vigilance, Gertrude Stein affects an almost nonchalant fatalism. While implausibly predicting that the Europeans would "probably" not fight another general war, she also insists that if they do, "then the writers will have to fight too like anybody else, some will like it and some will not" ("Situation" 41). Tellingly, Stein makes no attempt to justify fighting as distinct from liking it (or not), much less to admit that a writer has any obligation to assess or evaluate the case for war.

A comparably disengaged stand was taken by Allen Tate, an American poet and essayist who would become the nation's poet laureate in 1943. Tate had no interest in war or even in what form of government might circumscribe his life as a writer. "The writer, *as* writer," he says,

> has no responsibility when war comes. The responsibility that he may have as a citizen is something he must decide for himself. ... I doubt if a Marxist society would be any more favorable to literature than Nazism or finance capitalism. Nobody knows what kind of society is best for literature. ("Situation" 30)

Tate's detachment is breathtaking. In claiming that war has no relevance to the life of a writer and that one system of government is just as good for literature as any other, he assumes that wherever the writer lives and works, he or she will always enjoy the freedom of speech that Tate himself—like all his country-men and women—was then enjoying in capitalist America. Yet in spite of the First Amendment, not even American writers and speakers had enjoyed such freedom during World War I. On the contrary, the Espionage Act of June 15, 1917, passed shortly after the U.S. entered the war, criminalized any interference with the operation of its armed forces, including any criticism of the war effort. Under this law authorities arrested, tried, and convicted about 1,200 anti-war speakers including Eugene V. Debs, the perennial presidential candidate of the Socialist Party, who–at the age of sixty-two—was sentenced to ten years in prison for speaking against the military draft in Canton, Ohio, on June 16, 1918. (In 1921 he was released but not pardoned.) In the following year, the Espionage Act was unanimously upheld by the Supreme Court, and in spite of many challenges it remains alive to this day—though far less strictly enforced than it was during World War I.

Had it been strictly enforced in 1939, the very issue of *Partisan Review* that included Tate's comments would have been seized by the Postmaster for including a long article against war that I will examine below. Even Tate's linking of Nazism with "finance capitalism" might have laid him under suspicion. But to judge his comments more precisely in the context of their time, consider what the governments of Germany and the Soviet Union respectively did to two men—a renowned writer and a highly innovative theater director—at just about the time the summer 1939 issue of *PR* appeared.

In late February 1933, when he was thirty-five, Bertolt Brecht had been forced to leave Berlin right after the Nazis burned the Reichstag and blamed it on the Communists, whose members included Brecht himself. For the next six years, he lived peacefully and productively in Denmark on an island overlooking the Svendborg Sound. But the proofs of the poems he wrote there were destroyed in January 1939, two months after his Prague-based publisher had to leave the Nazi-occupied city, and Nazi pressure on Denmark forced Brecht himself to flee Denmark for Stockholm in April 1939.

A far worse fate befell Vsevolod Meyerhold, the renowned Russian theater director who had joined the Bolshevik Party in 1917, actively promoted Soviet Theater, and founded his own theater in Moscow in 1920. In January 1938, the Politburo closed this theater on grounds that it had never freed itself "from thoroughly bourgeois Formalist positions" (qtd. McSmith 231): the worst possible charge that the Politburo could bring against any artistic institution. While Russian Formalism began in the 1910s as a school of literary criticism that prized the distinctive, autonomous properties of literary language, Trotsky attacked Formalism in 1924 for neglecting the psychology of "living people" as well as their "social conditions" (Trotsky, *Literature and Revolution* 171). As a result, Formalism became a slogan for any kind of art that privileged art itself over the material world idolized by Social Realism. In the late 1930s, the impact of this difference on all Russian artists—writers, painters, directors—was literally a matter of life and death. While addressing an audience of theater directors in June of 1939, Meyerhold denounced "anti-formalism" in the theater and frankly confessed: "In my heart, I consider what is now taking place in our theaters frightful and pitiful." A few days later, the 65-year-old director was arrested by the secret police, imprisoned in Moscow, excruciatingly tortured until he incriminated himself, and shot on February 2, 1940 (McSmith 231). In short, whether or not "finance capitalism" is best for literature, or the arts in general, it is hard to imagine anything worse for artists of any kind than Soviet Communism in 1939.

Fortunately, the editors of and contributors to the *Partisan Review* could say at this time whatever they wished about war without risking prosecution under the Espionage Act, let alone risking their lives. This is one reason why the respondents take such diverse stands on what writers ought to do in time of war. While William Carlos Williams simply declares, "If war comes we've got to fight," James T. Farrell—a novelist best remembered now for the *Studs Lonigan* trilogy (1932–35)—finds war just a quarrel over "real estate" ("Situation" 33), and two others absolutely loathe it. "I am a pacifist," writes Katherine Anne Porter, whose third collection of stories—*Pale Horse, Pale Rider*—was just appearing. "If and when war comes," she says, the "prime responsibility" of the artist

is not to go mad. Madness takes many forms, it is the old deceiver. . . . If you are required to kill someone today, on the promise of a political leader that someone else shall live in peace tomorrow, believe me, you are not only a double murderer, you are a suicide, too. ("Situation" 39)

Henry Miller also loathed war. Writing from Paris, where he had been living since 1930 and where his third semi-autobiographical novel—*Tropic of Capricorn*—had just appeared, Miller declared:

> I refuse to go to war, whether for a just or unjust cause. If that means being killed by the government advocating war, then I am willing to be killed … I cannot say what the responsibilities of writers in general should be on the question of making war … To kill or not to kill, to defend myself or not to defend myself, are questions which each individual has to answer for himself. I see no problems confronting the world which might not be solved peaceably. … I believe that the most sane and practicable solution to the present impasse would be to scrap all forms of defense and expose ourselves absolutely to every risk. ("Situation" 51)

Among all the answers to the *PR* editors' question about writers and war, this one seems the most pacifistic of all. Yet it stops short of extreme pacifism because Miller speaks only for himself. Rather than denouncing war or even trying to argue against it, as Porter does, he claims not even to know what writers should be doing about war—except to say, as he does, that we should "scrap all forms of defense."

A far more thoughtful statement about the responsibilities of writers and artists in time of war came from Kenneth Fearing, a 36-year-old novelist and poet who had helped to found the *Partisan Review*. First, he says that if France is attacked, American writers should "duplicate the aid they gave to loyalist Spain"—presumably by means of donations if not by joining the fight. Second, if the war spreads, he "would personally urge that the U.S. give material aid to any and every enemy of the axis powers." Thirdly, and (I believe) most importantly, Fearing asserts that in wartime,

> the writer's responsibility is to tell the truth as he sees it. And that means today, that if democratic processes are to be preserved and extended … writers and artists are the decisive factor in their defense and development. The literature of today controls at least some of the guns of tomorrow. And finally, any writer who promotes the concept of freedom for larger and still larger masses of people is loyal to the democratic idea, while any who distorts, disrupts, or denies is a traitor to it. ("Situation" 35)

In thus urging writers to defend democracy, Fearing lays himself open to the charge made by Philip Rahv in the same issue of *Partisan Review* that in the early months of 1939, intellectuals are already backing a second "war to save democracy" when the first one failed ("Twilight" 3). Yet rightly or wrongly, Fearing was the only respondent to the *PR* questionnaire who declared that writers had a specific role to play in time of war. They were bound, he wrote, not only to tell the truth "as [they] see it," but also to use their words on behalf of freedom and in the face of guns. There is of course a fine line between using one's words on behalf of freedom and doing what Williams warned against: "becom[ing] a liar for propaganda's sake." More than two years later, in December 1941, the bombing of Pearl Harbor prompted several thousand American writers to join a domestic propaganda organization known as the Writers

War Board (Chasar). Telling the truth about the war was obviously not their highest aim.

Yet telling the truth while pursuing freedom and humanity was the highest aim of Bertolt Brecht, whose major works of the late 1930s—the *Svendborg Poems* and *Mother Courage*—I consider in Chapters 5 and 6. Here I wish only to note the impact of Brecht's poem, "Legend of the Origin of the *Book of Tao-te-ching* on Lao-tsu's Road into Exile" ("Legende von der Entstehung . . .," *Werke* 12: 32–34). First published on April 23, 1939 in the anti-Fascist Swiss newspaper *Schweizer Zeitung am Sonntag*, the poem tells the story of an old Chinese teacher who has learned—even in the face of growing wickedness—that soft water can eventually subdue stone, that "hardness succumbs" (st. 5). Soon after the poem appeared, it was read in Paris by Walter Benjamin, who wrote that the line about hardness expressed the "minimal program for humanness . . . at a time when this statement rung upon the ear like a promise nothing short of messianic" (qtd. Wizisla 138). Likewise, Hannah Arendt wrote that "speedily, like a rumor of good tidings, it travelled by word of mouth—a source of consolation and patience and endurance—where such wisdom was most needed" (qtd. Wizisla 139).

In the fall of 1939, it was needed above all by the German emigrés who had been rounded up and sent to French internment camps right after September 3, when France—along with Great Britain—had declared war on Germany. The Germans dispatched to internment in the once-feudal city of Nevers, 160 miles south of Paris, included Walter Benjamin, who not only circulated Brecht's poem among the other internees but also recited it several times from memory and explained it to the French officers guarding the camp (Wizisla 139–40). In another French internment camp, the German poet and philosopher Heinrich Blucher is said to have "treated the poem like a talisman with magical powers" (qtd. Wizisla 139). Much more recently, Antony Tatlow has described the source of its powers. The *Book of Tao-tê-ching* in the poem, he writes, "teaches survival in a dangerous age, triumphant subservience" (Tatlow 452).

It is almost impossible to find such teaching in what leading American writers told the *Partisan Review* in 1939. With the exception of Kenneth Fearing, who dared to claim that "the literature of today controls at least some of the guns of tomorrow," none of the writers even mentioned the power of literature to contest the devastating effect of war on its victims, to furnish anything like what Seamus Heaney has called "the redress of poetry." Porter and Miller take staunchly pacifist stands, as we have seen, and several others (including Fearing) insist that writers tell the truth in time of war, or at the very least not tell lies. But that is hardly the same as producing works of literature that speak to anyone who might be terrified, traumatized, or demoralized by war.

For the New York literati who answered *PR*'s question, of course, war was a transatlantic specter, a distant abstraction rather than—as it was for Brecht—a fearfully close threat. Yet something like the perseverance that Brecht's "Legend" commemorates can be found in James Laughlin's "A Letter to Hitler," a short poem that obliquely reprises the Nazi book burnings of 1933. (Like the comments on writing and war, it appeared in the Summer 1939 issue of *PR*.) Lacking firewood during the previous winter, Laughlin's speaker says, we burned "old books" taken from the attic, "just old / novels nobody would / ever want to read." But the burning pages fought back, twice setting the chimney afire, flaming up just when "you thought / the fire was all out," and even wafting their ashes "out all over the room" (Laughlin, "Letter" 69). In thus implying that the fire of literature is inextinguishable, the poem strikes a modest blow against Hitler and the Nazis even as it quite inadvertently foreshadows their immolation of the Jews.

If Laughlin turns the fire of book burning against itself, Brecht makes it signify the authenticity of what it consumes. "The Burning of the Books" ("Die Bücherverbbrennung," *Werke* 12: 61) was the first of his "German Satires for the German Freedom Radio," which were partially published in *Das Wort* from December 1937 through March 1938, possibly broadcast from outside Germany at about the same time, and eventually became Part V of the *Svendborg Poems* when they were published in June of 1939. Richly ironic, Brecht's poem makes burning an honor bestowed on authors who tell the truth. As cartloads of books are dragged to the bonfires, "a hounded-out poet, one of the best" is shocked to learn that his own books have been spared.[6] So in a flying rage he writes to those in power,

> Have I not
> Always reported the truth in my books? And now
> I'm treated by you as a liar! I order you:
> Burn me!

The last two words compound the irony of the poem by identifying the books of the banished writer with himself, so that he seems to be pleading for a fiery martyrdom. At the same time, given its obviously autobiographical import, Brecht's poem again reveals the gap between himself and those across the Atlantic: between an exiled, ever-threatened German writer and American writers free to say anything they pleased without fear of exile or immolation in any sense.

III

The *Partisan Review* exploited this freedom. Though a few of its pages made the case against Hitler as well as the case for war, its leading articles in the spring and summer issues of 1939 argued not only against war but also against both of the likely sides: the Fascists on the one hand, France and Britain on the other. (Russia's intentions were known only to Germany, which had been courting the Soviets since January). Given Hitler's unbridled lust for *Lebensraum* along with his brutal treatment of German Jews, the case for defending Western Europe against him at this time seemed overwhelming. But the intellectual case against this move was probably made nowhere else more vehemently than by Dwight McDonald and Philip Rahv in two successive articles.

In the first one, which I have already cited, McDonald charges that American intellectuals of all kinds are beating the drums for "a new world war to save democracy." Recalling that American intellectuals had urged the U.S. to fight for Belgium in 1917, McDonald finds the first quarter of 1939 nothing but a second act of war-mongering staged by a formidable if heterogeneous cast: Phi Beta Kappa, Communist groups, and leading commentators such as Dorothy Thompson and Walter Lippmann. Essentially,

McDonald argues, intellectuals have bolted themselves to the "capitalist war machine," siding not with democracy against fascism but rather with "democratic capitalism" against "fascist capitalism" (McDonald 10).

But just what was the "capitalist war machine"? Whether or not American intellectuals had sold their souls to capitalism and war-making alike, one of the strongest foes of war-making was also one of its richest capitalists: Joseph P. Kennedy, American Ambassador to England, whose stubborn opposition to fighting for Britain and France disgusted FDR so much that he would sack Kennedy in October 1940. Furthermore, both houses of Congress in 1939 were dominated by isolationists such as Senator Key Pittman, Democrat of Nevada and Chair of the Senate Foreign Relations Committee, who in March drafted a bill that barely modified the Neutrality Act of 1937. But not even this baby step toward intervention gained enough support to pass, and in mid-May Pittman shelved the bill because, he said, "the situation in Europe does not seem to induce any urgent action on neutrality legislation" (qtd. Watt 265). Not until two and a half years later, when the Japanese bombing of Pearl Harbor propelled the U.S. into war, did the case for "urgent action" finally vanquish the inertia of Congress and the American public.

In making the case for war in 1939, then, American intellectuals were arguably just as far-sighted as FDR, who—as noted above—was already signaling his inclination to fight. But McDonald saw nothing good in what he called this "crusade against fascism" (10). On the contrary, he blames capitalism for war. "Modern warfare," he writes, "must be regarded as the chief instrument by which the obsolete bourgeoisie retains their death-grip on the social order" (18). Given this conviction, he is appalled by the pro-war stance of what he calls "nominally Marxist" intellectuals. "[T]hey have been morally enraged against a scapegoat fascism across the ocean," he writes, "and to defeat it they have made common cause with the class and economic system that is preparing the next world slaughter" (19). In echoing his earlier prediction that "the next war will be an orgy of slaughter and destruction," McDonald sounds like Katherine Anne Porter and Henry Miller, who would passionately argue for pacifism in the next issue of *PR*. But McDonald offers a final riposte to intellectuals of every stripe, even those who thought—in the words of William Carlos Williams—that "we've got fight." "War," writes McDonald, "

> is a serious matter for intellectuals, who may have to die, and for capitalists, who may risk their property. But intellectuals have little to lose because they will stay behind the lines. (19)

Whatever the cogency of McDonald's case against America's joining the war, he was probably right here. Practicing medicine as well as writing poetry, Williams would certainly work behind the lines, and though Gertrude Stein insisted that "writers will have to fight too like anyone else," she had to know that as a woman of sixty-five she would never go anywhere near a battle. Neither would Dorothy Thompson or Walter Lippmann.

In the summer 1939 issue of *PR*, Philip Rahv seconded McDonald's essay with one of his own, "This Quarter: Twilight of the Thirties." But unlike McDonald, who mainly sought to scold Marxist intellectuals for supporting a "capitalist" war, Rahv addressed writers of fiction, poetry, and plays. Dismayed that Arnold Zweig had recanted his anti-war novel of World War I (*The Case of Sergeant Grischa*), and also that the American Writers Congress and many notable writers such as Thomas Mann were supporting war, he bluntly observed:

> War mongers speak in the name of literature and the arts. But they fail to note that every work of art that emerged from World War I is filled with loathing for war. ("This Quarter" 3–4)

The second point is hard to fault. In England alone, the literary work of men such as Robert Graves, Wilfred Owen, and Siegfried Sassoon showed how the brutalizing experience of combat in the Great War—and especially of trench warfare—demolished everything they might once have thought about the glory of fighting.[7] Postwar literature, Rahv contends, is driven above all by antiwar feeling, breathing "disgust with its counterfeit idealism, its predatory motives and aims," and "if literature is to survive another such experience, it will do so not by concealing but by exposing the real nature of war …" (4).

The problem with this antiwar agenda, however, is that it does not always serve the ends of literature as Rahv himself conceives them. Later on in the essay, he excoriates Andre Malraux's *Man's Hope* (1937–38). Though based on the author's experience and "generally regarded," Rahv writes, "as a truthful record of the Spanish [Civil] war," he finds it only a "party-pamphlet in the guise of objective fiction," a novelistic brief for the communist fantasy that brotherhood can transcend war. "[D]evoid of a single real character," it substitutes

> an imaginary drama of hope and fraternity for the black counter-revolution in Loyalist Spain that swept the anti-fascists to defeat. The only parts of the novel that are not false are the plainly reportorial descriptions of air battles and of the sensations of the combatants." (Rahv 7)

Rahv faults the novel, then, chiefly because it fails to foreground "the black counter-revolution in Loyalist Spain," above all the devastating setback suffered by the Republicans when they tried to seize Teruel, the capital of Aragon: in a battle lasting more than two months of the worst winter in twenty years (from December 15, 1937 to February 22, 1938), the Nationalists lost and then regained the city, inflicted far more casualties than they suffered, and thus sealed the defeat of the Republicans in the war as a whole.[8] Rather than trying to salvage some shred of hope from the Communist revolution in Spain, then, should Malraux's novel have simply exposed its futility— along with the futility of all war? Perhaps. Yet in commending the realism with which the novel describes "air battles" and "the sensations of the combatants," Rahv implicitly grants that fiction may thrive aesthetically on the sheer *frisson* of war, which hardly supports his antiwar prescription for literature.

This prescription goes well beyond urging the writers of his time to expose the brutality as well as futility of war. On the contrary, just after decrying the conformity of "today's younger writers," he asserts that "only one thing promised to revitalize literature in the past decade: the idea of social revolution as applied to culture, which gave rise to a new creative writing and Marxist literary criticism" (5–6). Surveying "A Variety of Fiction" in the previous issue of *PR* (Spring 1939), Rahv himself reviews a brand-new novel that would seem to exemplify the literary application of this revolutionary idea: Steinbeck's *Grapes of Wrath* (1939). Yet even though Rahv calls this book "an authentic and formidable example of the novel of social protest," it "fails," he says, "on the test of craftsmanship." Relentlessly goading our sympathies, it is also "far too didactic and long-winded," displaying "all the familiar faults of the 'proletarian' literary mode"; "the 'ornery' dialect spoken by its farmers . . . [is] less a form of human speech than a facile convention of the local-color schools": and "Steinbeck does not so much create character as he apes it" ("Variety" 111–12). In short, whatever this novel might do for the cause of "social protest" or "social revolution," it fails as literature.

By contrast, Rahv warmly commends a novel that subordinates social protest to individual psychology: Robert Penn Warren's first novel, *Night Rider*, published the same year as *Grapes of Wrath*. Marginalizing the conflict between tobacco farmers and the tobacco trust in 1904, *Night Rider* chiefly shows how Percy Munn leads the farmers while struggling to hold his identity together in time as well as place. In other words, while Steinbeck's Joad is pitifully victimized by ruthless banks, Percy Munn fights to the point of self-destruction a battle with himself. *Night Rider* voices neither antiwar sentiment nor—except marginally—social protest. Yet according to Rahv, it displays "an almost classic normality of form and rare qualities of a dramatic and pictorial order" with "at least half a dozen superb scenes of action" (112). Furthermore, since its author was just thirty-three years old, it belies the claims that Rahv makes in the next issue of *PR*: that younger writers are conformist, and that literature can be revitalized only by "the idea of social revolution" ("Variety" 5–6).

By themselves, none of Rahv's comments on the literature of the late thirties invalidates the case against war made by Rahv himself or by any of the other New York intellectuals. But in complicating the antiwar case, Rahv's literary analyses furnish a fascinating answer to the double-edged question that he and William Phillips posed to many other writers of their time for the summer issue of *PR*. Do Rahv's contributions to the spring and summer issues of *PR* amount to saying that a writer's job is simply to oppose the coming war and expose the horrors of all war? Or does he epitomize the dilemma of an antiwar Marxist who had not only come to loathe Stalin but also prized literature and literary craftsmanship just as much as any political agenda? In Hitler's Germany, Rahv writes, "all free and authentic creation as well as thought are forcibly repressed" ("Twilight" 5). Since Rahv recognized the plight of German writers and artists, and since he must have seen (among other things) the *Time* cover of January 2, 1939, with its appalling spectacle of Nazi victims splayed across a wheel, one wonders if he did not sometimes question his own insistence that the writer's only "responsibility . . . in time of war" was to wage war against war itself.

Whatever the answer to that question, the imminence of World War II in the early months of 1939 had already begun to change the direction of American literature. While Steinbeck's *Grapes of Wrath* encapsulated the misery of the Great Depression, the victory of fascism in the Spanish Civil War (1936 to 1939) prefigured the much greater war against fascism in Europe as a whole. In February 1939, two months before the Spanish war ended and seven months before the European war broke out, Ernest Hemingway started writing a novel about the former: a novel whose impact would rival if not eclipse that of Steinbeck's.[9] As the first major work of fiction inspired by the war that Hemingway himself called the "dress rehearsal" for World War II, *For Whom the Bell Tolls* deserves a chapter of its own in this book, and that is what follows.

Notes

1   See http://jamesheff.com/images/cover.png

2   Von Ripper was not the first to make this connection. In a photomontage published five years earlier and captioned *Als im Mittelalter, So im Dritten Reich* (*As in the Middle Ages, So in the Third Reich*), the German artist Helmut Herzfeld (aka John Heartfield) juxtaposed the photograph of a sculptured Catherine wheel (taken from the northeast side of the Tübingen Stiftskirche) with the photo of a naked man stretched across a swastika superimposed on a circle. Heartfield's picture, which I strongly suspect von Ripper knew, appeared in the magazine *AIZ* 13.22 (May 31, 1934): 352. See http://jamesheff.com/images/Wheel.jpg

    On the topic of hanging, "The Devil" in Part II of Brecht's *Svendborg Poems* includes a novel twist: right after Hitler blames the devil for starving the German people, the devil hangs Hitler himself.

3   "President Roosevelt to the German Chancellor (Hitler) [and the President of Czechoslovakia]," Telegram of September 26, 1938. https://history.state.gov/historicaldocuments/frus1938v01/d631

4   In his coast-to-coast tour of the United States from February to May 1938, Mann delivered a lecture that was published that year as *The Coming Victory of Democracy* (1938). See also *This War* (1940).

5   First coined in the seventeenth century to designate the leader of a war-party, the word "partisans" came to denote resistance fighters such as the Communists who fought the Fascists in the Spanish Civil War and who are called *partizans* in Hemingway's novel about that war, *For Whom the Bell Tolls,* which I examine in Chapter 2.

6   The poem was actually inspired by what a Bavarian writer named Oskar Maria Graf told the Nazis: they should burn his books, he said, rather than imply by sparing them that he had been lying for the regime (Midgley 20). But this hardly precludes the possibility that Brecht may also be referring to himself and his own books.

7   I allude here to the argument made by Paul Fussell in *The Great War and Modern Memory* (1975).

8   Thomas 773. For the Republicans, writes Laurie Lee, the Battle of Teruel "was meant to be the victory that would change the war; it was indeed the seal of defeat" (Lee 158).

9   With 430,00 copies printed by February 1940, *The Grapes of Wrath* was the best seller of 1939, won the Pulitzer Prize for Fiction, and was cited as a "great work" by the Nobel Prize Committee that gave the literature prize to Steinbeck in 1962 (Österling). But eight years earlier, Hemingway won the Nobel, and though not cited by the awarding committee, *For Whom the Bell Tolls* sold half a million copies within months (Meyers, *H:B* 335–38). It lost the Pulitzer in 1939 only because the *ex officio* head of the board found it offensive (McDowell).

The Spanish Civil War and Ernest Hemingway's
For Whom the Bell Tolls

In *The Battle for Spain: The Spanish Civil War 1936–1939* (2006), which is probably the most comprehensive history of its subject now available, Anthony Beevor gives eight packed paragraphs to the Segovia Offensive of May 30 to June 6, 1937 (Beevor 275–76). During this week, Loyalists fighting for the legally elected Republican government of Spain tried in vain to retake Segovia, about fifty-four miles northwest of Madrid, which had been captured by the rebel Nationalists. To forestall the Nationalists' assault on Bilbao in the north, they had been ordered by Indalecio Prieto Tuero, minister of defense, to attack the rebels at La Granja de San Ildefonso so as "to seize Segovia by surprise in an energetic attack." Since Prieto "was prepared to collaborate closely with the communists and follow their advice on military operations," the head of the I Corps of the Army of the Center was the Spanish Colonel Domingo Moriones Larraga, but its 35th division—one of three making the attack—was commanded by "General Walter," *nom de guerre* of a Polish and Soviet Red Army General named Karol Waclaw Świerczewski. Also participating were the XIV International Brigade under General Walter and a Byelorussian light tank brigade led by Kombrig D. G. Pavlov.

Besides stressing throughout the role of the Soviets, Beevor forecasts that Prieto "was to become one of their fiercest opponents later," highlights the farcical ineptness of the Republican air force (which for a dawn attack did not arrive "until eleven in the morning, and then bombed republican positions"), and documents the cynicism of General Walter. After the 69th Division managed to get part way to Cerro de Cabeza Grande, the "Big Head Hill" from which it could fire directly on the Segovia Road, Beevor writes,

> Walter ordered XIV International Brigade to launch a frontal attack, which left the pinewood hillside scattered with corpses. Walter's cynicism was revealed in a report back to Moscow in which he wrote, "the XIV, which heroically, but passively, allowed itself to be slaughtered over the course of five days."

Counterattacking on June 1 "with strong support from bombers and fighters," the Nationalists "forced the Republicans back from Cabeza Grande and threatened the whole advance on La Granja." On June 2, Walter "was relieved from operational command of the offensive" and on June 6, Colonel Moriones pulled back his troops. To delay "the nationalist assault on Bilbao ... by no more than two weeks at most," the Loyalists lost 3,000 men, including 1,000 from the XIV Internationalist Brigade. "The operation failed," Beevor explains,

> partly because the nationalists appeared to have got wind of what was being prepared, but mainly because the republican command had greatly underestimated the speed of the nationalists' reactions and the effectiveness of their air power. The nationalist Fiat fighter force ... even managed to machine-gun Moriones's headquarters.... Colonel Moriones in his report wrote, "Our own aircraft carried out bombing attacks from a great height and carelessly ... our fighters kept at a respectable distance and rarely came down to machine-gun the enemy ... enemy aircraft were highly active and extraordinarily effective."

Finally, Beevor notes, the International Brigade felt doubly abused by their superiors. Besides sacrificing them "for little benefit," their commanders brutally punished men who "broke in the face of strafing by nationalist fighters." One captain "designated five men at random and shot them, one after another, in the back of the head with his pistol in Soviet style," and before he was relieved, General Walter had ordered "the machine-gunning of those who pull back, executions on the spot, and the beating of stragglers."

From this summary of Beevor's account I have omitted one telling item. The attack he describes, he says, "was later used by Hemingway as the background for his novel *For Whom the Bell Tolls*" (Beevor 275). Just as Joe Rosenthal's photograph of the raising of the American flag on Mount Suribachi has become part of the history of the Battle of Iwo Jima, Hemingway's novel has become part of the cultural historiography of the Spanish Civil War.

But it remains a work of literature, and as such it prompts us to ask just *how* it uses the Segovia Offensive. For a start, quite obviously, Hemingway could not have used Beevor's historical account as a source. For all its comprehensiveness and depth of research (including access to Russian archives), Beevor's account was written more than sixty years after Hemingway's novel, and thus can merely serve as an alternative— and paradigmatically historical—way of representing the event. To some extent, it may also confirm the historical authenticity of Hemingway's novel, which reveals not only the Soviet Communists' domination of the Loyalist forces but also their ruthlessness.

Nevertheless, Beevor's account of the Segovia Offensive says absolutely nothing about what Hemingway's novel consistently foregrounds: guerrilla warfare.[1] There is nothing generically "unhistorical" about this kind of fighting. On the contrary, it gets its due in at least one notable history that Hemingway consulted while writing his novel: General Sir William Napier's *History of the War in the Peninsula* (1828–40), the war in which British, Spanish, and Portuguese forces—fighting from 1808 to 1814—ended the Napoleonic occupation of the Iberian Peninsula. According to Jeffrey Meyers, who learned about Hemingway's interest in this book while interviewing Martha Gellhorn, Napier's eyewitness account of the earlier war made the novelist see how it prefigured the later one.[2] Like the later one, which pitted German and Italian forces against those of Soviet Russia, the earlier one was international, and just as important, Meyers notes, it saw the emergence of guerrillas (Spanish for "little wars"), in which mobile bands of freelance fighters harassed the enemy and helped the allies defeat the French. (Meyers, *HPW*)

A much more recent history of the earlier war shows how much these nineteenth-century guerrillas resemble those portrayed by Hemingway. According to Ronald Fraser's *Napoleon's Cursed War* (2008), which Meyers cites, the early guerrillas were a small and above all *mobile* alternative to a regular standing army. Though somewhat heterogeneous—including women, outlaws, and even French army deserters—they formed cohesive bands mostly led by and composed of peasants who had been humiliated by the enemy or who had seen close relatives abused or killed (Fraser 346). They also operated behind enemy lines and sometimes resorted to "barbarous" reprisals (Fraser 336, 411).

Fraser's term for one kind of guerrilla band is notable. "Those who took up arms without any authorization from either civilian or military authorities," he writes, "could be called *partisans*" (344, my emphasis). The Russian version of this word—партизанский / partizanskiy—turns up in *War and Peace*, which "Hemingway had certainly read" by the time he wrote his own novel (Meyers, *HPW*). Tolstoy uses the word to explain what guerrillas did in the Spanish Peninsular War as well as in the Caucasus, where he himself had fought in 1852–53. One of the best ways of breaking "the so-called laws of war," Tolstoy writes, is to pitch scattered groups of men against massed armies:

> In such actions, instead of two crowds opposing each other, the men disperse, attack singly, run away when attacked by stronger forces, but again attack when opportunity offers. This was done by the guerrillas (partizanskiy) in Spain, by the mountain tribes in the Caucasus, and by the Russians in 1812.

This "guerrilla warfare," Tolstoy writes, breaks the rule which

> says that an attacker should concentrate his forces in order to be stronger than his opponent at the moment of conflict.
> Guerrilla war (always successful, as history shows) directly infringes that rule.
> (*War and Peace*, Book 14, Chapter 2)

Along with Fraser's account of the Peninsular War, Tolstoy's definition of guerrilla warfare is cogent in all respects except for his parenthetical comment that it "always" succeeds, which would be disproven in the twentieth century for reasons that Meyers succinctly explains. "In the Peninsular War," he writes, "the guerrillas had a unifying common goal and fought to support the regular armies; in the Civil War the Loyalists were not only overwhelmed by fascist military power, but rival militias also fought amongst themselves and the guerrillas disintegrated into brutal factions" (Meyers, *HPW*).

This factionalism may well explain why Beevor's account of the Segovia Offensive has nothing to say about its guerrillas. If the Nationalist defeat of the Loyalists can be explained by superior air power and the utter callousness of General Walter, what more need be said about guerrillas fighting among themselves? As a novelist, Hemingway answers this question by imagining a band of guerrillas who enact the central contradictions of the war in the concentrated space of just one battle zone and in the concentrated time of just seventy-two hours—three days. But above all, these contradictions plague Robert Jordan, the American college teacher of Spanish who has volunteered to join the Loyalist fight against fascism and do one specific job—blow up a bridge—with the aid of the guerrillas.

Paradoxically, the novel aims to tell the "truth" of the war even while representing just one battle through the eyes of an imaginary character and treating many actual figures—some of whom appear under their own names—with scant regard for historical accuracy. To unravel this paradox, however, we must first consider the history of the novel itself.

As much as it re-creates the history of the Spanish Civil War, *For Whom the Bell Tolls* reflects Hemingway's response to the wider history of his time—above all to the imminence of World War II. On this topic he was acutely ambivalent. In an *Esquire* article of September 1935, he flatly rejected any more American involvement in European wars, stating that no European country deserved defending and that it would be folly for the US to fight for any one of them again ("Notes on the Next War," qtd. Nilsson 81).

Yet soon after the Spanish Civil War broke out in July of 1936, Hemingway himself was sucked in. Given his long experience of Spain in the 1920s, which had inspired not only *The Sun Also Rises* (1926), his first novel, but also *Death in the Afternoon* (1932), his book on bullfighting, he knew both the country and its language, and for covering the war he was offered a juicy contract by the North American Newspaper Alliance (NANA).[3] Apart from the lure of this contract, his motives were mixed to the point of self-contradictory. On one hand, he had long loathed the brutality of war and the hypocrisy of the abstractions used to justify it. In *A Farewell to Arms* (1929), based on his own experience as an ambulance driver for the Italian army in World War I, Frederic Henry cannot accept a doctor's claim that getting wounded has made him a hero. In Henry's opinion, the whole idea of heroic self-sacrifice in war is no more glorious than the killing of animals in a slaughterhouse (*FA* 185). On the other hand, this gruesome conception of war did not keep Hemingway from prizing it as a quarry for literature. Writing to F. Scott Fitzgerald in December 1925, he stated that "war is the best subject of all. It groups the maximum of material and speeds up the action and brings out all sorts of stuff that normally you would have to wait a lifetime to get" (*SL* 176). And among the kinds of war that a writer might choose to re-create, he ranked civil war above all others. "Civil war," he wrote, "is the best war for a writer, the most complete" (qtd. Meyers, *H:B* 301).

Whether or not Hemingway foresaw that the Spanish Civil War would inspire his next novel, he told family and friends in February of 1937—just before leaving for Spain—that he mainly sought to make the case against intervention. "This is the dress rehearsal for the inevitable European war," he told the Pfeiffer family, "and I would like to try to write anti-war war correspondence that would help to keep us out of it when it comes" (*SL* 458). Yet keeping America out of war was hardly his sole motive. Four days before writing the above, he told the pro-Franco Harry Sylvester why he backed the Loyalists. "The Spanish war is a bad war," he wrote, "and nobody is right. . . . [B]ut my sympathies are always for exploited working people against absentee landlords even if I drink around with the landlords and shoot pigeons with them. I would as soon shoot them as the pigeons" (*SL* 456). It did not matter to Hemingway that the exploited workers were backed by the Soviet Union. "The Reds," he told the Pfeiffers, "may be as bad as they say but they are the people of the country versus the absentee landlords, the moors, the Italians and the Germans" (*SL* 458).

The intervention of the latter two steeled his commitment to back the Loyalists—the Republican government of Spain—even if this also allied him with the Communists. In August of 1936, just one month after the Spanish war broke out, Britain and France had persuaded twenty-seven nations—including Nazi Germany, Fascist Italy, and the Soviet Union—to sign a Non-Intervention Agreement pledging to stay out of the war. But Hitler was already sending planes and armored units to the Nationalists, and Mussolini would shortly be sending more aircraft as well as machine guns, artillery, and the Royal Italian Navy. Though Germany and Italy thus openly violated the agreement they had just signed, nearly all the other major signatories—including Britain, France, and U.S.—kept their pledge to stay out of the war. As Douglas Little notes, the Western powers reckoned that General Franco's conservative regime would be more promising for foreign investment than the revolutionary left, which—given the chance—might collectivize both industries and agriculture (Little 232). By the spring of 1937, furthermore, the revolutionary left—the Republican government of Spain—was firmly backed by Joseph Stalin's Soviet Union, the only foreign power that had significantly intervened on its side. The Soviets not only sent aircraft, tanks, and eventually more than 2,000 men, they also steered thousands of volunteers into the International Brigades and championed the Republican cause around the world (Nilsson 84). Within Spain itself, the Soviets took control of that cause. In the fall of 1936, Soviet military intelligence agents reorganized the Popular Army and thus gave the Kremlin a lasting grip on the Loyalists (Payne 160–73).

Choosing sides in the war, therefore, was no easy matter. Though Hemingway's sympathy for workers in any conflict with landlords led him to back the Popular Front, Ichiro Takayoshi rightly observes what this move entailed. "Expressing support for the Spanish Republic," he writes, "required American liberal writers, artists, and intellectuals to make peace with Stalinism one way or another." Since "moderate liberals, including Hemingway, had doubts about the Soviets," they couldn't simply "embrac[e] Communism all the way." Most, therefore,

decided to reassure themselves that their collaboration with Communists was an alliance of convenience, subject to renegotiation or annulment once they won their common objective, the defeat of global fascism. The Soviet conduct, however, taxed their creative credulity, as damning evidence mounted throughout the war. After all, the Spanish Civil War (1936–39) coincided with the Great Purge (1936–38), the period when Stalinism at last bared its dreaded lineaments. For these fellow travelers, the war in Spain meant as much an inner struggle against gnawing apprehensions about their Communist allies as an actual combat against Franco's rebel armies. (Takayoshi 102–3)

Hemingway's novel reflects this struggle much more than his reporting on the war does. His reporting was driven simply by his loathing of fascism, which he branded "a lie told by bullies" in a speech delivered to the American Writers Congress in Carnegie Hall on June 4, 1937 ("Fascism" 479). A little less than two years later, as already noted, Kenneth Fearing told the *Partisan Review* that "the writer's responsibility is to tell the truth as he sees it." Hemingway anticipated him. The writer's "problem," he told the Writers Congress, is to tell the truth so as to make readers feel they have experienced it ("Fascism" 479).

These two statements differ, however, in one notable way. For Hemingway, telling the truth is not a "responsibility" but a "problem," and to set his reporting on the war beside his novel about it is to see him wrestling with this problem. Ironically, as Milton Cohen has cogently demonstrated, Hemingway's novel reveals what his own reporting had buried or falsified. It thus demonstrates that a work of fiction can be not just "a record more truthful than history," as Graham Greene wrote of this novel (qtd. Sean Hemingway xx) but also more truthful than journalism—whether or not journalism is truly the first draft of history.

In reporting on the Spanish Civil War, Cohen writes, Hemingway steadfastly championed the Republican or Loyalist side as "a democracy fighting for its life against brutal fascism" (Cohen 43). He ignored or denied evidence that Soviet Stalinists not only took control of the Loyalist forces but also ruthlessly repressed other leftist parties such as the anarchistically Marxist POUM, which George Orwell supported, and assassinated Loyalists such as José Robles and Andru Nin.[4] So long as the war lasted, Hemingway felt bound to suppress such ugly facts, to write nothing about the war "which could hurt the Republic which [he] believed in" (letter of October 14, 1952, qtd. Cohen 43). But once the Republicans were decisively beaten, he was free to do what the protagonist of his novel aims to do but does not live to do after the war: "write a true book" (*FWBT* 167).

Its truth is clearly not historical. Though Jordan is partly based on Hemingway himself and almost always speaks for him, Hemingway's characters are creations rather than historically accurate portraits. If I risk stating the obvious here, it is chiefly because Jeffrey Meyers tends to make the latter claim in his otherwise highly informative account of the historical figures who stand behind Hemingway's characters and sometimes appear in the novel under their own names.[5]

Among the latter is André Marty, a leading French Communist who became Chief Political Commissar of the International Brigades during the Spanish war. In Hemingway's novel, Marty is portrayed as a bumbling fool—*loco*—who not only suspects everyone of treachery but also orders the arrest of two men bent on delivering a vital message from Jordan to his superior, General Golz, whom Marty also suspects (*FWBT* 365–69). But this portrait is hardly fair. According to one American reporter, Marty played a crucial role in getting weapons to the guerrillas, and according to another, he could not have appeared where Hemingway puts him because his "job was not at the front, it was at the base. . . . In all its physical details, the particular incident is untrue, and the slander is all the more glaring because Hemingway used a real, historic figure as the center of the incident."[6] Even allowing for the bias of reporters writing for Communist newspapers in the U.S., we must also recognize that Hemingway himself was anything but impartial or above the temptation to settle scores. Whether or not Marty had ordered two volunteers shot for panicking in the midst of combat, for which Hemingway called him a "swine" (Bolloten 294–95), Marty was the "goddamned bureaucrat" who kept Hemingway from the front in the Battle of Brunete—by signing an order that kept all correspondents away (qtd. Boyd 7). He was just as disgusted with Dolores Ibárruri, the Loyalist rabble-rouser known as La Pasionaria. In Hemingway's terse verdict on this woman, her blind adherence to the Communist party line "made me vomit always" (qtd. Baker, *EH:LS* 347). In the novel, one of the guerrillas deflates another's admiration of her by saying, "Do you know your Pasionaria has a son thy age in Russia since the start of the movement?" (*FWBT* 309).[7] Yet as Meyers observes, "Hemingway's statement (probably inspired by Fascist propaganda) is false, for Hugh Thomas writes that in October 1937 'her miner husband was all the time at the front with her son'" (Thomas 492; Meyers, *FWBT-CH* 94).

Nothing in Hemingway's novel, however, departs more radically from historical fact than his portrayal of Golz, who is based on the Soviet officer known as General Walter. As we have already seen in Beevor's meticulously researched history of the Segovia Offensive, Walter not only led to slaughter the XIV International Brigade but also treated his own men ruthlessly, and having ordered "the machine-gunning of those who pull back, executions on the spot, and the beating of stragglers," he was relieved of command just two days after the offensive began. Yet Hemingway admired this man so much that he used neither his real name nor "Walter" in the novel. When asked about this by Bronislaw Zielinski, his Polish translator, Hemingway said of Walter,

> He was such a splendid man and splendid soldier that I wouldn't dare to present him in fictitious situations, and put in his mouth fictitious words. (Letter of January 3, 1983 to Jeffrey Meyers, qtd. Meyers, *H:B* 605n16)

Nevertheless, Hemingway's Golz is a totally sanitized version of Walter. Whether or not the novelist ever learned what Walter actually did at Segovia (he could hardly have consulted Soviet sources, as Beevor did), Golz is simply the embodiment of military discipline, the "Général Sovietique" (*FWBT* 8) "who is the party as well as the army" (*FWBT* 162) and who gives Jordan his orders. To obstruct the movement of fascist cavalrymen against the Loyalists, Golz tells Jordan to blow up a bridge in the foothills of the Sierra de Guadarrama, a mountain range above Segovia, on the first day of the offensive.

Hemingway took pains to survey this site. Though he did not witness the Segovia Offensive himself, he and Martha Gellhorn toured the Guadarrama from late April to early May, shortly before the fighting occurred. With one exception, then, it seems plausible to infer—as Takayoshi does—that "the novel's descriptions of the terrain, troop movements, characters, and even the bridge must have been drawn from the actually existing things and people Hemingway witnessed" (Takayoshi 113). The one exception is the category of "characters," as already noted, since besides creating its central figures (such as Jordan, Maria, and Pilar), the novel misrepresents some historically documented facts about several others.

What kind of truth, then, does Hemingway's novel tell? Immediately after the United States entered World War II, Hemingway edited an anthology of stories about war that he thought would show how previous generations had fought and died. In his introduction to this anthology, *Men at War* (1942), he makes a startling claim:

> A writer's job is to tell the truth. His standard of fidelity to the truth should be so high that his invention, out of his experience, should produce a truer account than anything factual can be. (*MW* xiv)

If a work of fiction driven by the writer's commitment to the truth is "truer than anything factual can be," it must also be "a record more truthful than history," as Graham Greene wrote of *For Whom the Bell Tolls* itself (quoted above). Paradoxically, however, Hemingway believed that the surest road to truth was invention. While writing his novel in the spring of 1939, he repeatedly told Maxwell Perkins—his editor at Scribner's—that his best fiction was neither factual nor based on memory but rather "made . . . up" (*SL* 482, 479; Bruccoli 281).

This startling claim prompts a fundamental question about the nature of invention: what principles drive it? What, if anything, regulates it? In *For Whom the Bell Tolls*, Takayoshi argues, the answer is pragmatism:

> [T]o the extent that the character's pragmatism (his ability to fight well) is the author's pragmatism (his ability to write well), our knowledge about what Hemingway wanted should be derived from our knowledge about what Jordan wants. (Takayoshi 115)

The truth of Hemingway's novel, then, would lie not in its even-handedness, its revelation of the atrocities committed by all sides in the Spanish war, including Communists as well as Fascists, but rather in the wishes of its protagonist.

What he wants above all, it can be argued, is to blow up the bridge and thereby follow the orders of General Golz. In spite of major obstacles to this objective, Jordan obeys Golz to the very end, and thus accepts the Communist chain of command. As he tells himself at one point, he was "under Communist discipline for the duration of the war" (*FWBT* 163). Working with Communists, he thinks later on, made you a total believer, made you feel an "absolute brotherhood" with everyone else fighting beside you (*FWBT* 235).

Was Jordan himself a Communist? Early in the novel, when Maria asks him this question, he says, "No I am an anti-fascist" (*FWBT* 66). But in the original version of this passage, as Takayoshi notes, he answers "Yes." Likewise, "He was under communist discipline for the duration of war" originally read, "He was a Communist for the duration of war." Given these facts along with the other passages cited, Takayoshi argues that Jordan "is a Stalinist guerrilla, motivated as much by his political preference as by soldierly professionalism" (Takayoshi 119).

If this is true, it could well explain why Scribner's (Hemingway's publisher) asked him to suppress Jordan's Communism while the novel was in galley proof, in August 1940. By that time, as Takayoshi notes, "Communist" had ceased to mean "anti-fascist" in the world at large (Takayoshi 120). One full year earlier, in fact, the Soviet Union had signed a non-aggression treaty that secretly made it Germany's ally in a war on Poland, which they brutally carved up between them in September 1939. Yet the changes pressed upon Hemingway by his publisher do not really change what the novel says about Jordan's politics. Whether he calls himself "Communist" or "anti-fascist," he is "under communist discipline *for the duration of war*," which hardly differs from being "a Communist" for the same period. His commitment is neither permanent nor essential to his identity. It springs only from his conviction that the Communists can best lead the Loyalists to victory.

Nevertheless, since Jordan obeys Golz's order to blow up the bridge even after learning about the brutality of all sides, including the Communists, Takayoshi argues that he comes to embody a "soldierly pragmatism" which survives the demolition of his original faith in the Loyalist cause:

> The first rationale—the civil war as a "holding attack" against global fascism— prompts Jordan to volunteer in the first place and exhorts him to stay in the fight. The second, fallback rationale—soldierly pragmatism—helps Jordan rationalize the action he continues to take after the persuasiveness of the first discourse wears off. (Takayoshi 121)

Up to a point, this is perfectly plausible. If Jordan is judged simply by what he finally succeeds in doing—blowing up the bridge—he is indeed a pragmatic soldier. But along with his relentless self-questioning, several of his other deeds define him as a man of unresolved if not irresolvable contradictions. Like the guerrilla band that he struggles to persuade—but cannot command—for the sake of his mission, he is divided against himself, and thus embodies the divisions that split the Loyalists as a whole and doomed their cause. This is not the whole truth of the Spanish Civil War, which a Nationalist historian might read as a triumph of capitalist freedom and a Soviet historian might read as a story of betrayal—with Hemingway himself among the worst of its betrayers. But arguably, his novel is a true story of how the war *felt* to a particular kind of Loyalist: a soldier who was not only a pragmatist but also an acute observer and a relentlessly self-questioning thinker.

The final claim seems contradicted by the end of the very first chapter. After Jordan and an old man named Anselmo scout the bridge they are to blow up, Jordan tells himself that he must not think of anything but blowing up the bridge (*FWBT* 17). But Jordan never stops thinking. As self-interrogating as Hamlet, he repeatedly and obsessively weighs his orders—his duty to the cause, his duty to kill—against his aversion to killing and his gradual discovery of the ugly truth about his own side in the war.

Besides wrestling with this moral conflict, Jordan foresees that even if his mission succeeds, it will be suicidal. The night before the offensive begins, he tells Maria, who has just become his lover, "We'll be killed but we'll blow the bridge" (*FWBT* 379). Yet doing so seems to him pointless as well as suicidal. For one thing, he knows that the enemy is primed for the coming offensive and will hardly be deterred by the demolition of the bridge. Also, on the day before the battle is set to begin, Jordan's dynamite detonators and exploder are taken by a guerrilla named Pablo, who throws them down a gorge in hopes of preventing the demolition and thus forestalling fascist reprisals.

Combined with losing the advantage of surprise in the offensive, Pablo's treachery exemplifies another kind of surprise: the unforeseen setback that threatens to sabotage Jordan's mission—no matter how pragmatically pursued. This kind of setback heightens the suspense that Hemingway artfully weaves into the novel, as Meyers notes (*HPW*). Further heightening the suspense, Jordan sends a message to Golz, the Russian general in charge of the offensive, urging him to cancel the bridge-blowing. But since the message is hand-carried and the messenger repeatedly delayed by obstructive officials, it fails to reach Golz until just before dawn of the attack day—far too late for any changes. As a result, Jordan feels bound to blow up the bridge by using hand grenades to explode the dynamite and wires to pull their pins. Since this maneuver puts both him and Anselmo near the explosion, its flying shrapnel kills Anselmo, and soon after, when a shell from a big tank knocks over Jordan's horse, the fall breaks his left leg, leaving him painfully alive only long enough for a final sequence of thoughts and one last action.

Before judging that last action, consider what the foregoing sequence of events says about the cohesion of the guerrilla band and its place in the Soviet-dominated chain of command. First of all, the band exemplifies what Fraser writes about guerrillas. As already noted, he says they were "*partisans*" in the original sense: not Communists but freewheeling agents of resistance "who took up arms without any authorization from either civilian or military authorities." In other words, unlike Robert Jordan, they were *outside* all chains of command, responsible only to themselves, and therefore always subject to disruption. Though Pablo was once the leader of the band, he has been displaced by his wife Pilar, and he is so much afraid of fascist reprisals for blowing up the bridge that he does all he can to sabotage it. If Jordan were a Stalinist guerrilla, as Takayoshi claims, he would surely have assassinated Pablo, which is just what a gypsy member of the band urges him to do (*FWBT* 61). But instead of shooting Pablo, Jordan simply denounces him—silently—as a filthy traitor (*FWBT* 377) and then accepts his suggestion that they use a grenade—in place of the discarded explosives—to detonate the bridge. Just as notably, Jordan asks Golz to rescind his order, which is hardly the act of anyone who believes—like the doomed British cavalrymen commemorated by Tennyson—that "theirs was not to question why, / Theirs but to do or die."[8] So while Jordan's detonation of the bridge proves him a pragmatic soldier, he is in many ways a one-man band of resistance to the treachery, brutality, and thoughtlessness he finds all around him.

Nevertheless, his final act is to kill. After briefly considering suicide, he suddenly realizes that he can still do something: shoot the officer in charge of the troops coming into view just below him in pursuit of the guerilla band that has just left. Since the enemy officer, Lieutenant Berrendo, has recently ordered both the killing and the beheading of a guerilla band that had pledged to help with Jordan's mission, his final act—clearly implied by the ending, which has him simply lying in wait on the pine-needled ground—is an act of murderous revenge that will of course provoke his own death in retaliation.

Berrendo is the last of the many men Jordan kills. At one point he calculates that he has killed over twenty, including the 21-year-old cavalryman whom he shoots early one morning in the chest, just under the insignia of the Sacred Heart (*FWBT* 309, 270). Yet throughout nearly all of the novel, he struggles to face the truth about killing. Just after telling himself that he and his comrades kill "coldly," of necessity rather than desire, he tells himself that, like all who choose to be soldiers, he likes killing even if he claims otherwise (*FWBT* 292). In spite of this truth, however, Jordan feels deeply ambivalent about killing. In one of his searching self-interrogations, he admits that while killing is "wrong," he still does it and still believes in the righteousness of his cause. But he cannot stop there.

> [Y]ou mustn't believe in killing, he told himself. You must do it as a necessity, but you must not believe in it. If you believe in it the whole thing is wrong. (*FWBT* 309)

Yet to believe in the necessity of killing while disbelieving in killing itself hardly answers the questions that Jordan relentlessly puts to himself. Of the more than twenty he has killed, he calculates that only two were fascists, and he resolves never again to shoot even fascist prisoners by "necessity." By itself, he realizes, the bald abstraction "fascist" cannot justify killing anyone "unless it is to prevent something worse happening to other people. So get it straight and do not lie to yourself" (*FWBT* 309)

For Jordan, not lying to himself means contesting the pious abstractions that had once inspired him in the early months of the war, in the summer and fall of 1936: devotion to duty, the sense of total brotherhood with his fellow guerrillas, and the sheer joy of defending the whole world's poor against all tyrants (*FWBT* 240–41). By the spring of 1937, those ideals have collided with reality. When Jordan learns from one of the guerillas that the fascists shot four members of his family and also raped Maria after killing both her parents, he calls the fascists "barbarians" (*FWBT* 138). But when the guerrilla leader Pilar tells at length how her own husband Pablo ordered twenty-plus captured fascists to be flailed to death and then thrown over a cliff, she "made him see," we are told, the barbarity of the Loyalists (*FWBT* 139).

Furthermore, after one of the guerrilla band urges Jordan to assassinate Pablo, as noted above, Jordan jettisons his faith in the brotherhood of the Spanish revolutionaries. "If you had three together, two would unite against one, and then the two would start to betray each other" (*FWBT* 140). Later on, after learning that Pablo has thrown away the explosives needed to detonate the bridge, Jordan mentally curses all Spaniards, using "muck" to stand for a rhyming obscenity that Hemingway knew would be censored: "muck this whole … country and every mucking Spaniard in it *on either side* and to hell forever. … God muck Pablo. Pablo is all of them. (*FWBT* 377–78, my emphasis)

To be sure, Jordan soon recovers from this outburst. "If that were true," he asks himself, "what are you here for?" (*FWBT* 378). He is still driven by what he earlier felt was his "absolute loyalty" to the cause (*FWBT* 140), and even after admitting both the barbarity of the Loyalists and their readiness to betray each other, he remains determined to serve the cause as fully as he can. But he does so on condition that "nobody owned his mind," nor his eyes and ears, and not until "afterwards" would he judge anyone (*FWBT* 140).

Given this contradiction between his commitment to the cause and his determination to judge, independently, all the evidence he is now gathering about it, how should we judge his reaction to the tutoring he gets at Gaylord's Hotel from Karkov, the Soviet journalist who is actually a propagandist for Stalinism?[9] On one hand, Jordan recalls that before meeting Karkov, he was "too naïve" (*FWBT* 241). On the other hand, he is hardly amused when Karkov jokingly quotes a "beautiful" communiqué about "[o]ur glorious troops" advancing in Cordoba, where Jordan knew men who had died in the fighting (*FWBT* 243). To be educated by Karkov, Jordan suspects, is to be corrupted, and we can almost see him pretending to be duped. When Karkov insists that "destroy[ing]" unreliables is not the same as "assassinat[ing]" them, Jordan says simply, "I see" (*FWBT* 249), which could be construed as an elliptical way of saying, "I see your specious distinction for what it's worth."[10] He also seems to swallow Karkov's claim that the Spanish Communist party POUM was "a heresy of crack-pots" that had to be crushed by the execution of its leaders, including Andru Nin, who was actually tortured to death by Soviet agents in Madrid. But when Karkov says of Nin—in response to Jordan's question about him—that he is "In Paris, we say" (*FWBT,* 251), he seems to be not so much stating a fact as parroting an official Party line, or lie.[11] Since Jordan says nothing in response, we do not know if he truly swallows this lie, but in spite of his hatred of lying, we are told that he learns to "accept the necessity for all the deception" (*FWBT* 235). It is just one of the contradictions that roil his character.

In the end, Jordan also feels bound to accept the aid of a murderer. Though he knows that Pablo has just killed several of his own new recruits in order to seize their horses for a getaway after the bridge is blown, Jordan tells himself, "Don't make moral judgments" (*FWBT* 462). All moral judgments are finally trumped by the order to blow up the bridge, which Jordan feels bound to obey no matter the military value of its demolition, no matter its cost in morality or lives, including his own.

In assessing the novel for *Partisan Review* soon after it appeared, Lionel Trilling argued that *For Whom the Bell Tolls* fails to keep the promise of its title, which—in the sermon by John Donne from which it is lifted—counsels us not to seek "for whom the bell [of mourning] tolls" because we are all bound together in mortality. Instead of "celebrat[ing] the community of men," writes Trilling, the novel "actually glorifies the isolation of the individual ego" (Trilling 67). Does it, though? Besides devoting his ego to a cause much larger than himself, however riddled it may be with contradiction, Jordan thinks of his comrades to the very end. After insisting that they leave him behind so as to make their getaway before the enemy troop arrives, he rejects the impulse to kill himself and instead resolves to kill their lieutenant, which will at least delay the enemy's pursuit of the guerrillas. Also, since he does not take his own life— something Karkov recommends via poison for anyone captured by the enemy (*FWBT* 243)—he cannot be sure that he will not be taken alive and tortured to death for whatever information he might divulge about his comrades. So even though his initial faith in the "absolute brotherhood" of the revolution" has been sorely tested, he is hardly an isolated ego.

Does the ending tell us, then, what the novel finally says about war? According to Seán Hemingway, the novelist's grandson, he considered war "a crime against humanity" (Introduction xv), and Jordan himself clearly sees that both sides commit atrocities. Even his final act, which may help to save the life of his beloved Maria, may also save the life of a man he detests for murdering his own recruits. But if Hemingway's novel aims to expose the brutality of war, it also fully exploits the excitement of war, whose intensity, conflicts, and concentrated drama make it "the best subject of all" for literature, as Hemingway told Fitzgerald. Jordan himself turns this aesthetic into a formula for life itself. Just now, he tells himself at one point, you must squeeze all your life into the few days you have left (*FWBT* 173). And on his last night with Maria, he thinks, "Maybe I have had all my life in three days," and remembers her account of the last words spoken by her mother just after the fascists killed her father. "Yes," he tells himself, the woman's last utterance "was good because it made a tingle run all over him when he said it to himself" (*FWBT* 362)

In this moment of almost orgasmic arousal (Maria is sleeping beside him), Jordan's feelings exemplify the paradox of war, which generates the greatest possible excitement in the face of appalling atrocities and the unrelenting threat of sudden death. Since Hemingway took the title of his novel from a sermon by John Donne, we should recall that long before Hemingway, Donne tapped the erotic charge of the word "die," which in his time and place—early seventeenth-century England—could mean "have an orgasm" as well as expire. Addressing his mistress in "The Canonization," Donne writes, "We die and rise the same, and prove / Mysterious by this love." Jordan says nothing so metaphysical to Maria, but as they lie together, the tingle aroused within him by her quoting of her mother's last words resembles a sexual rush. Likewise, Hemingway's novel sometimes blurs the line between glorifying war and exploiting its emotional or even erotic impact for the sake of fiction.

How could it not? If Hemingway aimed to tell the whole truth about war, he had to recognize and reckon with its power to captivate fighters as well as to inspire writers. Before turning to literary scholarship, Samuel Hynes won the Distinguished Flying Cross for his service as a pilot in World War II. Decades later, having studied "many men's narratives from many wars," he concluded:

> most men do feel war's high excitement and romance, and even its beauty (to which there are many testimonies), and not only *before* they experience war but *after*.
>
> Some soldiers never lose that excitement. They are the war lovers, and we must acknowledge that they exist and always have. (Hynes 27)

In other words, this group of veterans loved fighting long after World War I had "discredited the rhetoric Cof patriotic sacrifice," as Joyce Wexler says (1), and shredded the ancient Horatian teaching that it is sweet and fitting to die for one's country ("Dulce et decorum est / Pro patria mori"). For some soldiers, the glory of the cause—whatever the cause—shrivels like so much bunting in the flame of purely personal excitement. In spite of the brutality, wastefulness, and sheer criminality of war, the thrill of fighting itself—what the novel calls the "the dry-mouthed, fear-purged, purging ecstasy of battle" (*FWBT* 241)—has never lost its grip on the feelings and imagination of fighting men.

Besides dramatizing this truth about all war, Hemingway's novel reveals a central truth about the Spanish Civil War. According to Jeffrey Meyers, Hemingway's story of the guerrilla band symbolically explains why the Loyalists lost: "Pablo's theft of Jordan's detonators," for instance, is said to symbolize "the difficulty of fighting without adequate war materiel" (Meyers, *FWBT-CH*). But above all else, as I have already argued, the novel's portrayal of the animosities within the band itself as well as the conflicts within the mind of Jordan symbolize the fundamental weakness of the Loyalist side. Even as they fought the Nationalists, they kept fighting each other.

Hemingway dedicated *For Whom the Bell Tolls* to Martha Gellhorn, an American journalist whom he had met in Key West in 1936 and come to know intimately the next year, when both of them were reporting on the Spanish Civil War. (They would be married on November 5, 1940.) In April 1939, Gellhorn joined him in Cuba, where they soon took up residence high in the hills above Havana in Finca Vigía (Lookout Farm), now a Hemingway museum. While he was writing most of *For Whom the Bell Tolls* there, she wrote a novel of her own about the plight of refugees in Czechoslovakia in the fall of 1938, right after the Munich Agreement allowed the Nazis to occupy its northwest frontier—the so-called "Sudetenland" of Germany. Gellhorn's novel is the topic of my next chapter.

Notes

1 Beevor's index has just one entry on this topic: "guerrilla warfare, under Franco regime."
2 According to Meyers, "the guerrilla warfare of the Confederate soldier John Mosby may also have affected his portrayal of Pablo's band" (*FWBT-CH* 87).
3 It promised to pay him "$500 for each cabled story and $1,000 for each mailed story (up to 1,200 words), with no limit on the number of dispatches he could send" (Meyers, *H:B* 302).
4 Payne 227–29. Unlike Hemingway, who simply reported on the war, Orwell joined an "anarchistically inefficient" militia for the Party of Marxist Unification (POUM) in early 1937 and fought in an "absolute fearless" way in Catalonia. But on May 20, 1937, in the midst of a skirmish on the Huesca front, a sniper's bullet hit him in the throat. After recovering in a Barcelona hospital (though he could never thereafter speak in more than a whisper), he discovered that the POUM had been declared illegal and that police were arresting all of its members—whereupon he escaped to France on June 23 (Meyers, *Orwell* 148–67).
5 Besides linking Jordan to Hemingway himself, Meyers writes that the novelist "based aspects of Robert Jordan on T. E. Lawrence," since both "are foreign technical experts who assume command of a guerrilla group operating behind enemy lines" (Meyers, *HPW*). Elsewhere Meyers also states that Hemingway's model for Pilar was "Gertrude Stein, a forceful and dominant lesbian who first introduced Hemingway to Spain" (*FWBT-CH* 87). Hemingway's description of Pilar resembles his description of Stein in *A Movable Feast*, as Meyers notes, but to claim that "Maria is based on Martha Gellhorn" (*FWBT-CH* 86) is quite a stretch. Though Gellhorn became Hemingway's

lover in the spring of 1937, just as Maria becomes Jordan's lover in the novel, Maria has nothing in common with the journalist—and novelist—whose ambition and independence rankled Hemingway and finally led to their divorce.

6   Art Shields, "Ernest Hemingway's Travesty on Spain's Fight for Freedom," *Sunday Worker*, New York, December 8, 1940: 1, and Steve Nelson, 'Hemingway Evades Some Great, Historic Truths', *People's World*, February 12, 1941: 3, both qtd. Boyd 6–7. Boyd also notes that a recent study of Marty by a French historian has found no evidence to support the epithet that he was the "butcher of Albacete" (Boyd 16).

7   Not incidentally, this sentence illustrates the peculiarity of diction in this novel, which is often meant to evoke the Spanish language. To indicate that his Spanish characters are using the informal "tu" with each other, Hemingway often uses "thou" and "thy" instead of "you," but in many places such as this one, he slides between one form and the other. For more on Hemingway's amalgamation of English and Spanish in this novel, see Fenimore.

8   Tennyson's "Charge of the Light Brigade" was prompted by the slaughter of 670 men of the British Cavalry Light Brigade on October 25, 1854, when they rode against 25,000 Russian soldiers during the Battle of Balaclava in the Crimean War.

9   He is based on Mikhail Koltzov, whom Hemingway admired for his candor as well as for his faith in Hemingway's own work. In a letter to Edmund Wilson of November 8, 1952, Hemingway wrote of Koltsov: "He knew I was not a Communist and never would be one. But because he believed in me as a writer he tried to show me how everything was run so that I'd give a true account of it" (*SL* 789). Nevertheless, Karkov's explanations of what the Soviets did in Spain are plainly disingenuous, as shown below.

10 Elsewhere, General Golz uses precisely this formula to propitiate a man he loathes—"Yes, Comrade Marty, I see your point"—before disagreeing with him (*FWBT* 370).

11 In the original version of this passage, Karkov says simply, "In Paris." Commenting on "We say," which Hemingway added while correcting the galleys of his novel in August 1940, Ichiro Takayoshi writes, "It is likely that by the summer of 1940 Hemingway had second thoughts about the party explanation for Nin's disappearance" (Takayoshi 128n54).

3

Prague After Munich: The Plight of Refugees in Martha Gellhorn's *A Stricken Field*

In virtually all histories of the Munich Agreement, Czechoslovakia is the lonely victim of Nazi aggression sanctioned by the acquiescence of Britain and France, its faithless and feckless allies. Meeting with Hitler in Munich on September 30, 1938, the prime ministers of Britain and France agreed to let German forces immediately occupy the so-called Sudetenland of Czechoslovakia: a ring of largely mountainous terrain fortified against invasion and surrounding the western half of Czechoslovakia, including Prague, like a giant claw. Since these lands had been largely occupied by ethnic Germans, Hitler had demanded the right to "liberate" them.

Addressing the Nazi Party Congress in Nuremberg on September 12, 1938, he ranted at length that Czechoslovakia had brutally persecuted the three and half million ethnic Germans living within its borders, and that "if these tortured creatures can find neither justice nor help by themselves, then they will receive both from us."[1] This thinly veiled declaration of war sprang from a gross distortion of facts. And the most authoritative history of those facts—as well as of Czechoslovakia's response to Hitler's uncompromising demands—is probably the one composed by Igor Lukes, *Czechoslovakia between Stalin and Hitler* (1996). Along with Martha Gellhorn's eyewitness report on Czechoslovakia in the fall of 1938 ("Obituary"), Lukes is my chief source for what immediately follows.

Among many other things, Lukes refutes Hitler's charge that the Czechs were persecuting and even torturing ethnic Germans. Even though the Czechs were torturing no one and had *accepted* nearly all the demands made by Konrad Henlein, the Nazi leader of the Sudetens, the Czechs had stopped just short of granting them complete autonomy. Here was Hitler's pretext for a war of liberation.

The Sudetens themselves made up the front line of this war, for as Lukes has shown, Hitler's Nuremberg speech gave the Sudeten German Party (SdP) all the signal it needed to launch an open rebellion against the Czech government. Armed with rifles and machine guns and already trained in Germany by the Wehrmacht and SS, its 40,000 paramilitaries—the Sudetendeutches Freikorps—wasted no time in wreaking havoc. By the morning of September 13, barely twelve hours after Hitler gave his speech, they had murdered at least four Czech police officers and kidnapped twenty-six others who were never heard from again.

By September 15, however, after calmly retaking several German districts that had been captured by the Freikorps, the Czechs declared the SdP illegal and issued a warrant for the arrest of Henlein, who promptly fled to Germany even while urging his followers to stay on and fight "Czech tyranny."[2] But with Henlein's fellow officers fleeing in his wake, the remaining Sudetens had no heart for fighting. According to Lukes, in fact, "leading members of the former SdP [now disbanded] publicly welcomed the restoration of order by the [Czech] authorities and proposed to cooperate with the Prague government" (Lukes 214). Could anything have more dramatically demolished Hitler's endlessly repeated claim that the Sudetens were tortured and persecuted, and desperately yearned to join the Reich?

Unfortunately, good news all too often trails bad. By the late evening of September 13, after French premier Edouard Daladier learned of the just-begun Sudeten uprising, he told the British that Hitler's invasion of Czechoslovakia had to be checked by means of negotiation, and through the British ambassador in Paris he begged Chamberlain to conduct it (Lukes 215). Shortly before midnight, then, Chamberlain cabled Hitler, and by the morning of the 14th Hitler had agreed to a meeting on the next day: the first of three meetings culminating in the Munich Agreement of September 30.

One of the many ironies of this agreement is that up to the day it was signed by four nations *excluding* Czechoslovakia, the Czechs had been fully prepared to fight. Right up to September 30, they were led by a president—Edvard Beneš—who did everything he could to defy Hitler's threats.[3] In spite of them, in spite of the fecklessness of the British and the French, and in spite of Neville Chamberlain's infamous dismissal of the Czech crisis as "a quarrel in a far-away country between people of whom we know nothing" (Self 321), more than a million Czechs stood ready to fight on September 28. The nation had spent 400 million dollars to build the Czech Maginot Line, and though the Germans would easily cross the French original nine months later, a German officer who walked through the Czech defenses in early October—right after the Munich Agreement—reckoned with awe that the Germans "would have lost hundreds of thousands of men getting through here, and maybe we couldn't have done it" (qtd. Gellhorn, "Obituary" 13). The Czechs had also spent 750 million dollars arming themselves and voluntarily donated another 20 million to the National Defense Fund (Gellhorn, "Obituary" 13). At 9pm on September 23, just after Britain and France told the Czechs they would no longer advise against mobilization, a government call for troops was answered in just three hours by 800,000 men who promptly left their nighttime jobs—as waiters, taxi drivers, streetcar conductors, or whatever else they did—to serve the nation. According to Gellhorn, "[t]hey were a fine army and they knew it; they were trained and disciplined and brave and they knew what they were fighting for." They would fight "to defend the land they had won back after three hundred years; they were going to fight for the democracy that they had spent twenty years patiently building" ("Obituary" 13).

But in the early hours of September 30 in Munich, Britain and France agreed to let Hitler's forces invade Czechoslovakia on the very next day, and by late morning on the 30th, Edvard Beneš finally realized that he could expect no help from Russia, which had once equivocally offered it, let alone from France or Britain. At 11:45am, government ministers and the nation's top general—Ludvik Krejči—joined Beneš at the Castle for what turned out to be his final response to the Munich Agreement. If Czechoslovakia chose to reject the agreement and fight on its own, said the general, it would be massacred as well as stripped of its independence. Given this prospect, all he could do was "suggest the acceptance" of the agreement (qtd. Lukes 254). By nightfall on September 30, the Czech army began withdrawing from the fortresses of the Sudetenland, and starting at 2pm on the following day, German troops planted a forest of Swastikas in Czech territory.

In this familiar story of how Germany devoured the Sudetenland in the fall of 1938, Czechoslovakia is simply the victim of Nazi aggression: heroic in its struggle to resist, helpless and utterly blameless in accepting a brutal occupation. But a much more recent history of Czechoslovakia in this period reveals not only what the familiar story omits but also what Martha Gellhorn highlights in her novel, *A Stricken Field* (1940): Czechoslovakia betrayed refugees from Germany, Austria, and even the Sudetenland—its own former territory—especially if they were Jews.

The ranking expert on this topic now is a native of Prague named Michal Frankl, whose numerous publications on Czech history include *Unsafe Refuge: Czechoslovakia and its Refugees from Nazi Germany and Austria 1933–1938* (2012), co-authored with Kateřina Čapková.[4] More recently, he has distilled the argument of this book in an article that has been published in English ("Prejudiced Asylum"). Drawing on the autobiography of Richard A. Bermann, an Austrian journalist who had dared to criticize the Christian Social authoritarian "Ständestaat" of 1934–38, Frankl begins his article with a story that is almost novelistic in its specificity and pathos:

> Shortly after midnight, on 12 March 1938, an unusually full train arrived at the Czechoslovak border station of Břeclav.... For endangered anti-Nazi activists and many Jews, the Czechoslovak border seemed to be the best way (and one of the last escape routes as well) to avoid Nazi rule. Richard A. Bermann ... recorded his excitement on arrival in the "free" Czechoslovakia: "Finally, I was able to breathe again. I was, we were saved." He therefore found it hard to believe what followed after the train pulled into Břeclav: the refugees were all forced out of the train and after a couple of hours of tense waiting returned to what had, in the meantime, become Nazi-ruled Austria. In Bermann's narrative, the image of freedom, both personal and of Czechoslovakia, turned into the description of an ugly and prison-like waiting room at the railway station. Rather than a description of a real place, this text can be read as a symbolic expression of profound surprise and disillusionment with the "democratic" Czechoslovakia. Before being returned to Austria, Bermann managed to send a telegram to the Czechoslovak president Edvard Beneš appealing to the "humanity of Czechoslovak democracy". His message ended up—without any reaction or answer—in the archives of the Ministry of Interior. (Frankl 537–38)

While Lukes casts Beneš as the heroic embodiment of a nation betrayed, Frankl finds him personifying a policy that betrayed the nation's own history—by closing the door to refugees in 1938. As recently as 1934, Frankl explains, Czechoslovakia had granted refuge to approximately 2,000 Austrian activists seeking asylum. But in March of 1938, more than six months before the Munich Agreement, Richard Bermann and his fellow refugees had to grapple with what Frankl calls "the most important shift of the Czechoslovak policy towards refugees in the twentieth century" (Frankl 538). Czechoslovakia had once tolerated both minorities and refugees "in the midst of the increasingly authoritarian and violent Central Europe," and "in the 1930s it was also the only [East-Central European country] to be represented with the High Commissioner for Refugees (Jewish and Other) Coming from Germany" (Frankl 539–40). Yet once refugees from Nazi Germany started coming to Czechoslovakia, Frankl explains,

> the Ministry of Interior jealously defended its freedom of action and resisted any attempts to put forward a clear definition of a refugee or a description of the rights of such a person. For this reason, Czechoslovakia never ratified the 1936 provisional convention on German refugees, although its diplomats took an active part in all preceding negotiations. (Frankl 543)

In Frankl's account of Czech refugee policy in the 1930s, several points indicate just how exclusionary as well as antisemitic it became. First, while Czechoslovakia had admitted some 25,000 Russian refugees by the mid-1920s, the total number of German refugees in the mid-1930s—including illegal immigrants—never reached 4,000 (Frankl 544–45). Second, the Czechs turned "a blind eye" to the activity of Gestapo agents who not only aimed to stifle the political activity of such refugees but sometimes blackmailed, abducted, and even assassinated them (Frankl 546). Third, the Czech authorities themselves sought to suppress refugee activism in 1937 and thereby "appease the Nazi state" by devising a plan to confine German refugees to "several poor and isolated districts in the interior of the country" (Frankl 547). Though international protests blocked this move, the Czech authorities had already begun to close the door on Jewish immigrants, and as Frankl explains, the German Annexation (Anschluss) of Austria in March of 1938 prompted the Czechs to shut it:

> the anti-Jewish turn in Czechoslovak refugee policy culminated in 1938 in the closure, without any public discussion, of the border to Jewish refugees from Romania, Austria, and—after the Munich Agreement—from the Sudetenland. (Frankl 549)

But Jews were not the only ones to suffer. In early October 1938, Czech authorities dispatched some 20,000 Sudeten refugees back to their newly occupied homelands. "Driven into the trains at the point of the bayonet," we are told, they now faced "deadly peril under the Nazis" (Warriner 210; London 149). On October 11, 1938, *The New York Times* reported that the Czechs were generally unwilling "to accept any Germans or Jews, whatever their politics and however loyally they may have stood shoulder to shoulder with the Czechs in defense of the republic and democracy in the exposed Sudeten frontier areas." Besides feeling "pressure from Germany, which is anxious to lay its hand on these refugees," the Czechs did not wish "to share what is left of their homeland with those who are not of Czech descent" (Gedye).

To be fair, the Czechs felt overwhelmed. According to Doreen Warriner, who spent the winter of 1938–39 working for the British Committee for Refugees from Czechoslovakia (BCRC), there remained in the country at the end of October something like 100,000 Sudeten refugees, including 90,000 Czechs and 10,000 Sudeten Germans. "Most of the Czechs," she writes, "were quartered on the peasants, and the Sudeten Germans were put into camps—that is, schools, castles or village halls" (Warriner 214).

By January of 1939, when a British MP named Eleanor Rathbone visited Prague, she concluded that the Czech government was "absolutely powerless" to protect any anti-Nazi refugees sought by Hitler (Warriner 220). Yet the government had no wish to protect Jews. "Before and after the Munich Agreement," Frankl writes, "most of the approximately 28,000 Jews living [in the Sudetenland] escaped or were expelled into the interior of the country." But even though Germany and Czechoslovakia had officially agreed that Sudeten Jews who were not "of German nationality" could "opt for Czechoslovak citizenship," they were denied that option: blocked by Czech police or stuck for days between Czech and German border posts (Frankl 549–50). Also, even though British officials pressed the Czechs to accept Sudeten Jews, the Czechs did not want even "Jews of Czech nationality" (London 145).

The Munich Agreement intensified this animus. "The national humiliation" of the agreement, Frankl writes, "triggered a wave of antisemitism and within a few days most of the Czech press participated in the antisemitic campaign" (Frankl 550). In January 1939, furthermore, the Czech government acted "to strip a significant proportion of Czechoslovak Jews of their citizenship" and thus turn them "into real refugees," which meant they would have to "leave Czechoslovakia within six months" (Frankl 551). Worst of all was the plight of Sudeten Jews who had "fled into post-Munich Czechoslovakia." Systematically denied the citizenship they were entitled to claim, they became stateless "with only a limited possibility to emigrate," and "[l]arge numbers of them were later deported to ghettos and concentration camps" (Frankl 551)—presumably with the acquiescence of the Czechs.

Measured against the familiar story that makes Czechoslovakia simply an innocent victim of the Munich Agreement, this grim history of Czech refugee policy in the 1930s is radically—even shockingly—revisionist. But it is largely confirmed by *A Stricken Field*, the novel Martha Gellhorn wrote after spending several weeks in and around Prague in the fall of 1938. Having made her name by reporting on the Spanish Civil War for *Collier's*, a weekly magazine whose circulation ran well into the millions, she investigated the plight of refugees in Czechoslovakia for an article—"Obituary of a Democracy"—that was published by the same magazine on December 10, 1938.

Like Hemingway, Gellhorn is sometimes inaccurate—or at the very least incomplete—in her reporting.[5] Read in light of Frankl's history, the most startling thing about her article is that it never mentions a single Jew, and the only Jews who appear in her novel are a doctor and his wife whose plight is briefly described near the end of it. Nevertheless, the novel communicates its own kind of truth. Besides dramatizing the plight of individual refugees by telling their particular stories, it swerves from historical narrative by immersing the author herself in their lives. Just as Hemingway makes us see the Spanish Civil War through the eyes of an American volunteer who to some extent speaks for the novelist himself, Gellhorn makes us see refugees through the eyes of an American reporter fictionally based on herself. And just as Hemingway's Robert Jordan is a central actor in *For Whom the Bell Tolls*,

Gellhorn's reporter—Mary Douglas—is a highly active participant in the story she narrates.

Like Hemingway's novel, *A Stricken Field* springs from extensive experience of its setting. Gellhorn first visited Prague when she was twenty-nine, in early June of 1938, shortly after the Prague government had partially mobilized the Czech army in response to reports of German military activity along the Czech border.[6] Though no attack occurred at that time, Gellhorn knew that war was coming and deplored the passivity of the Anglo-French response to Hitler's belligerence. After reporting from Paris and London on the disheartening run-up to their capitulation in Munich, she returned to Prague in early October to see just how the Nazis were killing a democracy for which she wrote her "Obituary."

But in *A Stricken Field*, a novel closely based on what she witnessed right after the occupation began, the Czech authorities in Prague routinely kill the hopes of refugees. "[E]ven those who were always loyal to the Czech republic," says one of Gellhorn's characters, "are driven back to the towns they escaped from," where they may well have fought alongside Czech police against the Sudeten Nazis—forerunners of the occupation. These returning refugees, therefore, may be "killed for Treason to the Third Reich" (*StF* 70). Thus speaks Rita, a Communist of about thirty-three who was jailed by the Nazis in 1933 and made to see her brother beaten to death because he would not talk about his comrades. Released after three years and given just two days to leave Germany, she fled to Prague, where now—in the fall of 1938—she lives in hiding while doing all she can for other refugees.

A Stricken Field thus swerves from historical narrative by individuating ordinary figures like Rita as well as by creating a narrator who speaks in many ways for Gellhorn herself. Though the novelistic story of Richard Bermann raises the curtain of Frankl's argument, he promptly proceeds to generalize about groups of refugees rather than dramatizing individual characters, let alone fictionalizing himself, as Gellhorn fictionalizes herself. Besides differing in this generic way from Frankl's history of refugees in Czechoslovakia, Gellhorn's novel differs in revealing ways from her own reporting. Like typical histories of what the Munich Agreement did to Czechoslovakia, Gellhorn's "Obituary" portrays both Czechoslovakia *and* the refugees who have fled to it as essentially the victims of Nazi aggression. The refugees, she writes, were "hundreds of thousands of Sudeten Germans" who had never belonged to the party of Konrad Henlein, Nazi leader of the Sudeten Germans and now ruler of the Nazi-occupied Sudetenland. These desperate people "were either in concentration camps or fleeing toward a brief uncertain safety in the remnant of Czechoslovakia" ("Obituary" 33). Their safety was brief and uncertain because that "remnant" had been crippled. Shorn of its encircling fortifications, which had now become the jaws of the Nazi occupation, Czechoslovakia had been pushed back to its "third line" frontier: nothing but a double row of barbed wire zig-zagging "across open indefensible country" ("Obituary" 12).

While occupying only part of Czechoslovakia, then, the Germans menaced the rest, including Prague, which now quite literally displayed what Churchill had predicted would happen right after the Munich Agreement: "Silent, mournful, abandoned, broken, Czechoslovakia recedes into the darkness" ("The Munich Agreement"). In the fall of 1938, the darkness of Prague was plainly visible to the eyes of Martha Gellhorn.

The cathedral spires, the opera house, and Hradsin Palace, she reported, no longer glowed at night "because the main electric power station [was] now in German territory" ("Obituary" 32). Gripped by fear as well as darkness, the people of Prague

> were afraid to talk in restaurants because who knew what kind of person was listening at the next table? Their mail was censored, and their newspapers. They could not take their money from the bank; they could not leave the country without permission. ("Obituary" 33)

The refugees were still more vulnerable. The Czech government could protect neither the Germans who had fled the Sudetenland nor the Austrian and German exiles who had mostly escaped from prison or concentration camps to seek safety in Czechoslovakia. "Even Beneš was not safe," wrote Gellhorn. "And besides, this small mutilated state cannot even temporarily house and feed and clothe hundreds of thousands of refugees. The economy of Czechoslovakia is as shattered as its military defenses" ("Obituary" 33).

Besides developing this point with the aid of ugly statistics furnished by an unnamed government official, Gellhorn also describes—as if rehearsing for her novel—individual refugees suddenly bereft of all they owned, of their families, or both. In the market town of Louny, near the new frontier and about thirty-six miles northwest of Prague, she met a man from the now occupied town of Chomutov, who told Gellhorn that he had lost his wife and their two children. Having fled to Louny with them after fighting *with* "the Czech gendarmes against the Henleinists when they started to terrorize our town," he and his family and nearly 1,200 others had been returned by train to Chomutov, where they were promptly imprisoned by the Henleinists. He got his wife and children transferred to another town by falsely claiming that they lived there, and having escaped by himself, he returned on foot to Louny. But he had lost his whole family. "I know nothing of my wife," he said. "And who will find our families for us?" ("Obituary" 28).

This poignant story prompts one question above all: who sent this family *back* from Louny to the brutally occupied territory they had just fled? The escapee never specifies, and Gellhorn does not say. But we know they were sent back from a town not yet occupied. Could this have happened without the authority or at least complicity of Czech officials?[7] It is hard to say for certain, since even the unoccupied "remnant" of Czechoslovakia had to live within the grip of Nazi power, and long before Prague was formally occupied on March 15, Beneš himself was forced to resign on October 5.[8] But as already noted, the crippled state of Czechoslovakia could not "even temporarily" absorb the flood of refugees who poured into it.[9] So the Czechs themselves helped to drive them back by means of a policy that Frankl explains at length and that plays a leading part in *A Stricken Field*.

Around the central figure of Mary Douglas—Gellhorn's alter ego—the novel deploys two sets of characters. One is the small group of writers and reporters with whom Mary regularly drinks, dines, and trades stories such as the one about workers living in the suburbs of Pilsen who must now cross Germany to work in the Skoda factory of Pilsen—even though it remains unoccupied (*StF* 20). Yet bits of information like this, tossed out over drinks with well-fed fellow expatriates, lead Mary first to wonder "how many coal mines had the Nazis taken" and then to recall the sight of Czech workers driven out of factories that had been seized by the Germans:

> you would see them on the roads, with bulging sacks over their shoulders, walking from place to place, looking for jobs that had disappeared forever behind an unreasonable line of barbed wire: the expanding Nazi frontier. (*StF* 21)

Far more desperate than these displaced workers, however, are the second set of characters ranged around Mary: the refugees from the Sudetenland and from Germany itself who are hiding in Prague after being granted just two days to return to what is now Nazi territory.[10] One of them is a little man that Mary and a fellow journalist named Tom Lambert accidentally knock down one Sunday morning as they drive through the city en route to Beneš's villa. The accident thus implicates Mary and Tom in the story she aims to report. By making the journalists themselves partly responsible for what happens to the victim of Tom's inept driving, the episode further exemplifies the difference between reporting (including Gellhorn's own) and fiction.

Earlier, when Mary tells another journalist sitting at a restaurant that she has seen Rita on the street, the novelist sitting with them asks, "Who's Rita?" and thus prompts Mary to wonder how the novelist might use her. He was, Mary perceives,

> hearing a name that meant a face, a story, something you could store up and later alter in your imagination until it had a shape. You could almost see him reaching and groping for a minor character, with that nervousness and groping of someone who would have to pull out of his brain, year after year, people and situations, whether he was able or not. (*StF* 26)

The first part of this passage might well describe how Gellhorn herself stored up the faces she saw and the presumably true stories she heard as a journalist and then re-shaped into fiction.[11] Yet for Mary, Rita is far more than an incidental figure whose "story" is remembered just well enough to furnish material for a "minor character" in a novel. In Gellhorn's novel, Rita is a major character whose fervent commitment to her fellow refugees leads Mary into not just writing about them but also taking up their cause. Ironically enough, Gellhorn later wrote that she was secretly ashamed to have "used two of my own small acts in that tragedy as part of the story"—her fictional story of the refugees' plight (Afterword 314). Yet she could hardly have avoided doing so, for as much as anything else, her novel shows how a journalist can be driven to participate in the "story" she tells, can be drawn right into it just as Mary and Tom—a pair of journalists—are irresistibly drawn into the life of the man whom their car accidentally hits.

The accident drives all three of them into the arms of the Czech police. Though the man is quickly helped to his feet and has evidently suffered only a short scratch across his forehead, Tom shoves him into the back seat of the car and heads to the hospital. But even as the obviously frightened man insists in German that his injury "is nothing" and tries to get out of the car, "the long pointed notes" of a police whistle bring tears to his eyes. Since he is just the innocent victim of Tom's careless driving, Mary cannot understand what he fears, or why he should be so eager to get away without any treatment for his wound or any compensation from them. Yet when Tom and Mary and the struck man reach the hospital with the policemen, who has joined them in the car, the officer's words—translated by a stout young woman into "stiff English"—sound ominous. "The wounded man," it seems,

> must follow the police. He will become treated. Then all must go again with the
> police to the police house, where must be given names and a statement. (*StF* 35)

Tom cannot understand why this prospect should mean any trouble for their victim—especially since Mary assures Tom that "nothing will happen to us" (*StF* 36). Though Tom has no driver's license, Mary offers to claim that she was driving the car on her international license, and both are protected by their well-respected American passports as well as by their status as journalists.

No such status shields the man they struck down. So instead of asking Tom and Mary for money at the police station, where he sits "as far from the policeman as possible," he can only sigh, "*Lieber Gott, Lieber Gott*" (Dear God, Dear God) (*StF* 36). When finally asked for his papers, he pretends to fumble for them before admitting that he is a democrat from Romberg in the Sudetenland, which means—as the policeman infers—that he must be a refugee. As such, he is told, he must return to the Sudetenland in two days (again that frighteningly short deadline) after registering with the Prague police. But even though he is sixty-two and has always owned a house in Romberg, where he was respectfully called "*Herr Brecht*," and even though he is now homeless in Prague, where he must sleep in the street, he would never return to Romberg, "where the people had gone mad, and hunted each other like animals" (*StF* 41).

Now the novel enters his stricken mind. While a journalist could merely paraphrase his spoken words, this journalist-turned-novelist imagines what he remembers about the ghastly metamorphosis of his hometown just before he left it:

> There was the butcher from the Hermannstrasse whom he had known all his life,
> and Plauen who ran a restaurant and Gutberg, the gymnastics professor at the high
> school, and he had seen them with crazy faces going through the streets, armed,
> walking as men could not walk but only as terrible hungry animals moved, going
> through their own streets in their own town after other people, his friends (but
> their friends too surely), to beat and torture and kill. (*StF* 42)

It is to this hideous world that the little man knocked down by the journalists must now return, and his desperation is nowhere more evident than in his frantic search for the non-existent papers that might save him. Ordered by the policeman to leave Prague in just two days unless he can produce such papers, he scours his pockets, "tearing at them, his back twisting and bending to find something that did not exist" (*StF* 40) and he also comes up empty-handed from his search for a non-existent train ticket to show Mary (*StF* 44).

A remarkably similar scene occurs in the opening pages of Olivia Manning's *The Great Fortune*, a novel based on her sojourn in Bucharest, Romania from September 1939 to June of 1940. On a train bound for Bucharest, Manning's protagonist Harriet Smith and her husband Guy notice the desperation of a German refugee. Asked for his ticket by the train conductor, he

> rose and felt in an inner pocket of his greatcoat that hung beside him. His hand
> lingered, he caught his breath: he withdrew his hand and looked in an outer pocket,
> then another and another. He began pulling things out of the pockets of the jacket
> he was wearing, then out of his trouser pockets. His breath came and went violently.
> He returned to the greatcoat and began his search all over again. (*GF* 9–10)

Dismayed by the behavior of this man whose "face had become ashen, his cheeks fallen like the cheeks of a very old man," Guy asks him what he has lost, and the man answers, "Everything. . . . My pocket-book, my passport, my money, my identity card . . . My visa, my visa!" (*GF* 10). We have no way of knowing whether he just now discovered his loss or was merely pretending to search for what he knew did not exist. Either way, he has been stripped of all he once owned, even his identity.

Like him, Gellhorn's refugee scours his pockets for a train ticket to Zurich that does not exist and could not get him there even if it did. And just as Guy and Harriet can offer nothing but some money to the refugee on the train, all that Mary can do for the man knocked down by Tom's driving is to give him—via Tom—the little over three hundred kronen she has with her: about $400 in present-day US currency.[12] After finally accepting the money from Tom, we are told, "the little man came to [Mary] and took off his hat and thanked her for her kindness to him and set off down the street" (*StF* 45). We are asked to imagine what Mary feels. Though Tom simply relishes their own good luck and Mary accepts his proposal that they call off their trip and go to the movies, the episode clearly leaves her with a residue of pain and guilt.[13]

She can assuage it only by doing whatever she can for other refugees, such as the group she meets in the next chapter: adolescents living on mattresses in a third-floor apartment, feeding on watery soup and dry bread and dreaming of flight to any land beyond the reach of the Nazis—such as Nicaragua, a tiny yellow dot that one of them finds in a colored map of the world. Their dreams seem hardly more fanciful than Mary's chances of doing anything effective for refugees. When Rita arrives (a little late) at this place, which has been appointed for their meeting, she tells Mary that she and her fellow journalists "must write about this . . . quickly, to make an opinion in your countries." Yet while Mary says, "All right," she does so

> without enthusiasm. After they had public opinion all properly shaped, what good
> did it do? It was immensely easy to make people hate but it was almost impossible
> to make them help. (*StF* 56)

The sense of futility conveyed by that sentence permeates the rest of the novel. Obviously, Mary feels that her moral as well as professional duty is to meet refugees where they live so as to write about them, as Rita urges. Yet having already played her inadvertent part in the expulsion of one refugee, she works almost hopelessly on behalf of the others. As a woman with a passport and a job, we are told, "[s]he only felt she was lucky and lucky and luckier than anybody could be, and you had to pay back for that" (*StF* 57). So the next morning, she and Rita ride off by taxi to the far-off suburbs of Prague in order to visit two houses.

At the first one, in the broken-windowed taproom of what seems to be an abandoned inn off a muddy, unpaved road, they find a group of seventy-two silent, huddled, immobile people who turn out to be the remains of what was originally 120. As Rita explains to Mary, they are all ethnic Germans doomed to be "sent back to Hitler" even though they are Czech citizens (*StF* 70). From the corner of the room a man mournfully reports that their wives and children have been taken "we do not know where and we will never see them again" (*StF* 69). A number of the men, however, have been told that their wives are "back home . . . wherever [the men] came from," in what is now occupied territory, and even though the men know that "home" will be a death trap, they return in hopes of saving their wives (*StF* 69). One such man is now known to be dead, and the seventy-two people left behind in this house, Mary thinks, are effectively "buried alive": sleeping on straw, feeding on scraps of donated food, knowing nothing of what may lie ahead for them (*StF* 71). Just before Mary and Rita leave, an angry tall man says to himself, "They will not get me" (*StF* 72), draws a knife from his pocket, opens the blade, and lays it against his wrist.

In the sea of despair that seems to surround the refugees, Mary finds two small islands of joy and hope. One is the sound of orphans singing "with joyful soaring voices" in the candlelit room of a bleak "hotel" housing German refugees of all ages (*StF* 80, 74). The other is the evening she spends over dinner in the small, spare, fourth-floor apartment of Rita and her husband Peter, who runs a Communist party weekly newspaper. Their mutual devotion, Mary sees, is more than equal to their common fear of being found out. Yet once Mary leaves to return to her hotel, Peter broods by himself. He does not tell Rita that two plain-clothed strangers—Gestapo agents—came to his newspaper office to say with infuriating smiles that "It will be a privilege to see you in Germany again" (*StF* 92). He knows too that he and Rita have just "four more days to disappear" (*StF* 94), that no one—let alone any free nation—will fight for them, and that they must somehow find a way to fight for themselves. Suddenly Rita screams in her sleep. Caught up in a nightmare of desperate flight as the streets of Prague turn into the streets of Berlin, she ends up in a room where uniformed men stand laughing at her. Back in the waking world, Peter does what he can to comfort her. But in telling her that they will not be caught before they leave for France, he knows that he is lying "with all his heart" (*StF* 97). He has to lie because he knows they are doomed to die.

The road to death leads through separation, dispersal, and isolation. Without waking Rita, Peter quietly leaves at 5am and takes a highly circuitous route to his newspaper office in order to elude followers. Rising later, Rita goes to the office of the Communist *Solidaritat*, but after a harrowing day spent with a crowd of refugees, she finds no one to comfort her. The windows of Peter's office are dark; Mary Douglas is not at her hotel; and when Rita returns to her apartment, it is ominously empty. As she vainly waits for Peter's return, she slowly sinks into a deep well of loneliness. Only in sleep can she smile, "dreaming that her head was on Peter's shoulder" (*StF* 154).

On that same night, Mary jettisons her duties as a journalist in order to do something for the refugees. Having learned that an Englishman named Lord Balham, Commissioner for Refugees of the Society of Nations, is briefly visiting Prague, she goes to the elegant hotel where—as she learns from other journalists—he has just announced at a press conference that he is delighted to meet the journalists and will return to London at noon the following day. This particular episode is historically plausible, since—according to Frankl, as already noted—"Czechoslovakia was the only [East-Central European country] to be represented with the High Commissioner for Refugees (Jewish and Other) Coming from Germany" (Frankl 540). In Gellhorn's novel, however, the Commissioner's bland announcement offers nothing for refugees. Since the countries he represents will take none of the refugees he is supposed to help, he knows that "he [has] no power" (*StF* 165)—that he can do nothing for them, that he is totally helpless against cruelty and corruption. But Mary decides to approach him. Seeking neither an interview nor a news story, she asks him if he will meet the Czech prime minister in the morning, so as to request a two week suspension of the expulsion order that would make refugees leave the country at once.

By now, the novel itself has shown us that neither the prime minister nor anyone else in the Czech government can or will do anything for the refugees. But stirred by Mary's youthful excitement as well as by his own desire to *look* as if he is doing something for the refugees, Balham agrees to see the PM if Mary will make the appointment. By posing on the telephone as Balham's secretary, she succeeds in doing so. Intoxicated by her success, she not only imagines that Rita and all the other refugees will be safe, but also offers to enlist the support of a French general named Labonne, who had resigned as head of the French Military Mission when France failed to honor its pledges to Czechoslovakia. Labonne is hardly sanguine about Mary's plan. Nevertheless, dangling Mary on a thread of hope, he agrees to meet the prime minister along with Lord Balham at 10am the next day.

The next day yields only crushing disappointment for Mary and Rita alike. At four in the morning, Rita is awakened by the return of Peter, as if her fitful dreams had suddenly come true. But after a brief spasm of lovemaking, he tells her that he must leave at once without her and assures her that Mary "will arrange somehow for you to go to Paris" (*StF* 192). A few hours later, however, just before Lord Balham leaves Prague, he and Labonne tell Mary that the PM would not even listen to their plea for the refugees.[14] Though Mary tells herself that she can "get [Rita] out," all she can really do is book a seat for herself on the next day's noon flight to Paris (*StF* 198–99). She can do almost nothing for anyone else. She cannot furnish passports and money for the radio technician who comes to her hotel room on behalf of himself and ten others, and all she can do for a Jewish doctor and his wife is to call a doctor who knows them when she gets to Paris.

Meanwhile, Rita learns that Peter has been arrested and dragged bleeding into 4 Valdstyn Street, the same house that earlier swallowed up another refugee. Though she manages to penetrate the basement of this house, all she gets for doing so is to hear from above the voices of Gestapo interrogators torturing Peter for his stubborn refusal to talk.[15] After he dies in the middle of the night, she makes her way to what is presumably the Vltava River, where she sits on a bench until she is found by a policeman who "must [take her] now to the station" and report her as a refugee "without papers" (*StF* 276). Doomed at best to a concentration camp, she is now bereft of both freedom and hope.

In the final chapter, Mary herself straddles the gap between her life as a journalist perpetually in motion and her passionate desire to do something for Czech refugees beyond simply reporting on their plight. Sitting in her hotel room just a few hours before her plane will leave for Paris, she is still trying in vain to track down Rita when she is called upon by another woman, who wants her to smuggle out a wad of typed reports: eyewitness accounts in German of what the Henleinists and the Gestapo have done to their victims. The testimonies set down in these papers differ radically from professional journalism, which must sound detached to be credible. Yet for Mary, the papers signify something invincible by the simple act of telling the truth:

> They have been defeated, Mary Douglas thought, and they will not accept defeat. This one comes alone with a sheaf of papers, and through her the others refuse defeat also. They are lost and buried, and they will not give up: each one has faith enough still to believe in the power of two or three typewritten pages that tell the truth. (*StF* 285)

Mary knows that the life of an American journalist is privileged. After spending just one week in Czechoslovakia, she is doing something impossible for any of the refugees she has met, including of course Rita: flying off to Paris, capital of a nation still free.[16] For this very reason, she feels bound to do something for those she cannot liberate, for the doomed refugees of Czechoslovakia. Though she tells her visitor that she "get[s] nervous about smuggling a pack of cigarettes," and though she jokes about pretending to be pregnant with the bundle, she finally understands what the bundle means: "proof that everyone is not beaten yet" (*StF* 285). No piece of journalism could match the power of such proof.

Mary knows she is taking a chance. Having stuffed the wad of papers in her square calfskin bag "beneath her cigarettes, powder, coin purse and notebook" (*StF* 296), she has no trouble opening her suitcase and typewriter for the customs inspector at the airport, but after he lets her pass she is alarmed to hear him call her name. For just a moment, she feels something like the fear that has constantly gripped the refugees hiding in Prague. But the fear evaporates as soon as she learns that the inspector simply wants to practice his English, to have "a nice talk with the American girl" (*StF* 298). Settling into her seat as the plane takes off, she finally admits to herself that she will never again see any of the refugees, but insists she will remember both Rita and Peter, wherever they "are . . . now" (*StF* 301).

A Stricken Field is the work of a journalist who discovered, paradoxically, that fiction alone could re-create the truth of what she had seen in Czechoslovakia, especially Prague, in the weeks immediately after the Nazis occupied the Sudetenland. The fictional journalist at the center of the novel makes a comparable discovery. Rather than simply reporting on the fear and misery she has seen, Mary Douglas must play some part in alleviating it, or at least in making sure it is not forgotten. Since her final act is to smuggle out of Czechoslovakia a sheaf of reports on the viciousness of the

Gestapo and the Henleinists, the ending of the novel seems to imply that what she has to offer to the West is simply more evidence of Nazi aggression. But the novel itself imaginatively confirms what Frankl historically documents: even in a Prague not yet occupied by the Nazis, the Czechs connived at the tactics of the Gestapo, shattered the hopes of refugees without papers, and—at the highest levels—refused to help them. While Gellhorn's novel plainly shows how the field of Czechoslovakia was stricken, it also shows how the Czechs struck back: not at their enemies, but at the most innocent and vulnerable among them.

Notes

1   In spite of Hitler's charge, the Sudeten Germans of Czechoslovakia had their own political party—a branch of the Nazi party—led by Konrad Henlein. In the Carlsbad Decrees, issued on April 24, the SdP demanded complete autonomy for the Sudetenland and freedom to profess Nazi ideology. Told by Hitler to make demands upon the Czech government that it could not accept, Henlein demanded autonomy for the Germans living there (Wikipedia). Because the Czech government declined (even while offering them more minority rights), Hitler charged that it was brutally persecuting them.

2   Lukes 212–13. Remarkably enough, the process of suppressing this armed rebellion took the lives of just eleven Sudeten Germans. Contradicting Hitler's incessant claims of their brutality, the Czech authorities exercised remarkable restraint.

3   According to Lukes, Beneš was totally in charge: "By the spring of 1938, the Czechoslovak parliament, the prime minister, and the cabinet had been pushed aside by Beneš. During the dramatic summer months he was—for better or worse—the sole decision-maker in the country" (Lukes 15).

4   Frankl works at the Masaryk Institute and Archives of the Czech Academy of Sciences in Prague. His book is in Czech and German (I have translated the German title), but the article from which I quote below was published in English.

5   For instance, having left Czechoslovakia after just a few weeks in the fall of 1938, she bases her novel on what she saw well before the spring of 1939, when the BCRC managed to arrange the departure and safe resettlement of about 250 Sudeten refugee families and 2,459 anti-Nazi Sudetens (Warriner 223).

6   Lukes 699. The partial mobilization was ordered on May 10. In response to longstanding debates over which side provoked the so-called "May crisis" of 1939, Lukes argues that Prague mobilized the Czech army because the Second Bureau of the army's general staff mistakenly thought a German attack was imminent (Lukes 700).

7   Michal Frankl informs me that since "a popular vote was planned" in occupied areas right after the Munich Agreement," the Czech authorities "wanted to keep anti-Nazi voters there" (email of April 2, 2022). But of course there was no popular vote—just prison for those sent back.

8   In the final paragraphs of her article, Gellhorn describes Beneš's departure on October 22, 1938. After driving with his wife to the town of Lany, twenty-six miles west of Prague, he knelt at the grave of Tomáš Masaryk, first president of Czechoslovakia (1918–1935), who died in 1937. "Perhaps," Gellhorn concludes, he "prayed in mourning for the democracy of all Europe" ("Obituary" 36).

9   In the novel, Rita says she does not think the expulsions are "the fault of the Czech government: I think they do this because they are ordered from Berlin and because they have no money to take care of thousands of homeless people" (*StF* 55).

10   At one point a German refugee is told that according to "the present rule," all refugees may stay in Prague for just "a pair of days" before "return[ing] to their own communities" after registering "with the Prague police" (*StF* 41). "A pair of days" may be Gellhorn's invention, since—as noted above—even Czech Jews stripped of their citizenship in January 1939 and thus turned into "real refugees" were given six months to leave the country.

11   The ambiguity of the word "story" blurs the line between reportage and fiction. In the world of journalists, the word "story" means "factual narrative." Yet however factual it may be, a good story about any actual person or event is always a *shaped* narrative, as Robert Darnton has shown.

12   See https://www.historicalstatistics.org/Currencyconverter.html

13   In the next chapter we learn that she thought of the refugee that night, that she woke "feeling it was all [her] fault, they would put him on the train and it was [her] fault" (*StF* 56).

14   In fact the PM (Syrový) responded just this way to Neill Malcolm, the League of Nations High Commissioner for Refugees. When Malcolm met the prime minister soon after reaching Prague on October 11, 1938, Syrový "refused his plea for a more benign policy towards German and Jewish refugees" (Michal Frankl, email to author of April 6, 2022).

15   It is hard to judge just how historically accurate this episode may be. On March 14, 1939, just before the Germans occupied all of Czechoslovakia, the Gestapo arrested a Canadian refugee worker named Beatrice Wellington, interrogated her for six hours, and accused her of illegal activities. But even though she defiantly stated, "Everything that you do is illegal," and refused to say anything about refugees, she was released unharmed (Warriner 237).

16   Before leaving the hotel she scratches a note telling Rita how to get visas for herself and Peter and promising to meet them at Paris's Bourget Airport, but she knows this effort is "too late" (*StF* 289).

4

Jan Karski, Patrick Hamilton, and W. H. Auden: Variations on September 1, 1939

On September 11, 2001, a series of suicidal attacks on the World Trade Center in New York and the Pentagon in Washington ignited what soon became an endless as well as worldwide war against terrorism. Likewise, the date that marked the outbreak of World War II reverberated far beyond its initial flashpoint. When Germany attacked Poland, the news soon traveled to London, where Neville Chamberlain promptly declared war on Germany, and across the Atlantic to New York, more than 4,000 miles from Poland, where it prompted a young English poet named W. H. Auden to write a poem called simply "September 1, 1939." I will shortly examine both the poem and a novel about life in England during the run-up to Chamberlain's declaration. But I wish first to consider an eyewitness report on what happened to Poland on September 1, supplemented by historical sources including what is probably the most authoritative history we have of Poland in the Second World War: Halik Kochanski's *The Eagle Unbowed* (2012).

I. Jan Karski and the Invasion of Poland

The eyewitness report comes from Jan Karski (born Jan Kozielewski), who was twenty-five years old on the day of the invasion and serving as a Lieutenant in the Polish Cavalry at an army camp near the factory town of Oświęcim, about forty miles west of Krakow in southwest Poland. Exactly one week earlier, he and thousands of other Polish reservists had been secretly mobilized: given just two hours to pack up and join their units for deployment against what seemed to be an imminent invasion of German troops. Posted to the 5th Regiment of Mounted Artillery, an elite unit serving in Poland's first line of defense, Jan was a superlative specimen of Polish manhood—a natural aristocrat destined to excel. After primary and secondary schooling by Jesuits, who reinforced the devout Catholicism that he had already imbibed from his mother, he studied law and diplomacy at Jan Kazimierz University in the eastern Polish city of Lwów, where he won a speech-making contest in his final year. He then became the very model of a citizen soldier. After graduating first in his class of cadet Horse Artillery officers in 1936, he went on to gain a First in Grand Diplomatic Practice and then—as of January 1, 1939—land a job that would normally have gone to someone much more experienced: administrative assistant to the Director of Personnel at the Polish Foreign Ministry.

When the mobilization order reached him at 5am on August 24, Jan was staying at the Warsaw apartment of his older brother Marian, and he was expected to reach the train station by 7am. But before doing so he went to see his boss at the Foreign Ministry, Tomir Drymmer. When Jan apologized for the suddenness of his departure, Drymmer told him: "You will be back here in a couple of weeks. All this stuff with Hitler will take care of itself. We just need to show him that we are not Czechs."[1] Jan thought likewise. Whatever the Czechs might have done if they had not been sold out at Munich, Jan knew that the Poles were determined to fight—just as an American journalist had reported in the *New York Times*.[2] Jan also knew that Poland's armed forces were widely admired for their discipline and gallantry, that its leaders—including foreign minister Józef Beck, who had served in Jan's own regiment—were confident of winning, and that Britain and France had guaranteed their support. But he should also have known that Poland was not only surrounded on three sides by the Wehrmacht but also handicapped by a border more than 1,750 miles long, with no natural defense lines (Olson and Cloud 51). Furthermore, whether or not these disquieting facts ever crossed his mind, there were many things that neither Jan nor anyone else in Poland knew about—or seriously thought about—in weighing its chances against a German attack.

First of all, in spite of the commitments they had made to Poland in May, the French had no intention of attacking Germany (with one slight exception) either on the ground or from the air.[3] Nor did the British. Though Chamberlain had promised British support back in March, he had been told by his own Chiefs of Staff that "Britain could offer no practicable help to Poland in the event of a German attack" (Kochanski 49–50). Compounding this defection, neither France nor Britain delivered any planes to Poland before the war even though the Polish government had bought 160 fighters from France and 100 Fairey Battle light bombers from Britain (Kochanski 53). Secondly, Poland's own forces were dwarfed by Germany's. On September 1, 1939, Poland had about a million men under arms with another million in reserve, and in the year leading up to September 1939, it had spent almost half its national budget on its armed forces—over a billion zloty. But that was about one-*tenth* of what Germany had spent on its air force alone, and one-fiftieth of its defense spending as a whole. Furthermore, Poland's thirty-seven infantry divisions were just over a third of Germany's one hundred (Kochanski 53, 55).

Besides this gigantic gap in military spending and strength, Poland was woefully under-prepared to fight a modern war. It had no heavy tanks at all—just over 300 medium and light tanks in the armored brigades and 500 "tankettes" attached to infantry divisions. Also, with only 6,000 trucks in the whole country, half the number needed to transport its troops, the infantry still relied heavily on horse-drawn wagons—and horse-riding officers—as if still living in the nineteenth century. Even though Polish leaders had come to see that its battles could no longer be fought and won by cavalry charges, and that cavalry officers could hardly withstand an armored attack, they still made the cavalry part of the nation's first line of defense and drew its officers from the aristocracy as well as—in Jan's case—their very best men (Kochanski 53). Neither Jan nor his superiors knew how devastating modern weapons could be, or how fast the German Panzer tanks could move. Worst of all, the Polish air force lagged far behind the German Luftwaffe. Poland had only about one-seventh of the combat planes of Germany, and at an Air Force exercise in early August, the American journalist William L. Shirer found them "dreadfully obsolete" (qtd. Olson and Cloud 45). By comparison, the German Messerschmidt fighters were ultramodern: faster, better armed, and capable of higher flight (Kochanski 54; Olson and Cloud 46–47).

Knowing nothing of these disparities, young Polish men who answered the call of duty in the early morning of August 24 had no idea what lay ahead of them. Braced with confidence, Karski reached the mobbed railroad station in the center of Warsaw and boarded a train headed toward Krakow. As the train chugged south, he caught a disturbing omen at each station: hordes of weeping women on the platform bidding farewell to their husbands and sons. But once he joined his unit, Jan found his fellow officers sharing his optimism: all the Poles had to do was show Hitler they could fight.

The fight was already starting. On the night of August 24, Jan's very first night in his barracks, southwest Poland became a hot spot. With Czechoslovakia now under German control, Poland had to defend itself against Slovak as well as German troops, and after crossing the Slovak border into southern Poland about forty-two miles south of Krakow, both sets of troops attacked the Jablonka railway tunnel in the Carpathians. Though the Poles repelled this attack, it was only the first of many overtures to the full-scale assault on September 1.

At 5am that day, Lieutenant Karski rose from his cot in the army barracks near Oświęcim. Expecting yet another uneventful day, he stooped over to peer into the bathroom mirror and carefully shaved a face still carbuncled by some adolescent acne. At 5:05, almost before he could have finished shaving, two massive explosions shook the camp, and for the next three hours a herd of Panzer tanks rolled in to pulverize the ruins. Altogether, the invaders wrought such death, destruction, and havoc as to make resistance impossible. Though Jan and a few other officers remained miraculously unhurt, the uncontrollable state of the horses left the Polish soldiers no way of hauling artillery against the invader, especially since the Luftwaffe kept raining incendiary bombs on the camp (Wood 5–6; Karski, *SS* 6).

Elsewhere in Poland, the cavalry was likewise overwhelmed. During battles fought in the village of Mokra near Jan's hometown of Łódź and in Pomorze, north of Warsaw, Polish horsemen actually charged and routed German infantry. But when the Germans counter-attacked with machine guns, artillery, armored cars, and tanks, they cut down the cavalry in minutes (Kochanski 63). Altogether Poland was struck from three directions—the northwest, south, and southwest—and indiscriminately bombed. On the first day, the Luftwaffe bombed a hospital, a school, churches, and shops in the farming town of Wiehun near Łódź, killing over 1,600 people—10% of its population. Elsewhere the Luftwaffe also bombed railways, towns, ambulances clearly marked with red crosses, ambulance trains, and passenger trains, and on the ground, fleeing passengers were machine-gunned (Kochanski 62). German forces thus began to implement Hitler's command to annihilate the Poles.[4]

At his army barracks near Oświęcim, Jan Karski soon realized that retreat was the only option. With the German Fourteenth Army pounding away at the artillery batteries of the Polish Army of Krakow—including Jan's cavalry regiment—Jan and his fellow officers organized their men for withdrawal to the local railroad station. But as they marched through the town of Oświęcim, which was heavily occupied by

Volksdeutsche (Poles of German descent, the Nazi Fifth Column), the Polish troops were fired on from houses and buildings. Though the officers kept their men from setting fire to the town in retaliation, Jan never forgot the last thing he saw as the train pulled out of the station: "the treacherous windows of Oświęcim" (Karski, *SS* 7), a town whose Germanized name would later be used for the nearby concentration camp known as Auschwitz.

Crawling east through the night at what must have been no more than walking speed, the train did not even make the forty miles to Krakow by dawn. It was then an easy target for a group of German Henkel 111 bombers that smashed and strafed the boxcars for over an hour, leaving hundreds of men dead and dying amid the smoking wreckage. Miraculously, Jan's boxcar was not hit. But all that he and the other survivors could do was leave the mess behind, walking east and picking up other soldiers just as dazed as they were. Their plight typified that of the Polish army as a whole. In the north, where two regiments of the Army of Pomorze had been obliterated by the Luftwaffe while being driven from the corridor, so few soldiers remained alive that "in reality the . . . Regiments had ceased to exist" (Kochanski 64). Likewise, Jan wrote later, the Army of Krakow—his own army—had become "no longer an army, a detachment, or a battery, but individuals wandering collectively toward some wholly indefinite goal" (Karski, *SS* 7).

Jan's own wandering eventually took him into the arms of the Soviet Army, which— by pre-arrangement with the Nazis—had invaded Poland from the east on September 17. Thereafter his story is almost miraculous. Though railroaded deep into the Ukraine and imprisoned there, he got himself sent back to Nazi-occupied Poland, escaped his captors by having himself thrown head first out the window of a slow-moving train in the middle of a rainy night, became a courier for the Polish Underground, was recaptured during his second trip to France, escaped from a hospital after nearly committing suicide, and—after the fall of France—travelled to England and then America, where he published in English a book titled *Story of a Secret State* (1944): his eyewitness report on the Nazi invasion of Poland, its brutal occupation (including concentration camps), and the struggles of its Underground.[5] I will have just a little more to say about him at the end of this chapter.

II. Patrick Hamilton's *Hangover Square*

As already noted, neither Britain nor France made any effective move to deliver the help they had promised to Poland if it were attacked. The only thing they did was to declare war on Germany two days after September 1. As we shall see more clearly later on, this was merely the start of the "joke war"—a period of about seven months in which (with one small exception) the French and British armies made no contact with German troops, let alone entering Poland. But since Britain played a major role in forging the Munich Agreement as well as in declaring war and thus confirming the global impact of what happened to Poland, I wish to consider what led up to the declaration in light of a novel by Patrick Hamilton (1904–1962). A prolific English novelist and playwright, he is probably best remembered now as the author of two plays—*Rope* (1929) and *Gas Light* (1938)—that were both turned into well-known films. Though admired by Graham Greene, J. B. Priestley, and Doris Lessing, who called him "a marvellous novelist," Hamilton remains in our time "grossly neglected," just as Lessing said he was in 1968.[6] Nevertheless, his novel is worth recovering for the peculiar light it sheds on the mood of Britain in the run-up to World War II. Its ending coincides precisely with Neville Chamberlain's declaration of war against Germany on September 3, 1939, which the doomed protagonist hears on the radio just after murdering a man and a woman in her flat.

Hangover Square (1941), a black comedy often considered Hamilton's finest novel, tracks the last eight months in the life of a 34-year-old man named George Harvey Bone: a lonely, jobless, borderline alcoholic periodically stricken by "'dead' moods" (Hamilton 3) that leave him wholly oblivious to what he has done for as long as the previous twenty-four hours. Since the novel takes him twice to the seaside town of Brighton, where he spends much of his time drinking, wandering aimlessly, and plotting murder, *Hangover Square* has been likened to Graham Green's *Brighton Rock* (1938), whose protagonist is a murderous gang leader named Pinkie. But Hamilton's novel, I believe, can be just as fruitfully read as a commentary on the imminence of war—a topic first broached in the opening chapters.

En route back to Earl's Court, London, just after spending Christmas of 1938 visiting his aunt on the Norfolk coast, Bone asks himself:

> what had next year, 1939, in store for him? Netta, drinks and smokes—drinks, smokes, Netta. Or a war. What if there was a war? Yes—if nothing else turned up, a war might. (Hamilton 20)

War is one of many things that divides him from Netta, the femme fatale who endlessly excites both his unrequited desire and his homicidal rage. Like her friend Peter, she believed "there wasn't going to be a war at all." Unlike Bone himself, who "hadn't fallen for all this 'I think it is peace in our time' stuff," she and Peter

> went raving mad, they weren't sober for a whole week after Munich—it was just in their line. They liked Hitler, really. . . . And old Musso too. And how they cheered old Umbrella! Oh yes, it was their cup of tea allright, was Munich. (Hamilton 20)

Just before scoffing at Peter and Netta's infatuation with Hitler, Mussolini, and old Umbrella (aka Neville Chamberlain), who cravenly traded Czechoslovakia for "peace in our time" at Munich, Bone mines all the implications of the name of his *belle dame sans merci*:

> Netta. The tangled net of her hair—the dark net—the brunette. The net in which he was caught—netted. Nettles. The wicked poison-nettles from which had been brewed the poison that was in his blood. Stinging nettles. She stung and poisoned him with words from her red mouth. (Hamilton 16)

Coursing three times through this onomastic riff on a woman's name, the word "nettles" echoes what Chamberlain said just before he boarded the plane that took him to

Munich on the morning of September 29: his third trip to Germany in barely two weeks. To catch the full force of Chamberlain's statement, consider its context.

Early in the morning of September 28, the day before his trip, he had drafted a fresh appeal to Hitler: "one more last letter," he called it: "the last last." He was ready, he wrote, to come to Berlin once more and to discuss the transfer of the Sudetenland with representatives of France and Italy as well with Hitler and the Czechs themselves. Certain they could "reach agreement in a week," he added: "I cannot believe that you will take [the] responsibility of starting a world war which may end civilization for the sake of a few days delay in settling this long standing problem" (qtd. Self 322). To buttress his appeal, he also asked Mussolini to support a conference aiming to "keep all our peoples out of war" (qtd. Kershaw, *H* 119). Mussolini furnished the key that unlocked Hitler's mind. As a result of his intervention, Hitler postponed the invasion of Czechoslovakia by twenty-four hours (Kershaw, *H* 120).

Later on the 28th, at exactly 2:54pm London time, Chamberlain began a long speech in the House of Commons without yet knowing what Hitler had decided. But after speaking for nearly ninety minutes, he was handed the message that furnished his dramatically unexpected conclusion. "I have now been informed by Herr Hitler," he said,

> that he invites me to meet him at Munich to-morrow morning [September 29]. He has also invited Signor Mussolini and [French prime minister] M. Daladier. Signor Mussolini has accepted and I have no doubt M. Daladier will also accept. I need not say what my answer will be. We are all patriots, and there can be no hon. Member of this House who did not feel his heart leap that the crisis has been once more postponed to give us once more an opportunity to try what reason and good will and discussion will do to settle a problem which is already within sight of settlement. Mr. Speaker, I cannot say any more.

As the House erupted in tumultuous joy, the 69-year-old prime minister—who might surely have aged another ten years after what he had just been through—was rejuvenated by this "news of . . . deliverance" arriving just in time: "a piece of drama," he shortly called it, "that no work of fiction ever surpassed" (qtd. Self 323). Exactly two weeks earlier, when Henry Channon MP learned at a banquet in Geneva that Chamberlain was headed to Germany for his first meeting with Hitler, he euphorically concluded that Chamberlain had already "saved the world." Now, marveling at Chamberlain's "amazing spirits . . . as he stood there, alone, fighting the gods of war single-handed and triumphant," Channon thought "he seemed the incarnation of St. George" (qtd. Self 324).

The next morning he seemed more like the embodiment of British pluck. Standing by the stairs to his plane at Heston Aerodrome, to the east of what is now Heathrow, he gave a little parting speech—obviously prepared beforehand—to the press and to members of his cabinet, who had nearly all come to cheer him off on his third trip to Germany. "When I was a little boy," he said, "I used to repeat: If at first you don't succeed, try, try, try again. That is what I am doing. When I come back, I hope I will be able to say as Hotspur says in *Henry IV*, 'Out of this *nettle*, danger, we pluck this flower, safety'" (my emphasis).

Like "Peace for our time," the phrase he would soon pronounce on his return from Munich, Chamberlain's valedictory words bristled with irony. For one thing, he evidently had no idea that someone at the Foreign Office had already concocted a parody of his boyhood motto: "If at first you can't concede, Fly, Fly, Fly again" (Self 321). Secondly, in quoting the words of Hotspur from Shakespeare's play *Henry IV, Part I* (2.3.9–10), the old statesman flying off again in quest of peace takes his cue—strangely enough—from a young hothead thrilled by nothing so much as riding headlong into battle, as his name suggests. Having joined a conspiracy to overthrow King Henry, Hotspur gets a letter warning him that his purpose is "dangerous." Though Hotspur testily replies that he will pluck the flower of safety from the nettle of danger, he ends up dead on the battlefield, where his rebellion is crushed. The words quoted by a would-be wise old statesman, therefore, are those of a reckless, fatally self-deluded young man.

In Hamilton's *Hangover Square*, Geoffrey Bone is a middle-aged man fatally deluded—again and again—by the hope that he can pluck the flower of love from the nettle named Netta: that he can persuade this dangerous woman to go away with him alone, if only for a few days. Chronically broke because she cannot land anything more than bit parts to feed her acting ambitions, she manipulates Bone with a cunning worthy of Hitler. Just as Hitler lured Chamberlain to various sites—Berchtesgarten, Bad Godesberg, and finally Munich—with tempting promises that he would soon break, Netta repeatedly undercuts the expectations she arouses. First, though she allows Bone to buy her dinner at a posh West End restaurant, her only aim in going is to be spotted by an important theatrical agent; second, though she agrees to spend a weekend with Bone in Brighton (at his expense, of course), she sends him on ahead and then turns up with two other men, one of whom she beds for a night; and third, after agreeing to go to Maidenhead with Bone, again at his expense, she puts him off with a story about a sudden crisis in her family and uses his money for a trip back to Brighton, where she vainly tries to ingratiate herself with the theatrical agent. In the end, roused by the "wicked poison-nettles from which had been brewed the poison that was in his blood," Bone takes his revenge by quite literally grasping the feet of the nettle called Netta while she is taking her bath, forcing her head underwater until she drowns, and then killing Peter with a golf club to the temple.

Though Peter is described as a "blonde fascist" (Hamilton 271) just before he is fatally struck, I am not sure what to infer from the fact that Bone's last day—the day on which he kills both Netta and Peter and then himself—is plainly identified as "September the third nineteen hundred and thirty nine" (Hamilton 268). But in the late morning, when Bone turns on the radio in Netta's flat so as to cover the noise of anything he might do with the two corpses, the voice of Chamberlain declaring war at 11am (readily audible now on YouTube) weaves its way into his thoughts:

"*. . . prepared at once to withdraw their troops from Poland*" he heard, "*a state of war would exist between us . . .*"

That was old Neville: he knew that voice anywhere.

"*I have to tell you now . . . that no such undertaking has been received . . . and that consequently this country is at war with Germany . . .*"

Oh, so they were at it, were they, at last! Well, let them get on with it—he was too busy.
"*You can imagine what a bitter blow this is to me …*" (Hamilton 273)

As Chamberlain declares international war, Bone concludes his private war with his tormenters, Peter and Netta, who have relentlessly demeaned and derided him. Since he takes his own life shortly afterwards, his victory is Pyrrhic, but since Chamberlain's own Chiefs of Staff had predicted a two months' hailstorm of German bombs if war broke out (Self 317), Chamberlain's declaration of war may itself have sounded suicidal.

III. Auden's "September 1, 1939"

Just as one radio delivers the voice of Chamberlain to the ear of Hamilton's doomed protagonist, another radio brought the same voice to the ear of W. H. Auden in New York. But Auden first learned of the invasion of Poland from a newspaper, and soon afterwards he started work on a poem that eventually came to be titled "September 1, 1939."[7] Unlike the novels of Hemingway and Gellhorn, Auden's poem is not based on any set of events that would later be recorded by historians. Though Auden had traveled extensively—to Berlin, Spain, and China—before writing the poem, he knew very little about the invasion of Poland as Karski and various historians would later record it. Yet the poem itself is an event in the history of literature as well as of the relation between literature and political history. To see what Auden brought to the making of the poem, I would like first to glance at his earlier life and then scrutinize the elegy he wrote on the death of William Butler Yeats in January of 1939.

In 1929, the 22-year-old Auden spent seven openly gay months in Berlin, whose political ferment and wide-open boy brothels furnished much of the material for his most important poem of the period, "1929" (Deer 25–26). A few years later, after launching his literary career in 1930 with his first volume of poems, he did some observing of war. In 1937, he spent seven weeks in Spain in the midst of its civil war, and in 1938 he not only traveled to China during its war with Japan but thereby gathered impetus for a travel book of prose and verse entitled *Journey to a War* (1939), which includes a sonnet sequence titled "In Time of War," later "Sonnets from China." So by September of 1939, when news of war reached Auden in New York, he had already begun bearing witness to the tumultuous history of his times.

The literary history of Auden's time included the death of William Butler Yeats. By late January 1939, when Yeats died at the age of seventy-three in Menton, France, he had made himself not just the greatest poet of Ireland but a poet whose international renown had been confirmed by the Nobel Prize for Literature in 1923. Yeats seldom wrote poetry about either politics or historically notable events. But in "Easter, 1916" he commemorates the agonizing birth of the Irish Republic: the abortive uprising against British rule that took place in Dublin on Easter Monday, April 24, 1916. While historians tell us that the uprising was crushed and most of its leaders executed for treason, Yeats's poem captures the enduring impact of the event. On one hand, he voices his aversion to violence and to several of the uprising's leaders, whom he personally knew and hardly idealized: he calls one a shrill-voiced "ignorant" polemicist and another a "drunken, vainglorious lout." On the other hand, he salutes the daring of their deed, which he presciently construes as a birth pang of independence: the freedom from British rule that Ireland would finally gain just a few years later, in 1922. No matter what Yeats had thought about violence or the leaders of the uprising, no matter how much he personally disliked them or how reckless they may have seemed, he now finds

> All changed, changed utterly:
> A terrible beauty is born.

As I have just noted, however, Yeats was not a political poet. Even though the Easter Rising—a landmark event in the history of Ireland—inspired one of his most powerfully prophetic poems, he was a cultural rather than a political nationalist, a man who felt that poetry should be apolitical. Paradoxically, however, the title of his very last lyric is simply "Politics." Written on May 24, 1938, it is headed by an epigram from Thomas Mann: "In our time the destiny of man presents its meanings in political terms."[8] Nevertheless, the speaker of the poem itself is irresistibly distracted by desire:

> How can I, that girl standing there,
> My attention fix
> On Roman or on Russian
> Or on Spanish politics,
> Yet here's a travelled man that knows
> What he talks about,
> And there's a politician
> That has both read and thought,
> And maybe what they say is true
> Of war and war's alarms,
> But O that I were young again
> And held her in my arms.

The poem is political insofar as it passingly alludes to the Spanish Civil War, Italian Fascism, Russian totalitarianism, and finally to Hitler and the looming threat of German aggression: "war and war's alarms." But even though Yeats wrote this poem at the age of seventy-three, he had been sexually rejuvenated four years earlier by a hormone operation, which may partly explain why he now rejects both politics and war in favor of love. To that end, he takes his inspiration not from any war but from an anonymous sixteenth-century English lyric called "The Western Wind" and the longing lament of its singer:

> O Western wind when wilt thou blow
> That small rain down can rain:—
> Christ, that my love were in my arms
> And I in my bed again.

Echoing this stanza in the last lines of "Politics," Yeats returns to the girl of the opening line with a lament of his own:

> O that I were young again
> And held her in my arms.

Is Yeats speaking for himself here? Literary critics often caution us not to make this kind of assumption, not to construe the words of a poem as the expression of the poet's own thoughts and feelings. A poem, we are told, is voiced by a "speaker" whom the poet creates and who speaks for the poet no more than Juliet or Iago speak for Shakespeare. But like many of the Romantic poets who came before him, Yeats often *does* speak for himself—as he most certainly does in "Easter, 1916." In "Politics" also, the old poet reveals not only his re-awakened desire for young women but also his longing to escape both politics and war. When he wrote the poem in May 1938, officials in London were already recruiting air raid wardens for a possible war with Germany. But Yeats did not expect that war would break out, and if it did, he told a friend, he might move to Cornwall, in southwest England, to escape the violence (Maddox).

Yeats died not in Cornwall but in France, as already noted, on January 28, 1939. One day later, news of his death reached Auden in New York, where he had arrived just two days before. Leaving his native England even as war clouds gathered over Europe, he had crossed the Atlantic by steamship with another young English writer named Christopher Isherwood, whom he had known since prep school, who had co-authored *Journey to a War*, and whose own experience in Weimar Berlin had already inspired a short novel called *Goodbye to Berlin* (1939) and two autobiographical novellas called *The Berlin Stories* (published later, in 1945), which in turn inspired the well-known musical *Cabaret* (1966).

In late January, the news of Yeats's death roused Auden to compose an elegy "In Memory of W.B. Yeats." Far from the site of that death in France, Auden views it in light of a New York winter, when "snow disfigured the public statues" and "the mercury sank in the mouth of the dying day." In the long tradition of pastoral elegy exemplified by Milton's "Lycidas," nature is typically said to mourn the death of a beloved friend, especially a poet. But in a world purged of mythology, it is mere coincidence that Yeats "disappeared in the dead of winter," that "the day of his death," as the poem repeatedly states, "was a dark cold day." Traditionally, the recompense for the death of a poet is the immortality of his words, which in this case are said to live on in the hearts of his admirers; no matter how "silly" Yeats became or how much he decayed in old age, Auden writes, "your gift survives it all." But the value and meaning of that gift is beyond control of the giver, for "the words of a dead man," Auden writes, "[a]re modified in the guts of the living." In leaving England just as a second Great War threatened to engulf it, Auden might seem to have followed the example of Yeats, who bade farewell to both war and politics near the end of his life. But in his elegy for Yeats, Auden turns him into a prophet of chaos. Just as Yeats's "The Second Coming" had decried the anarchy "loosed upon the world" by World War I, Auden now sees in Europe nothing but darkness, hatred, and canine rage:

> In the nightmare of the dark
> All the dogs of Europe bark,
> And the living nations wait,
> Each sequestered in its hate.

For Auden, however, Yeats's poetry remains an antidote to hatred and heartlessness: "the seas of pity . . . / Locked and frozen in each eye."

In spite of the postwar anarchy that Yeats himself lamented and the prewar darkness that Auden now beholds, he sounds a final note of regeneration:

> In the deserts of the heart
> Let the healing fountains start . . .

If applied to Auden's own life, these lines could be read as forecasting something like a re-enactment of Yeats's turn from war and politics to love. By March of 1939, when Auden's elegy first appeared in print, his literary reputation had brought him invitations to lecture in his adopted city of New York. Shortly after giving a talk on the Spanish Civil War at the Commodore Hotel, he met an 18-year-old Jewish-American poet named Chester Kallman and promptly became his lover. He also wrote the first of "Ten Songs" that juxtapose the newly coupled pair with the rumblings of imminent war:

> Thought I heard the thunder rumbling in the sky;
> It was Hitler over Europe, saying, 'They must die.'
> We were in his mind, my dear, we were in his mind.

(Auden, CP 210)

Perhaps in part to get Hitler out of their minds, Auden and Kallman decamped to California in the late spring for what Auden later called "the eleven happiest weeks of my life" (qtd. Galvin 29). Having written this down on August 30, 1939, the day he and Kallman returned to New York, he then added the following as part of the very first entry in a journal-diary that he would keep for the rest of the year:

> The prospect of war seems slightly less. It is curious how the knowledge of being loved can change one's attitude so completely. Last September in Brussels, I was really hoping there would be a war: the miraculous Second coming. This year the possibility of having to leave C[hester] if war breaks out, made me burst into tears while listening to the radio-news. I realize that for the last four years a part of me at least has been wanting to die. I say a part, because when I was in Spain and could have joined up, a little voice said, "no." That afternoon at Sarinyena [Sariñena] I realized that the other half wanted desperately to live. It had faith, and how right it was, bless it, though, God knows the bad half did its best to prevent its ever being so. But I wonder how many people there are in Europe who feel as I did last Sept? (qtd. Galvin 29)

Here is a fascinating self-portrait of a 32-year-old English expatriate newly in love and newly conscious of how much being so has changed his view of the coming war. Historians will never be able to answer Auden's final question—to count the number of Europeans who felt as much of a death wish as he did in September of 1938. But I think it is probably safe to say that he was part of a miniscule minority. Among the millions in France and England alone who dreaded the coming of a second Great War, how many would have welcomed its "second Coming," as Auden calls it, clearly thinking of Yeats's poem as well as of the Book of Revelation, the Second Coming of Christ, and the Last Judgment of the world?

Auden himself felt deeply divided in the late thirties. Though tempted in 1937 to join the fight against Spanish Fascism at Sariñena, where the Republican Air Force held an airfield until it was lost to the Nationalists in 1938, he suddenly realized that he "wanted desperately to live." Since that time, his faith in the possibilities of life had been rewarded not only by the pleasures of love, as he plainly indicates, but also—as he surely implies—by the poetry he had lived to produce. As a pacifist, Auden would never have signed up for combat, and he was such an erratic driver that one of his friends thought it "a mercy for the wounded" that he never even joined the ambulance corps (qtd. Galvin 29). "People have different functions," he told another friend some months after his time in Spain. "[M]ine is not to fight; so far as I know what mine is, I think it is to see more clearly, to warn of excesses and crimes against humanity whoever commits them" (qtd. Deer 29).

In light of these comments, consider what he wrote about poetry in a section that he added to his elegy for Yeats in the early spring of 1939, sometime between its first appearance (in *The New Republic* of March 8) and its second (in the *London Mercury* of April):

> . . . Mad Ireland hurt you into poetry.
> Now Ireland has her madness and her weather still,
> For *poetry makes nothing happen*: it survives
> In the valley of its making where executives
> Would never want to tamper, flows on south
> From ranches of isolation and the busy griefs,
> Raw towns that we believe and die in; it survives,
> A way of happening, a mouth. (my emphasis)
>
>   "In Memory of W.B. Yeats" (*CP* 197)

Auden's famous disclaimer (here italicized) has been endlessly debated, but its context is crucial. On one hand, Yeats's poetry has not made Ireland sane, any more than Shakespeare's plays made England sane in the early seventeenth century, when Roundheads and Royalists were gearing up for civil war. On the other hand, Yeats's poetry "survives / In the valley of its making" as "A way of happening, a mouth": a voice that bears enduring witness to the madness of his native land. While Yeats's poetry never cured Ireland's madness or allayed its grief, neither one ever choked his voice, which goes on singing from beyond the grave.

But if poetry makes nothing happen, if no poem can *be* an historical event, what is its relation to history? The closest Auden came to answering this crucial question was in a 1972 interview:

> Write a poem if you feel moved to because of circumstances. But what you must not imagine is that you can change the course of history by doing so. I wrote several things about Hitler in the thirties, but nothing that I wrote prevented one Jew being gassed or shortened the war by five seconds. . . . Because when it comes to social and political evils, only two things are effective: One is political action, of course, and the other is straight journalistic reportage of the facts. You must know exactly what happened. This has nothing to do with poetry. It is a journalist's job which, of course, is very important. (qtd. Galvin 39)

Unlike poetry, reportage *does* make things happen—as our own time freshly confirms. Again and again in the months after Donald Trump became President of the United States on January 20, 2017, investigative articles in the *Washington Post* and *The New York Times* (to say nothing of other media) led to resignations and indictments of key figures linked to his campaign, his administration, or both. But in the age of Hitler as in the age of Trump, nothing historical—nothing that counts as an historical event— was ever changed by poetry.

Yet to say so much, or to exclude literature altogether from the record of global or national "events," is to handicap our understanding of the past. Like the "whole truth" that courtroom witnesses routinely swear to tell, the whole truth of the past can never be recovered by anyone, historian or not. Whether or not any particular poem ever made anything happen, some poems bear witness to the impact of a particular event or particular moment on a mind capable of calibrating its significance *at the time it occurred*: of saying—as Wordsworth said of the early years of the French Revolution— how it felt then, how it touched a human heart, why it mattered to the human race. While no poem can ever count as an historical event, some poems become part of the memorable past.

Consider then the poetry Auden wrote at the outbreak of World War II. By the end of August, he and Chester Kallman had returned from their "honeymoon" trip to California and taken an apartment on 1 Montague Terrace in Brooklyn Heights, looking across the Promenade and the East River to the southern tip of Manhattan. With an ocean guarding him from the perils of European war, Auden knew very well how lucky he was. On August 31, the day before Hitler's invasion of Poland, he wrote in his new journal, "I must never forget that I am probably among the five hundred luckiest people in the world" (qtd. Galvin 24). But feeling still, perhaps, a tinge of guilt for having fled the scene of conflict, he quotes a line from a seventeenth-century English devotional poem in which George Herbert casts himself as undeserving of the very blessings he seeks: "all this not for my desert" (Herbert).

If Auden could find words for his feelings in a seventeenth-century poem, he was nonetheless keenly aware of his own time. The poetry he wrote in 1939—above all "September 1, 1939"—springs in part from his avid consumption of the latest news from all parts of the world. Though not at all a journalist, he listened to the radio whenever he heard it and read every newspaper he could find. He not only ingested the news; he curated it, turning it into a journalistic collage. The very first set of entries in his journal exemplifies what T. S. Eliot once wrote about the mind of a poet. When "perfectly equipped for its work," Eliot writes, "it is constantly amalgamating disparate experience[s]" that are "always forming new wholes" (Eliot 2406). Besides the entries quoted just above, Auden's journal of August 31 amalgamates two quite different news items:

Good news for the day
The A.A.S. [British Association for the Advancement of Science] meets in Dundee [Scotland] in the middle of the war-scare and discusses the world of sixty million years ago, and how to improve co-operation during war between scientists. If only artists had as good a record of co-operation, but then scientific language is translatable.

Today's Madness
Jacques Pericord in L'Intransigeant [right-wing French newspaper]. "Japan, Germany, Poland, have their volunteers of Death. It is time France had one. You have only to have one arm to fly a plane and release bombs after flying such a distance that there is not enough gasoline to return. Then tuberculars can go out to cut barbed wire. The first cuts a strand, and a second two more and so on. A hundred old men might save the lives of young men facing death on the first attack on a block house." I wonder how old Monsieur Pericord is. (qtd. Galvin 34)

The first of these entries records an event that surely belongs in the history of science, if only as a footnote; the second shows plainly that at least one citizen of a country whose leaders were doing all they could to stay out of war thought getting in well worth the sacrifice of "a hundred old men"—some of whom may well have lost an arm in the first World War. Is the gericidal proposal of a single Frenchman known to us only by his name worth the attention of an historian? Surely not. Yet it caught Auden's eye as a specimen of the madness that war itself exemplifies. And in juxtaposing the imminence of war with news of scientific inquiry and cooperation even "during war," Auden implicitly shows us how much the received histories of world events leave out.

Still more striking is the combination of personal dreams, war news, and scientific invention that Auden records in his journal for September 1, the very first day of World War II:

Woke with a headache after a night of bad dreams in which C. [Chester Kallman] was unfaithful. Paper reports German attack on Poland.

Good news. A scanning microscope has been invented, using electron beams passing through electrostatic and magnetic fields theoretically capable of a 100,000 × magnification. Professor Lawrence of California has made a cyclotron for the production of radio-active substances. (qtd. Galvin 37)

Under the heading of good news, Auden probably refers to two things: from 1938 to 1942, engineers at the RCA Laboratories in Camden, New Jersey, developed a Scanning

Electron Microscope; in 1931, Ernest Lawrence, Professor of Physics at the University of California, built a cyclotron that accelerated hydrogen ions up to more than a million volts, and his achievement would gain him a Nobel Prize in November of 1939. Though both items first caught Auden's attention on September 1, most physicists probably knew about the cyclotron well before then, and the invention of the scanning microscope was clearly an ongoing project. Yet insofar as these bits of news open a window to Auden's mind, their timeliness does not matter. What matters is that here, as in the entry for the previous day, he finds scientific activity just as important as the advent of war, and thus reminds us that not even the outbreak of war in Poland can arrest the course of other events—even consequential events—in other parts of the world.

Just as revealing is the combination of items in the first entry, which clearly belongs under the missing headline of <u>Bad News</u>. The only thing that would interest a historian in this entry is the German attack on Poland. Yet Auden couples this momentous event with a morning headache probably sharpened if not induced by jealous dreams about his young lover, whose frequent infidelity would eventually lead to their breakup. Auden thus reminds us that just as war cannot eclipse every other event of possible consequence that may be happening at the same time, it cannot monopolize the thoughts and feelings of everyone, and certainly not of a poet. In forming new wholes from disparate impressions, Auden's entries make up a part, however tiny or "irrelevant," of the memorable past.

Have I abandoned history for biography at this point? Only if history has absolutely nothing to do with the lives of individuals, or with the lives of individuals known for neither political, diplomatic, nor military feats. Let us then consider Auden's highly individual take on the outbreak of World War II in the most explicitly historical poem he ever wrote: "September 1, 1939."

In spite of its fame, we must face one awkward fact about this poem: Auden himself came to loathe it. Reading it a few years after it first appeared in the *New Republic* (October 18, 1939) and then in his collection *Another Time* (1940), he recoiled at what had become its most famous line: "We must love one another or die." "That's a damned lie!" he said to himself. We must die anyway!" (qtd. Fuller 292). As a result, he cut from his *Collected Poetry* of 1945 not just the lying line but the whole stanza ending with it, and though he allowed the stanza in Oscar Williams's *New Pocket Anthology of American Verse* (1955), he changed the line to "We must love one another *and* die" (my emphasis). Yet that one change was not enough. Eventually he decided the whole poem "was infected with an incurable dishonesty—and must be scrapped."[9] When asked for permission to include it and another political poem—"Spain 1937"—in a 1964 anthology *Poetry of the Thirties*, he agreed only if the editor would say that Auden considered both poems "trash which he is ashamed to have written" (qtd. Sullivan 16). Thereafter, "September 1, 1939" never appeared in any edition of Auden's collected poems, including the posthumous collection edited by Edward Mendelson and published in 1976.

Proving, however, that lines of poetry truly deathless cannot be slain by even the poet himself, the original version of Auden's poem—unaltered and uncut—can now be readily found online, as shown in the Bibliography. But why should I wish to revisit—

much less try to explicate—what Auden finally called "trash"? In spite of that verdict, I believe these lines still have enduring value. Paradoxically, much of that value springs from their *impermanence*: their expression of what the poet thought and felt at the time he wrote them. To that extent, they take their place in the cultural history of 1939 as well as the history or biography of Auden himself.

Reading them requires some adjustment. Though the poet begins by placing himself on September 1 "in one of the dives / On Fifty-second Street" in Manhattan, he actually wrote the poem some days after that momentous date while visiting the father of Chester Kallman in New Jersey (Mendelson, *LA* 531n74). Also, rather than literally reporting what Auden did or may have done on September 1, the opening lines echo the opening of a poem by Ogden Nash, best remembered now—if at all—for his comically pedestrian verse:

> As I sit in my office
> On 23rd Street and Madison Avenue
> I say to myself
> "you've a responsible position,
> haven't you." (qtd. Galvin 27)

If a poet is always forming new wholes, as Eliot says, from the bits of verse that stick to his memory as well as from the bits of news he picks up each day, Auden's opening is a perfect example. While doing something as commonplace as sitting in a mid-town Manhattan dive on a September night, he fearfully contemplates the fate of Europe, where "the clever hopes expire / Of a low dishonest decade." Roughly adapting the short, blank-verse lines of Yeats's "Easter, 1916," he concentrates this moment of history into just nine words. After years of false promises and assurances by French prime minister Édouard Daladier and British prime minister Neville Chamberlain as well as by Hitler, the "clever hopes" for peace enshrined in the arduously negotiated terms of the Munich Agreement have expired. Less than a year after seizing all of Czechoslovakia and thus breaking his promise to take only the Sudetenland, Hitler has killed all hopes for peace by invading Poland. As a result,

> Waves of anger and fear
> Circulate over the bright
> And darkened lands of the earth,
> Obsessing our private lives....

Like almost every other memorable poem, this one springs from many sources—private as well as public. "The day war was declared," Auden said later, "I opened Nijinsky's diary at random (the one he wrote as he was going mad) and read: 'I want to cry but God orders me to go on writing'" (qtd. Fuller 291). A few days earlier, Auden himself had "burst into tears" on hearing a radio news bulletin, as he wrote in a letter of August 28 (qtd. Mendelson, *LA* 77). But now he too feels bound to "go on writing" by exposing the contradictions of love even in time of war. To do so, he mines another passage from Nijinksy's diary: "Some politicians are hypocrites like Diaghilev, who does not want universal love, but to be loved alone" (Nijinsky 44). Since Auden knew only too well how war shreds platitudes and abstractions such as universal love and universal peace, he bluntly charges every one of us with hypocrisy:

> The windiest militant trash
> Important Persons shout
> Is not so crude as our wish:
> What mad Nijinsky wrote
> About Diaghilev
> Is true of the normal heart;
> For the error bred in the bone
> Of each woman and each man
> Craves what it cannot have,
> Not universal love
> But to be loved alone.

Behind this passage lies the Most Important Person of 1939, *Time*'s Person of the Year just past: Adolf Hitler, who repeatedly posed as a man of peace while relentlessly preaching "militant trash"—the gospel of intimidation and war. And since "universal love" would surely guarantee "universal peace," the former phrase reminds us that Hitler did everything he could to crush them both with hatred. But ironically enough, this stanza subordinates the Most Important Person to a mass of unimportant persons: each of us. The "normal heart," writes Auden, wants "universal love" no more than Diaghilev or even Hitler does: instead, it craves the gratification of *being* "loved alone," loved exclusively—above all others. Shortly before writing this stanza, as already noted, Auden had suffered a bad dream about the infidelity of his new young lover. While he nowhere alludes to this dream in the poem, he universalizes his craving for fidelity as not only an "error bred in the bone" of all humankind but also as something cruder than the "windiest militant trash" shouted by demagogues like Hitler. It does not matter that Auden's claim is implausible, that the "error" of wanting to be loved exclusively is probably no more universal than love itself. Nor does it matter even that Auden wound up disowning his whole poem, including of course this stanza. In spite of all that, the stanza flouts public—or what might even be called "historic"—speech with private truth, baring the anything-but-normal heart of a poet as he contemplates the outbreak of a second Great War.

Yet so far from being purely subjective and therefore *un*-historic, the poem as a whole is driven by Auden's sense of history. To be sure, his account of its stages is sweeping, leaping, and speculative. Cultural detectives, he supposes, can unearth what "has driven a culture mad," can explain how Hitler's "psychopathic" godhead sprang not only from "what occurred at Linz" during the fraught years of his childhood in that Austrian city but also from the legacy of Luther, whom Auden held ultimately responsible for German nationalism. Elsewhere Auden blames Luther (as well as various other early modern thinkers) for spawning Economic Man: a being life-threateningly riven by the gap between the individual and society, feeling and thought, conscience and the rest of himself (Fuller 291–92). Is this indictment just? Auden does not care. Setting it almost aside, he explains the origin of the new war in terms that would be perfectly understood by Hitler himself, who repeatedly claimed Germany's right to retaliate for the humiliations inflicted upon it at the end of World War I by the Treaty of Versailles. "Those to whom evil is done," writes Auden, "Do evil in return." It does not matter if the punishments imposed on Germany were justified, or, as Chamberlain and his fellow appeasers thought, unjustified and therefore "evil." Auden is not taking sides here. He simply avers that this war springs from the lust to retaliate—just as today's war in Ukraine is Putin's retaliation for its defiance of thje Soviet Union.

Though hardly a dispassionate historian, Auden ransacks the past. Turning back to the father of history in ancient Greece, he claims that Thucydides knew all "the elderly rubbish" spouted by dictators "to an apathetic grave," all "the habit-forming pain, / Mismanagement and grief." Yet even as Auden recalls the pains of the ancient Peloponnesian War, he unmistakably alludes to the pains of a war still raw in modern memory: "we must suffer them all again."

As war begins anew, what then does this poem have to offer? Only "a voice / To undo the folded lie," which probably alludes to the folded newspaper borne by the "man-in-the street," the "dense commuters" of the previous stanza (Fuller 292). Long before President Donald Trump denounced nearly all news as "fake," Auden implicitly charges that no newspaper ever tells the deep truth about human existence, especially in time of war:

> There is no such thing as the State
> And no one exists alone;
> Hunger allows no choice
> To the citizen or the police;
> We must love one another or die.

In spite of its seeming clarity, the last line of this cryptic passage is the most problematic line in the whole poem—for us as for Auden. For that very reason, we must carefully study the lines that just precede it. The State, he reminds us, is an abstraction with no life apart from the human beings who populate it; yet paradoxically, none of those beings is self-sufficient.[10] While both citizens and the police are constituted as such by "the State," they are both driven by "Hunger," by the need, instinct, or compulsion to love. Here is part of the reason for which Auden eventually disowned the whole poem. Not long after writing it, Edward Mendelson tells us, he came to hate the reduction of love to instinct (Mendelson, *EA* 477). Yet at the time he wrote it, he was still newly in love with Chester Kallman, newly compelled by a desire that must have seemed the only alternative to the hatred expressed by war. The last line, then, was true to his feelings in September 1939 even though—as a generalization about all of us—it came to seem flagrantly false.

The final stanza prompts another kind of objection. Since it ends by setting "an affirming flame" against "negation and despair," it courts a charge of poetic compulsion: having envisioned a world benighted and stupefied by war, the poet may have felt bound to say something compensatory or even redemptive about "points of light." Yet here perhaps Auden speaks better than he knew. As an English expatriate living more than an ocean away from the bombs and bullets of European combat, as one of the "five hundred luckiest people" in a world newly rocked by the outbreak of a second Great War, he could not have known anything about a young Polish cavalry officer named Jan Karski, who—when the poem was first published—was enduring all the privations and brutality of a Soviet prison camp, and would soon thereafter become a prisoner of the Nazis. Yet by the end of 1939, Jan Karski had not only survived his ordeal and escaped from the Nazis but had also vowed to do all he could to revive his native land. Viewed by the literary critic, the "affirming flame" of Auden's last stanza might be no more a stock trope, a conventionally "poetic" light against darkness. But had Karski been able to read it, it might well have struck him as a perfect metaphor for his burning aspirations at a time and place of devastation and suicidal despair.

Notes

1   Qtd. Wood and Jankowski 4. Though Karski does not mention his meeting with Drymmer in *Story of a Secret State*, he recalled it in an interview with Thomas Wood on October 5, 1993 (Wood and Jankowski 257).
2   "For good or ill . . .," wrote Walter Duranty, "I found no trace of defeatism anywhere in Poland" (qtd. Olson and Cloud 45).
3   On July 26, 1939, the British General Sir Edmund Ironside told his diary: "The French have lied to the Poles in saying they are going to attack. There is no idea of it" (Ironside 85).
4   At a meeting of his high command at the Berghof on August 22, 1939, Hitler had declared that Poland must be wiped out. Reminding his hearers that "Genghis Khan led millions of women and children to slaughter," he called for the "physical destruction" of the enemy, meaning first of all the merciless annihilation of "men, women, and children of Polish derivation and language" so that Germany might gain the *Lebensraum*—the living space—it needed (Lochner 1–4).
5   For the full story of this extraordinary man, see Karski as well as Wood and Jankowski.
6   https://en.wikipedia.org/wiki/Patrick_Hamilton_(writer)
7   When it first appeared in the *New Republic* on October 18, 1939, it was titled simply "September-1939." Not until later was it variously titled "1st September 1939" and then—for the canonized version—"September 1, 1939" (Sansom 30–31).
8   Probably quoted from a newly published essay by Archibald MacLeish (545–46), who declared in the same essay that "Yeats's later poetry is poetry of the world" (544). MacLeish uses no quotation marks and gives only Mann's name as his source.
9   Qtd. Fuller 292. For another analysis of Auden's deeply problematic line about love and death, see Sansom 268–69.
10 For more on the fictional status of states and nation-states, see Harari.

5

Bertolt Brecht's *Svendborg Poems*

Refuged beneath this Danish thatched roof, friends,
I follow your struggle. I send you now
As from time to time in the past, a few words, aroused
Through bloody visions over Sound and foliage.
Use what reaches you with caution!
Yellowed books, fragmentary reports
Are my sources. If we see each other again
I will gladly go back to work as an apprentice.
　　　　　　　　—Motto for the *Svendborg Poems*, *Werke* 12: 7[1]

Like James Joyce, Bertolt Brecht was an exile for much of his life, especially in the 1930s, when he wrote the *Svendborg Poems* and—in the fall of 1939—*Mother Courage*. Published in June of 1939, the *Svendborg Poems* voice his sympathy for the "struggle" of his friends and readers in Germany, his hatred of Hitler's belligerence, his loathing of fascist propaganda, and ultimately his faith in the coming of a time when man becomes "a helper to humankind" and thus triumphs over the war to come. But just three months after his *Svendborg Poems* appeared, the German invasion of Poland and the shocking revelation that Soviet Russia had joined it prompted Brecht to write one of the greatest antiwar plays of all time: *Mother Courage*. I treat the poems first in this chapter, and the play in Chapter 6.

The *Svendborg Poems* track the full complexity of what Brecht saw, felt, and thought as he watched his country gearing up for war. He watched from a distance. In early August 1933, a few months after the advent of Hitler's regime forced him to leave Germany in flight from persecution, he bought a house in Denmark and moved in with his second wife, the actress and director Helene Weigel, and their two young children, Barbara and Stefan. Brecht was then turning his celebrated *Threepenny Opera* (a huge hit in Berlin in 1928) into *The Threepenny Novel*. So along with money from various other sources, Brecht and Helene used his advance on the novel to buy a large, thatch-roofed fisherman's cottage overlooking Svendborg Sound from the island of Funen in south-central Denmark. The refugees thus found safe refuge—until forced to leave in April of 1939 by the imminent threat of Nazi troops arriving.

In the 1930s, exile was the defining condition of the modernist writer. It was memorably articulated by James Joyce, who—speaking through Stephen Dedalus, his fictionalized younger self—vowed to forge his art by means of "silence, exile, and cunning" (*Portrait* 247). But like Auden, who left England for the United States in January 1939, Joyce *chose* to live and write abroad for all of his adult life. Along with writers such as Ezra Pound and Ernest Hemingway, Auden and Joyce were "self-exiled," as Byron once called his alter ego Harold. But as Tom Kuhn rightly stresses, Brecht was never that kind of exile. Like all the other anti-fascist exiles of his era, he was "part of a mass enforced political exile" (Kuhn 50). Virtually obsessed with this condition, he implicitly broaches it in the very first poem of this collection, where he calls himself "refuged" in Denmark, and near the end he comments "On the Label Emigrant" ("Über die Bezeichnung Emigranten," *Werke* 12: 81). Rejecting the label for himself and everyone else who did not freely choose to leave their native land, he declares, "displaced persons are we, banned." "Vertriebene sind wir, Verbannte" (line 7).

Brecht's consciousness of exile haunts the *Svendborg Poems*. In "Visit to the Banished Poets" ("Besuch bei den verbannten Dichtern," *SG, Werke* 12: 35), an unnamed "he" dreamily enters "the hut" of would-be exiles ranging from Euripides, Ovid, and Po Chü-i through Dante, Shakespeare, and Voltaire right up to the German Romantic Heinrich Heine. Not all of these poets were actually banished: Shakespeare never left England, for instance, and Heine chose Paris for the last twenty-five years of his life. But since Brecht's poem springs from his obsession with banishment, he paints all of these figures with that brush, and beneath the running theme of banishment, the poem reveals the poet's deepest anxiety: to be not just banished, but forgotten—with his works annihilated.

This was no idle fear. In November 1938, as I have noted in Chapter 1, the proofs of the poems that Brecht wrote in Svendborg as well as two volumes of his *Collected Works* lay in Prague with his publisher, Wieland Herzfelde. But since the Nazis had already occupied part of Czechoslovakia and now threatened Prague, Herzfelde fled the city, and two months later—in January 1939—the proofs of the *Svendborg Poems* were destroyed and the two volumes "lost forever" (Parker 387). In April, when Nazi pressure on Denmark forced Brecht to move to Stockholm, he left behind the only other copy of these proofs that existed. When the poems finally appeared in June, it was only because this copy was taken to Copenhagen by Brecht's good friend Ruth Berlau, a Danish writer and actress, and published there. But before that happened, Brecht urged Berlau to "learn his poems by heart" (qtd. Parker 387)—presumably because he thought that only in such mental, immaterial form could they be safely preserved.

Against this highly personal background, the final words of "Visit to the Banished Poets" resonate with particular force. After speaking with all the poets mentioned above, the visitor finally hears a cry from the darkest corner of the hut:

> "Hey you, do they also know
> Your verses by heart? And those who know them
> Will they escape pursuit?"—"Those
> Are the forgotten," said Dante quietly,
> "Not (*nicht*) only their bodies, but also their works were annihilated (*vernichtet*)."
>
> (lines 26–30)

The resounding double *nicht* of the long final line—*nicht* and *vernichtet*—underscores the prospect of total annihilation: a prospect which, in spite of his fame, Brecht seems to have conjured up for himself and his works as war loomed ahead. Not even memorized poems would survive the capture of the memorizers.

The prospect of literary oblivion was inextricably bound up with the threat of war, which—no matter how tranquil his refuge—Brecht could never ignore. Living scarcely thirty miles from the German border, he could hear German warships exercising in the Kiel Bight, on Germany's northeast coast (Midgley 16), and thus could almost physically identify with Germany's fearful inhabitants. In the motto quoted above, he tells his readers, "I follow your struggle (*Kampf*)," which surely alludes to *Mein Kampf*, Hitler's story of his drive toward an absolute power against which his subjects now struggled in vain. In Auden's elegy for Yeats, who died in January of 1939, he writes, "Mad Ireland hurt you into poetry" (Auden, *CP* 197). In the motto written just a few months earlier, Brecht writes that his own poems had been "aroused / Through bloody visions over Sound and foliage." Of course Brecht could not literally see across the thirty miles of water separating him from Germany. But he devoured all the news he could get from radio broadcasts as well as print.[2] From these and other sources—"Yellowed books, fragmentary reports"—he could imagine something of what his fellow Germans were suffering. Yet he also writes that if he sees them again, he will gladly serve as an apprentice in die Lehre to the work of their lives.

The poems Brecht wrote in Svendborg sprang first of all from his hatred of fascism.[3] In the summer of 1938, he shared this hatred with Walter Benjamin, a German Jewish cultural critic whom he had first met in the spring of 1929 and who had since become his great friend and admirer. During the last of Benjamin's three summertime visits with the poet in Denmark, Brecht denounced the fascists fiercely. "They don't think small," he told Benjamin. "They plan thirty thousand years ahead. Horrendous things. Horrendous crimes. They will stop at nothing. They will attack anything. . . . They are planning immense devastation" (qtd. Parker 380). Politically, the only alternative to fascism that Brecht could see at this time was Communism, so in the mid-1930s he strongly supported the Soviet Union. In 1935, the hope of arranging major productions of his plays in Moscow led him there to see his friend Sergei Tretyakov, a playwright, and the producer Erwin Piscator (Midgley 17). Though the productions never took place, he agreed in March of 1936 to co-edit a new German language monthly in Moscow, *Das Wort* (Parker 357).

In that same year, however, Stalin launched a series of show trials that would last up to the summer of 1938, when Brecht learned that several of his Moscow friends and admirers, including Tretyakov, were being liquidated for allegedly supporting Leon Trotsky, who had dared to criticize Stalin. In Brecht's eyes, then, the Soviet Union had become a grotesque monarchy (Parker 380–81). To serve this monarchy, the Communist Party in Moscow was now imposing on writers the doctrine of Socialist Realism formulated at the Soviet Writers' Congress of 1934. Since Socialist Realism taught that "art must inspire the masses with uplifting images of society in its revolutionary development" (Parker 326), it had no place for the complexity of Brecht's drama or poetry.

In Moscow, the idolatry of Social Realism sparked attacks on Formalism. Founded in 1914 as a literary movement led by Viktor Shklovsky, Russian Formalism aimed to defend the autonomy of poetic language and literature. But Trotsky's critique of

Formalism in *Literature and Revolution* (1925) virtually demonized the term. It came to mean any kind of art or literature that aimed to serve the purposes of art itself rather than promoting the social good, above all the aims of the Russian Revolution. In the summer of 1938, Brecht told Benjamin that he considered this way of thinking about art "a catastrophe for everything we've committed ourselves to for 20 years" (qtd. Parker 380).

As already noted in Chapter 1, the animus against Formalism as Trotsky redefined it is best exemplified by the gruesome fate of Vsevolod Meyerhold, the actor and daringly experimental stage director who was tortured to death for publicly criticizing the anti-formalist movement in Soviet theater. Fortunately, Brecht was never punished with anything more than verbal attacks for daring to defy the Soviet custodians of culture, and in spite of his loathing for Social Realism, his devotion to the working class deeply informed his dynamic conception of realism. Rejecting "the extraordinarily narrow definition of the term 'Social Realism' in the Soviet journal *Internationale Literatur*" (Parker 385), Brecht likewise argued—in a long critique of György Lukács— that realism could not be epitomized for all time by one particular kind of historical novel—such as those of Balzac or Tolstoy. "Our concept of realism," Brecht wrote, "must be wide and political, sovereign over all conventions."[4] Brecht aimed this dynamic concept of realism directly at what he called "the people." "It is in the interest of the people, of the broad working masses," he wrote, "to get a faithful image of life from literature, and faithful images of life are actually of service only to the people, the broad working masses, and must therefore be unconditionally comprehensible and helpful to them—in other words, popular" (*A and P* 80).

By a singular irony, however, one of the most remarkable poems in the Svendborg collection seems to flout these requirements. When Brecht showed the poem to Walter Benjamin on July 24, 1938, probably soon after it was written, Benjamin did not "get its point" on first reading—even though he had become such an intimate friend of Brecht that the Svendborg volume includes his commentaries on some of its poems. This one is definitely not "unconditionally comprehensible." Ostensibly based on the song of an Egyptian peasant in 1400 BC, it is titled "The Peasant's Address to his Ox" ("Ansprache des Bauern an seinen Ochsen," *Werke* 12: 52) and reads as follows in English:

> O great Ox, godly plow-puller,
> Deign to plow straight! Lead the furrows
> Kindly not into confusion. You
> Go ahead, O leading one, gee-up!
> We have stood bent over, to cut your fodder
> Please deign now to eat it, dear bread-winner! Do not worry,
> While chomping about the furrow, feed!
> For your stall, you protector of the family,
> Have we groaning dragged the beams. We
> Lie in the damp, you in the dry. Yesterday
> You had a cough, beloved pacemaker,
> We were beside ourselves. Will you perhaps,
> Before the sowing, kick the bucket, you dog!

On first reading the poem, Benjamin was baffled and then alarmed by what it might mean. "At first I didn't get its point," he wrote, "and when a moment later the thought of Stalin passed through my head, I did not dare entertain it" (*A and P* 96). Brecht himself had made a daring move. Even though he caustically surmised that leaving Stalin's name out of a poem was "already considered an intentional omission" (qtd. Parker 382), he was now preparing an entire book of poems that nowhere mentioned Stalin by name and addressed him only as an ox. According to Benjamin, his own shock at this move "was more or less the effect Brecht intended, and Brecht explained what he meant in the conversation which followed," wherein "he emphasized, among other things, the positive aspects of the poem. It was indeed a poem in honour of Stalin, who in his opinion had achieved great things" (*A and P* 96). Regrettably, Benjamin says nothing about his own reaction to Brecht's preposterous claim, for this would-be "poem in honour of Stalin" is a merciless satire.

In treating Stalin as a "godly" ox who must be reverently addressed, fed, and housed by self-sacrificing peasants, the poem sounds almost worshipful. As Hodgson observes, the peasant's fawning epithets for the ox—"godly plow-puller" and "protector of the family"—recall what Stalin's sycophants called him, "leader and teacher" (Hodgson 76). But in calling the ox "leading" (*Führender*), the poem also links this Stalinesque beast with Germany's Führer, thus implying that Stalin is just as ruthless.

Still more savagely ironic are the lines about feeding. By widely confiscating household food in the 1930s, Stalin starved to death at least five million people, mostly in the would-be "counter-revolutionary" republic of Ukraine (Applebaum). In Brecht's poem, the peasant not only reports that he and his fellows have "stood bent over" to cut the ox's fodder; he also tells the ox not to worry about plowing straight and keeping the furrows in order—probably a metaphor for good government by this would-be "beloved peacemaker." But instead of plowing straight or feeding any family that he supposedly protects, the beast can simply feed himself. It is the peasant families, of course, who protect the ox by laboriously building his stall, gathering his food, and fretting about his cough—until the prospect of his dying prompts a final burst of undisguised disgust at his uselessness. He is hardly better living than dead.

"The Peasant's Address to his Ox," then, plainly shows that Brecht was anything but an apologist for the Soviet dictator. Though Brecht's loathing of fascism led him to embrace the promises of Communism in the early 1930s, just as Orwell and Hemingway (among so many others) embraced them for the same reason in the mid-1930s, the undeniable evidence of Stalin's dictatorial ruthlessness had clearly turned Brecht against him by 1938, when he wrote the poem about the ox. Yet the rich irony of the poem, which baffled even Benjamin at first, also points to something crucial about the Svendborg collection as a whole.

In the words of the motto for Part II, it reflects "dark times" (*Werke* 12: 16). As Ronald Speirs observes, the *Svendborg Poems* not only show how a fascist Germany is spreading "war and disinformation across the continent," but also express "the poet's determination to bring the light of reason to bear on these dark times" (Speirs 2). But could this light reach all eyes? If poems such as "The Peasant's Address to His Ox" baffled Walter Benjamin even briefly, could they be "unconditionally comprehensible" by "the broad working masses," as Brecht claimed? It seems unlikely, for Brecht's ambition to illuminate "these dark times" led him to use everything he knew about the art of poetry—above all its power to unsettle and surprise readers as a means of enlightening them.

In Part II of his elegy for Yeats, as noted above in Chapter 4, Auden wrote that while poetry "makes nothing happen," it is "a way of happening, a mouth." Echoing Auden, Tony Davies writes that Brecht's "ultimate commitment [was] not to party or cause but to the idiosyncratic 'way of happening' of poetry" (Davies 91). No matter how bad or dark his times became, Brecht never abandoned his commitment to the art of poetry. Consider what he does with rhyme in a distich from "Bad Time for Poetry" ("Schlechte Zeit für Lyrik," *Werke* 14: 432), which did not get into the Svendborg volume but was written in the spring of 1939, shortly before the volume was published:

In my song a rhyme
Would strike me almost as presumption.

By 1939 Brecht no longer thought that his poetry needed either rhyme or meter (*Poems* 469–70). But liberating poetry from rhyme and meter is hardly the same as attacking anything in literature that smacks of art—of artistic complexity, subtlety, or form. "Bad Time for Poetry" exhibits all three. Ostensibly, it seems to say that during the "bad time" of an imminent war, poetry must clip its own wings, blind itself to the visible beauty of the world, and swear off rhyme as a useless, irrelevant indulgence. As Davies puts it, the poem reveals "the political price exacted by Nazism, the necessary asceticism of political art" (Davies 92). Yet as Davies also notes, Brecht's would-be renunciation of poetry is itself "a lyric, with its characteristic pleasures" (Davies 92–93). Most ironically of all, the first line of a distich in which the singer faults the use of even one rhyme ("ein Reim") mischievously flaunts a triple rhyme in the original German:

In *mein*em Lied *ein Reim*
In my song a rhyme
Would strike me almost as presumption.

Hiding in plain sight, this trio of rhymes and near rhymes (*mein / ein / Reim*) undermines the ostensible message of the distich just as much as the would-be renunciation of traditional lyric imagery is undermined by its undeniable presence in the poem. As he gazes out on the beauties of Svendborg Sound and of his own seaside garden, the speaker claims to see only the crippled tree, the village woman who walks with a stoop, and the torn nets of the fishermen—while seeing nothing beautiful:

The green boats and the joyous sails of the Sound
I see not.

Nevertheless, the poem makes plainly visible the green boats, the joyous sails, and—in the last stanza—the beauty of "the blossoming apple tree" ("den blühenden Apfelbaum").

This kind of beauty repelled the mandarins of Marxism known as the Frankfurt School, who—starting in Frankfurt in 1923 and then moving to the U.S. ten years later—developed "a critique of bourgeois consciousness and the capitalism that produced it" (Lyon 258). Though sharing Brecht's Marxism, they thought him "vulgar, materialistic, and overly devoted to the working class," while he in turn disdained "their stilted, abstract language, their elitism, their isolation from human affairs, and their wrong-headedness."[5] Theodor Adorno, for instance, a leading member of the Frankfurt School, deplored any mention of nature's beauty in poetry written while Hitler reigned. "[E]ven the tree which blossoms," he wrote, "is a lie as soon as one sees its blossoming without the shadow of horror" (qtd. Leeder 217). Yet in Brecht's field of vision, not even Hitler could kill the beauty of the tree or falsify its truth. By the time we reach the final stanza of Brecht's "Bad Time for Poetry," we feel anew the truth of Yeats's dictum that while we make rhetoric (such as Adorno's) from our quarrel with others, poetry springs from our quarrel with ourselves (*Per Amica*, Chapter 5):

> In me contend
> Rapture at the blossoming apple tree
> And horror at the speeches of the white-washer.
> But only the second
> Drives me to my desk.

Suggestively, Brecht's mental battle pits sight against sound, the beauty of the blossoming apple tree against the manic stridency of the white-washer's speeches (*die Reden des Anstreichers*). He must have heard Hitler's voice on the radio almost every day. On April 1, 1939, for instance, he could have heard Hitler declare that the forthcoming eleventh Congress of the Nazi Party (scheduled to start on September 2) would be called the "Party Rally of Peace" because "Germany does not dream of attacking other nations" ("Speech … at Wilhelmshaven"). Three years earlier, in the spring of 1936, Brecht had exploded this sort of claim in a poem that plainly links it to white-washing, "When the white-washer (*Anstreicher*) speaks of peace through the loudspeaker" (*Werke* 12: 11). Anticipating what would happen to the "Rally for Peace" that was cancelled when Germany invaded Poland just before its opening date, the poem describes foundry workers listening to Hitler fulminate about peace even as bomber planes rumble overhead.

Brecht first used his favorite epithet for Hitler in 1933, the year he came to power. In "The Song of the White-washer Hitler" ("Das Lied vom Anstreicher Hitler," *Werke* 11: 215), the new German chancellor takes "a bucket of fresh whitewash" and paints "the whole German house anew" (st. 1). The poet then asks,

> O White-washer ("Anstreicher") Hitler,
> Why were you no builder? Your house
> If the whitewash gets into the rain,
> The dirt underneath comes out again,
> The whole shithouse comes out again. (lines 15–19)

Though Brecht's epithet for Hitler is "Anstreicher" ("Housepainter") rather than "Weißwäscher," his very first use of "Anstreicher" makes it clear that this particular housepainter uses whitewash. To catch the full force of Brecht's mockery, we need to know that Hitler was once an artist who produced at least a thousand sketches, watercolors, and oil paintings, and in the preface to a special edition of his watercolors published in 1935, he was actually called "the first artist of our Reich" (qtd. Werckmeister 275). But as a genuine artist himself, Brecht would never call Hitler a "Kunstmaler" (artist painter) or even "Maler," which can mean either "artist painter" or "housepainter." Instead of using "Maler," Brecht calls Hitler "Anstreicher," which never denotes a bona fide painter of any kind but rather connotes something like "hack painter."[6] To sharpen the edge of this insulting term, Brecht clearly shows this particular housepainter using whitewash to fill the holes and cracks of the German "house" (the German economy) so as to make it look new—even though the whitewash may soon be washed away to expose the dirt and the shithouse beneath it.[7]

The epithet "Anstreicher," then, encapsulates Brecht's contempt for Hitler's chicanery, for all the whitewash of lies about peace and the glories of nationalism that he spreads over his ruthless belligerence and spouts over the radio or loudspeaker. Speaking, for instance, from Berlin's cavernous Sportpalast on September 26, 1938, months after he had resolved to seize Poland as well as all of Czechoslovakia, he swore via radio to a global audience of millions that the Sudetenland—the northwest tier of Czechoslovakia—would be "the last territorial demand which I intend to make in Europe" ("Speech in the Sportspalast").

Besides unmasking the hypocrisy of Hitler's pretensions to peace, Brecht's "Song" of 1933 forecasts what is to come in Part I of the *Svendborg Poems*, "German War Primer." Normally, a primer is a book designed to help children learn to read. Yet in place of the sunny stories typically told in primers, these poems tell short, grim tales about the privations of a people consumed by preparations for war, even primed for it. In "The Workers Cry Out for Bread" ("Die Arbeitter schreien nach Brot," *Werke* 12: 10), the imminence of war levels even the barriers between merchants and workers, the unemployed and the employed. Just as the workers cry for bread, the merchants cry for markets, and just as the unemployed once went hungry, the employed go hungry now. But rather than producing bread or anything edible, they are wholly occupied with weapons. With hands that once lay quiet stirring again, "They make grenades."

The Germans had been making *Stielhandgranaten* ("Stalk hand grenades") since 1917, but in 1924 they introduced the M24, made by attaching a long wooden handle to a metal charge cap shaped somewhat like a top hat. The hand-held explosive known as a *grenade* (in German *Granate*) got its name because it looks like a pomegranate, but since the German word *Granat* (without an "e") means "garnet" or "jewel," Brecht may be punning on the two words—as if to suggest that what German workers are now making is neither edible nor beautiful, good only for destruction and murder.

Against such murderous devices Brecht deploys verbal weapons of his own. In "When the Drummer Begins His War" ("Wenn der Trommler seinen Krieg beginnt," *Werke* 12: 14–15), a poem that takes its title from *The Drummer* (*Der Trommler*), the newspaper of the Hitler Youth Movement (Speirs 9n14), the drummer is Hitler himself. When he "begins his war," Brecht tells the reader, it will not be "your war," for as Brecht implies, you will wage that *against* the Führer. Surrounded by enemies on all sides, he will face even marchers driven by his own S.S., the elite "Personal Squadron" of more than fifty thousand men meant to serve as Hitler's bodyguard but now marching "against him." In this "German War Primer," Hitler's war is thus made to confront the war against Hitler. Echoing the opening address to his readers, which turns Hitler's *Mein Kampf* into "your struggle" (*euren Kampf*), Brecht concludes the final poem of his first section by declaring: "Brave will he be, who struggles against him" (*ihn*). While *ihn* could mean either Hitler or "it," the war he made his own, the final line clearly predicts that "Only he who defeats him [Hitler] can save Germany."

This line could well be read as meant for members of the *Widerstand*, the German Resistance. Whether or not Brecht knew anything about this organization, it had already made one major move against Hitler in late September 1938, just before the Munich Agreement. Its plot to assassinate Hitler—the Oster conspiracy—had been led by Lieutenant Colonel Hans Oster, a highly decorated veteran of World War I who now ran the Abwehr, the counter-intelligence section of the military High Command. Hating Nazism, Oster did all he could to dethrone its god until his own execution in 1945. At a secret meeting held in his apartment on September 20, between Hitler's first and second meeting with Neville Chamberlain, Oster discussed final plans for the coup with his "inner circle," which included General Erwin von Witzleben and Captain Friedrich Wilhelm Heinz, head of the assault team. Having recruited "fifty to sixty anti-Nazis from a wide variety of opposition factions," they decided that with Heinz at the head of these commandoes, Witzleben could arrest Hitler at the Reich Chancellery as soon as he ordered an attack on Czechoslovakia (Parssinen 132–34).

In the early hours of the morning of September 28, just before Chamberlain's final meeting with Hitler, Heinz summoned his commandoes to the Army headquarters of the Berlin Military District and gave them automatic weapons, ammunition, and hand grenades. He had only to wait for news that German troops were on the move (Parssinen 181), and it seemed all but certain that Hitler would order them to attack. Four days earlier, right after his second meeting with Chamberlain had achieved nothing and right after all Czech men under forty had been mobilized, Hitler declared—via the Godesberg Memorandum—that if the Czechs did not cede the Sudetenland by 2pm on September 28, Germany would take it by force.[8] But about noon that day, just two hours before the deadline, Hitler accepted Chamberlain's proposal for a four power conference at which Germany would be allowed to take the Sudetenland on October 1 without attacking it—or consulting Czechoslovakia. As a result, General Franz Halder—the operational leader of the coup—was utterly demoralized. At the very end of September, when he learned what Chamberlain and French prime minister Édouard Daladier had done at Munich, he reportedly "collapsed over his desk" (K. Klemperer 109). Once Hitler gained the Sudetenland without firing a shot, he became politically invincible, the resistance lost heart, and the assault squad was dispersed. "What are we supposed to do now?" Halder asked. "He [Hitler] succeeds in everything!" (qtd. K. Klemperer 112).

Indeed he does—or did. In thwarting the conspiracy, Hitler dodged assassination for the twenty-sixth time in his life. Diabolically lucky in his adversaries as well as his timing, he succeeded at Munich only because the powers that could have stopped him overestimated German strength and underestimated—or willfully understated—their own. In April of 1946 at Nuremberg, Field Marshal Wilhelm Keitel, Supreme

Commander of the German Armed Forces for most of World War II, was asked if Germany could have attacked Czechoslovakia in the fall of 1938. He answered no. "From a purely military point of view," he testified, "we lacked the means for an attack which involved the piercing of the frontier fortifications" (Avalon, *NTP*).

Brecht had no way of knowing the relative strength of the Wehrmacht at this time, and his letters give no hint that he knew anything about the plot against Hitler in September 1938. Given not only the failure of this plot but the demoralization of the German Resistance, it might be argued that Brecht's prevision of Hitler's defeat confirms Auden's assertion that "poetry makes nothing happen." Yet as Speirs argues, the *Svendborg Poems* embody "Brecht's notion of 'interventionist thinking,'" which requires that each individual should play some part in "determining the outcome of developments" (Speirs 6). Though it neither determines nor predicts the outcome of the war ahead, the final poem of "German War Primer" precisely defines the war that had to be fought for the salvation of Germany: a struggle (*Kampf*) against the tyrannical author of *Mein Kampf*, a victory by whoever "defeats him" ("*ihn besiegt*") over the ubiquitously broadcast voice of "Hail, Victory!" ("*Sieg, heil!*").[9]

Of all the weapons Brecht himself wields against Nazi tyranny, one of the most potent is irony, and the second section of the *Svendborg Poems* includes a striking example. Like Hemingway's *For Whom the Bell Tolls*, it was prompted by the Spanish Civil War, and specifically by what the Condor Legion of the German Luftwaffe did for Franco's Nationalists—most notoriously in bombing the Basque town of Guernica in April of 1937. In "My brother was a flyer" ("Mein Bruder war ein Flieger," *Werke* 12: 22), the speaker explains that his brother flew south one day, presumably with the Condors, as "a conqueror":

> Our people need more room
> And getting hold of ground and soil, is
> With us a long-time dream.
>
> The space my brother conquered
> Lies in the Guadarrama Mountains
> It is one meter eighty [centimeters] long [about six feet]
> And one meter fifty [centimeters] deep [about five feet].

Here is what might be called the final solution to Germany's quest for *Lebensraum*—more living space. Though Germany's support for the Spanish Nationalists had nothing to do with this quest, *Lebensraum* had indeed been Germany's "long-time dream," a geopolitical goal of Imperial Germany in the first world war and its chief justification for Nazi aggression during the run-up to the second.[10] The Guadarrama is the mountain range north of Madrid where, as we saw in Chapter 2, the guerrillas of Hemingway's novel had to contend with bombers as well as cavalrymen. But Brecht's speaker imagines that his flying brother has fatally crashed into the mountains and thereby conquered what might be called his *Grabraum*—grave room, room enough for his corpse.

While "My Brother was a Flyer" takes ironic aim at Germany's vaunted Luftwaffe, another Svendborg poem takes much more subtle aim at its whole obsession with war,

Krieg. Written in July of 1938 and first published the following January in *Internationale Literatur* (9.1), this poem makes no direct reference to Germany, the Soviet Union, or the coming war. It is based on an ancient Chinese legend about the power of water to overcome stone or—according to Benjamin—about the power of friendliness to defeat hardness (*Poems* 572–73; Benjamin, *Understanding Brecht* 72–73). But in Brecht's hands the "Legend of the Origin of the *Book of Tao-te-ching* on Lao-tsu's Road into Exile" ("Legende von der Entstehung . . .," *Werke* 12: 32–34) becomes a lesson in patient resistance to war.

Leaving a country that has lately been deteriorating, an old man takes only his pipe, a book, and some bread, and rides off on the back of an ox led by a boy. When a customs officer at the border asks him if he has any valuables to declare, the old man says "None" (*Keine*), and the boy says simply,

> "He taught,"
> And so too was that explained. (st. 4)[11]

There is something slightly comic about the boy's stunningly terse explanation, which plainly implies that a life of teaching leaves one broke, as in Nazi Germany it often did.[12] And when the customs officer cheerfully asks the boy, "Did he get anything out of it?" ("Hat er was rausgekriegt?"), the answer has nothing to do with money:

> "That soft water in its movement
> With time the mighty stone defeats (*besiegt*)
>   [i.e., soft water defeats the mighty stone]
> You understand, hardness succumbs (*unterliegt*)." (st. 5)

Ostensibly, the lesson taught by the old man, tersely summarized by the boy, and now delivered to the reader, is that patient, gentle pressure will eventually prevail over stony force. But to grasp the full effect of the stanza, we must see what it does with the unusually strict rhyme scheme of the whole poem.

In the fifth stanza of "Legend," Brecht uses three end rhymes: *rausgekriegt, besiegt, unterliegt*. Embedded in the first two words is the language of war: *krieg* and *sieg*, war and victory.[13] But subverting what was surely Hitler's favorite word, the boy's answer to the officer's question may well imply, for Brecht's readers at least, that Hitler's stony obsession with victory ("*Sieg, heil!*") can be ultimately overcome ("*besiegt*") by soft water—such as the language of poetry itself. There is nothing monotonous or "lulling" about these rhymes, as Brecht says of rhyme elsewhere. Instead, by incremental repetition—by the steady pressure of their rhyming sounds—they linguistically besiege the stony core of Hitler's war machine.

In July of 1938, when Brecht wrote this poem, James Joyce was finishing the "work in progress" that he had started sixteen years earlier, soon after *Ulysses* appeared. Published in May of 1939, just four months before Germany invaded Poland, *Finnegans Wake* says nothing explicit about Hitler, but one passage in particular makes it clear that besides thoroughly sharing Brecht's contempt for the Führer, Joyce knew exactly how to mobilize Hitler's own words against him.

Joyce viewed Hitler through the lens of historical cycles. For Joyce, the rise of Hitler and his would-be thousand-year Reich could not check the cyclic force that would one day throw him down. I do not mean that *Finnegans Wake* makes a specific prophecy, as Yeats does in "Easter 1916." But Joyce's last great novel sprang from the mind of a writer who could look upon Hitler with comic detachment rather than either anguish or admiration. By the late 1930s, Richard Ellmann writes, Joyce "had surveyed the rise of German nationalism without sympathy: the world of discipline, anti-Semitism, and national frenzy was not his" (Ellmann 675). The tone with which Joyce appraised them all is exemplified by his comment on the failure of the Nazi coup against the government of Austria in late July 1934. Writing to Harriet Weaver, his patroness, on July 28, 1934, he not only jokes about the coup but also makes fun of Wyndham Lewis, whose admiring book about Hitler was published in 1931, and Ezra Pound, who (unlike Lewis) remained both pro-Nazi and antisemitic until the last years of his life. Apropos the failed Nazi coup, Joyce mockingly writes, "I am afraid poor Mr. Hitler-Missler will soon have few admirers in Europe apart from your nieces and my nephews, Masters W. Lewis and E. Pound" (qtd. Ellmann 675).

By January of 1939, Hitler's gains had made him harder to mock. But in *Finnegans Wake*, Joyce not only refers to Charlie Chaplin as "Chorney Choplain" (*FW* 351: 13) but also anticipates the mockery with which Chaplin would play the Führer in *The Great Dictator* (1940). Though Joyce mentions Hitler nowhere properly, he name-twistingly alludes to him as the builder of the German Autobahn—"them new hikler's highways" (*FW* 410: 8) —and as the manic voice of the Third Reich endlessly asserting the oneness of its nation and people ("Ein Reich! Ein Volk!) and endlessly demanding to be hailed as its one and only ruler "Ein Führer!" In Joyce's novel, Hitler becomes the would-be "helper" who cannibalistically devours everything and everyone: "heal helper! One gob, one gap, one gulp and gorger of all!" (*FW* 191: 7–8).[14]

Just as Brecht turns Hitler's favorite words (*krieg* and *sieg*) against him, Joyce ridicules Hitler's assumption that words themselves can have only one meaning: the one he gives them. Tolerating no dissent, no resistance or *Widerstand* to his rule, Hitler expected that every member of his German *Volk* should hear and heed no other word but his own—the Word of the Führer. Joyce repudiates this word. In exploiting the polysemy of language, in loading words like "funferal"—a wild mashup of "fun for all" and "funeral"—with radically dissonant meanings, he undermines Hitler's univocism and asserts the irrepressibly creative power of the human spirit. Against the threat of war and annihilation, Joyce proclaims—in his own inimitable way—the power to re-create language, to ridicule dictatorship, and to rise again—like Finnegan (Finn again).

From the Olympian viewpoint of Joyce, then, the rise and fall of empires—including Hitler's "thousand year" Reich—was no more world-shattering than the rise and mortal fall of a hod carrier named Tim Finnegan. In the Irish ballad from which Joyce takes the title of his book, Finnegan's death is followed not only by his wake but also—thanks to the whisky spilled on his corpse in the midst of it—by his miraculous re-awakening. In other words, while Auden's "September 1, 1939" bemoans the prospect that all the horrors of World War I must be suffered "again," the very title of Joyce's novel punningly proclaims his faith in cyclic regeneration, in the prospect that the world at large—like Finn himself—will rise "again." Hence the voracious dictator who had already devoured

Austria and much of Czechoslovakia by the end of 1938 and who now threatened to consume the rest of Europe makes only a fleeting appearance in *Finnegans Wake*. In the cycles of history, Joyce implies, this great gulper will himself be eventually gulped.

Brecht did not share this Olympian confidence. Though he knew *Ulysses* (as shown by his Journal of February 1939, *J* 21), and though he repeatedly deployed his own verbal weapons against Hitler's speeches and Nazi propaganda, the *Svendborg Poems* show him periodically caught in the nadir of an historical cycle that has hit bottom with no assurance of turning back up, no promise or prospect that gloom will give way to light. In the untitled Part IV of the *Svendborg Poems*, he descends into what Speirs calls "the darkest section of the whole collection" (Speirs 5). "The darkness grows" ("Die Finsternis nimmt zu"), he says in the opening poem (*Werke* 12: 47), and the second one shows even more chillingly how a corrupt regime can eventually force almost everyone to lie. Originally broadcast from Moscow in 1935, "To Those Who have been Brought into Line" ("An die Gleichgeschalteten," *Werke* 12: 47) peels away the layers of lies told by those fearful of losing their bread if they tell the truth. While the poem makes no direct reference to war, it brilliantly exemplifies both the intolerance of truth that is required to justify a war of sheer aggression and the fear that such intolerance generates.

In the first stage of evasion, those bent on saving face while not starving to death resolve "to tell no more the truth / About the crimes of the regime" (lines 4–5). But keeping silent about such crimes means normalizing them, treating them as something so "unremarkable ... / and so unpreventable as the rain" (lines 24–25). Furthermore, those who remain silent are soon forced to lie, and when "the will to lie" (line 58) becomes no longer enough, they must lie with "passion" (*Leidenschaft*, line 59), surpassing all others in praising their oppressors—precisely because they are suspected of having once scorned oppression. Those who know the truth, therefore, become "the wildest liars" until someone "convicts" them

Of having once had honesty, once decency, and then
They lose their bread. (lines 68–72)

On September 27, 1938, three years after Brecht wrote this poem and just a few days before Nazi troops invaded Czechoslovakia, Hitler himself was dismayed by the kind of silence Brecht describes. The night before, during his globally broadcast speech at the Sportpalast, Hitler lied about his plans for conquering Europe, as already noted, but he also inadvertently told the truth in declaring "that the German People wishes nothing else than peace." To his consternation, he found this claim confirmed the very next day. "To impress foreign diplomats and journalists with German military might," as his Luftwaffe adjutant later recalled (Kershaw, *The "Hitler Myth"* 118), Hitler ordered a "grand parade" with a motorized division rolling through the capital at dusk. But as hundreds of thousands of Berliners filled the streets on their way home from work, they quietly staged what the American journalist William Shirer called "the most striking demonstration against war I've ever seen." In the workers' quarters the motorized troops were reportedly greeted with "clenched fists," and when a bareheaded Hitler stepped out on the balcony of the Wilhelmstrasse Chancellery, a tight-lipped crowd of less than two hundred kept "icy silence" without raising a single arm. Utterly disgusted, Hitler turned back inside and poured out his rage to Goebbels. "I can't lead a war with such a people!" he said (Shirer, *BD* 399; V. Klemperer 106; Andreas-Friedrich 2).

What they did—or rather failed to do—could actually have been punished, for according to Ian Kershaw, the Nazi salute was mandatory for German civilians (Kershaw, *The "Hitler Myth"* 60). Like the hapless hungry people of Brecht's poem, they were required to speak out, to shout out, to lie with passion (*Leidenschaft*) by acclaiming the Führer's lust for war. Yet in a later poem enumerating "The Fears of the Regime" ("Die Ängste des Regimes," *Werke* 12: 68–70), we learn that these fears include not only the brownshirts' fear "of the man whose arm does not fly up" (lines 21–22) but also the rulers' terror of free speech, "the open word" (line 37). In a regime built on lies, truth is the greatest threat of all.

In Part V of the *Svendborg Poems*, "German Satires," Brecht tells the truth by means of nineteen satirical lies originally written for the German Freedom Radio and meant for broadcast in the late 1930s.[15] Of all the satires in this section, the most incisive is "The Necessity of Propaganda" ("Notwendigkeit der Propaganda," *Werke* 12: 65–67), which targets the practice of spreading lies everywhere about everything.[16] When a thousand people are murdered on a single day, the propaganda minister commends the patience of the Führer for waiting so long to have them killed. "A good propagandist," we are told, "turns a dungheap into a star attraction" (lines 36–37). Plainly anticipating the Party slogan "War is peace" in George Orwell's *1984* (1949), Brecht's propagandist turns every instrument of war into its opposite:

> Every new tank is a dove of peace
> And every new regiment is a new proof
> Of the love of peace. (lines 49–51)

But words, the poem ruefully adds, cannot do everything. The words "meat" and "clothing" cannot fill us up or keep us warm. On the contrary, the poem concludes,

> Always the more propaganda there is in our country
> The less there is of anything else. (lines 63–64)

Brecht was fascinated not only by the language of Nazi propaganda but also by certain words linked to Hitler: not only *Sieg* and *Krieg* but also "program" (*Programm*), which commonly denoted the 25-point Program of the National Socialist German Workers' Party (NSDAP) that Hitler publicly proclaimed in Munich on February 24, 1920. He did not stick with this program long. It helped to launch his career by mobilizing the masses on his behalf, but once he came to power in 1933, its demand for such things as land reform and "breaking the shackles of finance capital" served only to embarrass him because, among other things, he sought to court capitalists by demonizing Communists. Even in *Mein Kampf* (1925), he cites his 25-point program only as "the so-called program of the movement" without quoting any of its points (Turner 77). By 1937, therefore, when Brecht wrote "Words which the Führer Cannot Bear to Hear" ("Wörter, die der Führer nicht hören kann," *Werke* 12: 74), he could be quite sure that "program" stood high among them.

Well before 1937, however, another version of Hitler's program was skewered by a German artist named John Heartfield in a picture daringly published just a few months after Hitler came to power. Heartfield's picture targets a long speech that Hitler delivered on May 1, 1933.[17] While the Communist International had long celebrated May 1, May day, as a day of strikes and working-class protests against capitalism, Hitler set out to rebrand it as a day of united, classless German *Volk*. Though addressing his

Figure 1 John Heartfield, "Hitlers Programm," *AIZ Magazine*, 12.19, May 18, 1933. Artists Rights Society / The Heartfield Community of Heirs.

hearers as "Volksgenossen," "Comrades," he insists that May 1 will no longer symbolize "class conflict, . . . never-ending strife and discord" but rather "*völkisch* solidarity," a new kind of comradeship ("Volksgenossen") that supersedes Marxism. Demanding manual labor from all, he decreed "a work which will put German structures and buildings back in order and thus provide work for hundreds of thousands."

In his 1933 "Song of the White-washer Hitler," Brecht may well have alluded to this building program, for as noted above, the poem flays Hitler for whitewashing the rotten German economy instead of rebuilding it. Heartfield does likewise. Beneath a gigantic, cup-shaped paintbrush set against an elegantly fenestrated facade, his two-line caption reads:

The people (*Volk*) were luckily swindled (*angeschmiert*),
Now must the buildings be smeared (*angeschmiert*)!

Besides echoing *Volk*, a word Hitler used *ad nauseam* throughout his May day speech, Heartfield puns on the double meaning of the verb "anschmieren," which can mean either "swindle" or "smear." So far from rebuilding Germany in any sense, Heartfield's swindling Hitler is not even good enough to paint a wall.

In the "German Satires" of the *Svendborg Poems*, Hitler is not only a swindler but also a war-crazed dictator just as merciless to his own people as to his enemies. The final stanza of "The Cares of the Chancellor" ("Die Sorgen des Kanzlers," *Werke* 12: 75–76) assures us that

Sure, when he has thrown our land into war
He will cry like a child.
When your sons and husbands fall
He will sigh. When you eat grass again
He will look serious.
Thereby will you know
That you have a good Chancellor.

Brecht turns the knife still further in the very next poem, "Consolation from the Chancellor" ("Trost vom Kanzler," *Werke* 12: 76). Besides feigning solicitude for his people, we are told, the Chancellor typically revives them "through a great speech" (line 2) after fate has struck them down. But in the last two lines of this very short poem, his revived followers are likened to standing corn:

The reaper too, it is said,
Loves the upright ears. (lines 4–5)

Brecht probably alludes to Hitler's long history of cutting down anyone who stood in his way. And since Hitler was cruelest to German Jews above all, the next poem—"The Jew, A Misfortune for the People" ("Der Jude, Ein Unglück für das Volk," *Werke* 12: 26)—takes its cue from Hitler's ubiquitously echoed charge that all the misfortunes of "our land" (implicitly not at all *their* land), can be blamed on them. But the ending of the poem turns this charge upside down with a brilliant stroke of logic:

> Everyone knows
> That the regime is a misfortune for the people, so if
> All misfortune comes from the Jews,
> The Regime must come from the Jews. That is obvious!

In Part VI, the final section of the *Svendborg Poems*, Brecht turns from satires on Nazi propaganda and Hitler's maniacal belligerence to poems more personal and introspective, even autobiographical. They are epitomized by the very last poem in the collection, "To Those Born After" ("An die Nachgeborenen," *Werke* 12: 85–87). Each of its three sections is spoken by a first-person narrator who oscillates between persona and self: between wearing the mask assumed by virtually all narrators of the previous poems and unmasking the poet's true feelings.

The title alone invites some reflection. Implicitly, it banishes the anxiety voiced at the very end of "Visit to the Banished Poets," where Dante tells the visitor about poets whose works were annihilated along with their bodies. Since Brecht wrote "Visit" in the late thirties, about the time that all proofs of his *Svendborg Poems* were destroyed in Nazi-occupied Prague, Dante's grim statement may well reflect Brecht's anxiety about the survival of his own work, as already noted. Yet even though "To Those Born After" may also date in part from the late thirties (*Poems*, Notes 574), its very title presumes that his poems—or at the very least this one—will survive until "after" the Nazi era, will outlive the horrors of the "dark times" that he chronicles for the sake of future generations, who will presumably live in brighter times.

The phrase "dark times," which ends the very first line of the poem, echoes the beginning and end of the motto of Part II of the *Svendborg Poems*: a motto plainly addressed to the poet's contemporaries and telling them what *will* happen in the dark times to come. Ostensibly, "To Those Born After," especially Section I, aims to describe for future generations the dark times of the past. But the tense of the verb in the first line—"Truly, I *live* in dark times!" ("Wirklich, ich *lebe* in finsteren Zeiten!")—is present, and in spite of its title, the poem speaks not only from the present but also *to* the present, as Karen Leeder observes: to the poet's contemporaries, his first readers (Leeder 214). The double audience partly explains the oddity of the speaker's reference to himself alone—"*I* live"—as if his plight were solitary, and he its only witness. While the motto of Part II implies that everyone including the poet will be shadowed by the "dark times," the very first line of "To Those Born After" seems to say that the speaker of the poem speaks only or chiefly for himself.

Yet most of the lines that follow in Section I clearly imply that the dark times he solitarily inhabits have vexed his contemporaries just as much as they have vexed him. The original version of Section III, written about 1937 and in any case before Section I, includes a stanza that is all about himself *and* his contemporaries: "We two-faced people!" who, in the raging belligerence of "our summonses to battle . . . / / Could not ourselves be wise" (*Poems* 573–74). Likewise, the first two stanzas of Section I plainly invite the speaker's contemporaries to share his dismay at the insensitivity of those whose laughter means they have not yet heard the "terrible news" (line 6), and also at the callousness of the man ignoring his friends in need while calmly crossing the street (lines 11–13). Between these two examples of insensitivity, however, he asks:

> What times are these, where
> A conversation about trees is almost a crime
> Because it includes a silence about so many misdeeds! (lines 8–10)

Is a conversation about trees truly criminal? In "Bad Time for Poetry," as noted above, Brecht himself salutes the beauty of a "blossoming apple tree" even while proclaiming the uselessness of lyric poetry—including its images—in a "bad time." In the lines just quoted, is he deploring the criminality of a conversation about trees or—as implied by the first line—the perversion of values that *makes* it "almost a crime" to talk about them?

The latter alternative could easily criminalize poetry itself, which is why the passage subtly adumbrates the speaker's sudden re-assertion of his standing as a poet, and not at all a starving one. Right after deploring the insensitivity of the man who ignores the needs of his friends while calmly crossing the street, he admits, "I still earn my living" (line 14). Yet his comfort deeply discomfits him. He doesn't deserve it; it's "only luck" (line 15). And even though "[t]hey tell me" to eat and drink, to be glad for what I have, he writes, "how can I eat and drink, when / I snatch what I eat from the starving, and / My glass of water fails a thirsty man?" (lines 20–22). To this rhetorical question, which tendentiously presumes that the mere act of eating and drinking robs the poor of sustenance, he has no answer, only a bald statement of fact: "And yet eat and drink do I" ("Und doch esse und trinke ich," line 23). By ending both the line and the stanza with an *ich* that would normally come before the verbs ("And yet I eat and drink"), he punctuates his self-indictment.

Like the final stanza of "Bad Time for Poetry," then, Section I of "To Those Born After" stages the speaker's Yeatsian quarrel with himself. In the last stanza of this section, he ponders a third alternative to the conflict between filling his belly and empathizing with the hungry: the ancient wisdom of transcending "the strife of the world" (line 26), eschewing violence and fear, forgetting his desires, and repaying evil with good. But the way of such wisdom is closed to the speaker:

> All that can I not [do]:
> Truly, I live in dark times! (lines 32–33)

In closing the section by repeating its first line, the speaker gives it a fresh meaning: he lives in bad times because he can neither vanquish the guilt he suffers from eating while others starve nor follow the ancient way of wisdom, which is essentially renunciation. He cannot renounce the strife of the world or any of his desires, starting with the bedrock urge to eat and drink. He is caught up *in* bad times that leave him quarrelling endlessly and inconclusively with himself.

Section II, which started its life as a self-contained poem in 1934, is a piece of self-mythologizing that builds on "Driven out with Good Grounds" ("Verjagt mit gutem Grund," *Werke* 84–85), the next-to-last of the *Svendborg Poems*, which in turn recalls and rewrites a poem called, "Of Poor B.B." ("Von Armen B.B.," *Werke* 11: 119–20), written between 1922 and 1925. In the earlier poem, whose title puns on *bébé* ("baby"), "I, Bertolt Brecht" claims to have been conceived in the black forests but carried off in the womb to the "asphalt city," where he now puffs cigars, sips brandy, talks to men and women with a combination of "eccentricity and cynicism" (Speirs 205), and grimly imagines what "earthquakes" will do to the would-be "indestructible" houses of the city.[18]

In the much later "Driven out with Good Grounds," Brecht reconstructs his fictional self as simply "ich," "I," rather than "I, Bertolt Brecht." Since Brecht's father worked his way up to managing director of a huge paper mill in Augsburg during the years of Brecht's childhood and adolescence, the poem is autobiographically accurate in identifying the speaker "as the son / Of well-to-do people" (lines 2–3). But the speaker also claims to have repudiated such wealth. Betraying his class, he joined "the lowly people" (line 11), exposed by his writing how the rich deceive and oppress them, and thereby gave his parents "good ground" (line 41) to drive him out.

In portraying himself as a writer who has exposed the wrongs of the upper classes, Brecht plainly identifies the Marxist strain in his work. But he gives no hint of the complexity of his Marxism, of the fame and wealth he has gained by means of his writing, or of the considerable difference between being driven out by bourgeois parents and deliberately moving to the comfort of a large, seaside farmhouse in Denmark. All this complexity informs Section II of "To Those Born After," where he implicitly claims to be speaking from beyond the grave after a life of ultimately fatal as well as futile resistance. Coming into the cities "at a time of disorder" (line 35), when hunger was rising and mankind rising up, he joined the revolution, ate between battles, slept with murderers, made love heedlessly, and viewed nature "without patience" (line 44). Though Brecht had actually rebelled only in thought, this brutishly mythical autobiography contains a kernel of truth: he fought the powerful with words. Language, he goes on to say, "betrayed me to the butcher" (line 43).

So he died without reaching "the goal" (line 53), which lay far off, clearly visible even if hardly attainable. In the original poem that stands behind this section, the goal is identified as "a better-living mankind" / "eine besser lebende Menschheit (*Poems* 573).[19] But the absence of any such definition here recalls the quandary expressed at the end of the first section. The only thing definitely stated near the end of this one is the curious hope that "the authorities / would sit more securely without me" (lines 49–50), which clearly implies that he had made them less secure during his lifetime. In these dark times, is that all he could hope to leave as his legacy for those "born after"? Whatever the answer, Section III speaks directly to them:

> You, who will come up from the flood
> In which we have sunk
> Think
> When you speak of our faults
> Of the dark time
> Which you have escaped. (lines 60–65)

Speaking now as an apologist for his generation, the poet argues in effect that he and his fellow Germans were more sinned against than sinning. This claim remains and will probably forever remain undecidable—largely because Brecht could not foresee in 1939 all that future generations would have to remember about his own, especially how many of his generation would become what Daniel Goldhagen has called Hitler's willing executioners. The original version of this stanza seems to fault his generation only for "our" raging belligerence, as if—like a disease—"we" had caught Hitler's lust for blood.[20] But the final version of Section III makes a more complicated charge. After first implying that everyone (rather than a small minority) shared his experience of exile, "changing countries more often than our shoes" (line 66), the speaker laments both his generation's failure to fight the class war *and* the passions that gripped them:

> Through the wars of the classes, despairing
> When there was only injustice and no rebellion.
> Yet we know well:
> Even hatred against meanness
> Distorts the features;
> And even anger at injustice
> Makes the voice hoarse. (lines 67–73)

Regretting both the failure to fight and the passions of belligerence, these lines verge on self-contradiction. But in the final lines of Section III, the speaker identifies what his generation lacked above all: friendliness. We who sought to bake the bread of kindness, he writes, "could not ourselves be friendly" (lines 74–75). The word "freundlich" echoes not only Brecht's address to his "friends" in the opening motto of the whole collection but also what Benjamin judged the key lesson of Brecht's poem about Lao-tsu's road into exile: just as water can overcome stone, friendliness can overcome hardness. Hardness includes, of course, all the insensitivity deplored in Section I: everything that drives one man apart from—or against—another. Finally, not just addressing future generations but also envisioning a time when "man is a helper to humankind," he pleads:

> Think of us
> With forbearance. (lines 77–79)

From the utopia of altruism imagined at the end of the very last poem in the collection, the poet may well expect not only forbearance but empathy, the deepest kind of friendliness. Together, Brecht implies, these two qualities embody everything that may ultimately triumph over the war to come.

Notes

1   All translations are mine unless otherwise indicated.
2   On his radio listening, see Walter Benjamin's account of evenings spent in front of Brecht's radio during his summer visits to the poet in 1934, 1936, and 1938 (Benjamin, *SW* 1: 854).

3   Joyce Crick does well to note that the *Svendborg Poems* are "a selection out of a
    tremendous number of poems Brecht wrote during this astonishingly prolific
    decade . . ." (Crick 115). But assuming they constitute a representative selection, I have
    largely confined my discussion to them.

4   *A and P* 81–82. "Whether a work is realistic or not cannot be determined merely by
    checking whether or not it is like existing works, which are said to be realistic, or were
    realistic in their time. In each case, one must compare the depiction of life in a work of
    art with the life that is being depicted (instead of comparing it with another
    depiction)" (*A and P* 85).

5   Lyon 260. Though Brecht occasionally socialized with the Frankfurt Schoolmen in Los
    Angeles after moving there in 1941, he seems to have done so chiefly in order to gather
    material for his satirical novel about them, *Tui*. In May 1942, for instance, after
    lunching at Horkheimer's with the Austrian composer Hanns Eisler, Brecht picked up
    from Eisler a plot suggestion based on the fact that the Frankfurt School was founded
    with funds furnished by Hermann Weil, who at the beginning of the twentieth century
    was "the biggest grain trader in the world" (http://www.rsw.hd.bw.schule.de/shal/
    drweil/heimat.htm). In Brecht's account of Eisler's circular plot for Brecht's *Tui* novel,
    "a rich old man (Weil, the speculator in wheat) dies[;] disturbed at the poverty in the
    world, in his will he leaves a large sum to set up an institute which will do research on
    the source of this poverty, which is, of course, himself . . ." (*J* 230).

6   My thanks to O.K. Werckmeister for this information (email of September 25, 2018).

7   "In typescript the poem bears the title 'Frühjahr 1936' [Spring 1936] followed by an
    asterisk referring to the following (deleted) note: 'in many of his poems Brecht calls
    Hitler THE HOUSEPAINTER, because instead of tearing down the rotten building of
    the German economy, he only whitewashed the cracks on the outside, the holes and
    chinks'" (Speirs 14n13, my translation of the deleted note).

8   *Life* magazine, April 26, 1948: 74.

9   According to Speirs, the poem "foresees the time when 'the drummer' will have begun
    to wage 'his' war but when politically enlightened Germans, following Lenin's
    injunction to transform imperialist war into civil (i.e. *class*) war, will show their
    patriotism precisely by sabotaging Hitler's plans" (Speirs 4).

10 At his Obersalzberg home on August 22, 1939, just nine days before the invasion of
    Poland, Hitler told his Wehrmacht commanders that Germany needed it for living
    space (Lochner 11–12).

11 Ronald Speirs notes that Brecht is punning on "erklären," which can mean either
    "explain" or "declare" to a customs officer (email to author of February 7, 2019).

12 On July 9, 1933, for instance, less than six months after Hitler came to power, a
    Professor of Romance Language at the Technical University of Dresden found himself
    "entirely bereft of money," facing bills he could not pay and expecting a salary cut in a
    month or two (V. Klemperer 24).

13 Ronald Speirs objects that in this case, "krieg" is just the last syllable of "rausgekrieg,"
    which means "get [something] out" (email of February 7, 2019). But in rhyming this
    word with the verb "besiegt," which typically means "defeats," Brecht plays up its final
    syllable, which also gets the final accent ("*raus*-ge-***kriegt***") at the end of the line. When
    rhymed with "be-*siegt*," I believe, the syllable "krieg" may at least intimate war.

14 For more on Joyce's allusions to Hitler in *FW*, see John Gordon, "Joyce's Hitler".

15 Though eight of them were published in *Das Wort* from December 1937 to March
    1938, they were broadcast (if at all) only from stations outside Germany (*Poems*
    567–68n294).

16 See also the fine things said about war preparation by the Ministry of Propaganda in "The War Shall be Well Prepared" / "Der Krieg Soll Gut Vorbereitet Sein" (*Werke* 12: 72).

17 See http://der-fuehrer.org/reden/english/33-05-01.htm

18 This "Bertolt Brecht" is almost wholly fictional. Brecht's parents both came from the Black Forest to the industrial city of Augsburg well before he was born, and in 1922 he himself had recently moved to Berlin. But aside from the brandy and cigars, the speaker of this poem has nothing to do with the promising young dramatist whose *Drums in the Night* opened in Munich and Berlin in 1922 and won the prestigious Kleist Prize—all well before he finished writing this poem.

19 Willett, Manheim, and Fried render the German as "a better life for mankind," but this, I think, misses the polysemy of the original, which envisions mankind living better in every sense: not just eating and drinking more, but acting more humanely.

20 Yet as I have already noted above, few Germans shared Hitler's belligerence in the late thirties, when Brecht wrote the *Svendborg Poems.*

6

The Invasion of Poland and
Bertolt Brecht's *Mother Courage*

War came into Poland
In 1939
And there was only a wasteland
Where house and home had been.

—Bertolt Brecht, *Children's Crusade 1939*

Prophecies made by poetry are seldom if ever fulfilled. As we have just seen, the final section of the last of the *Svendborg Poems* envisions a time when "man is a helper to humankind." On September 1, 1939, scarcely three months after the *Svendborg Poems* were published, Hitler launched an invasion of Poland that in just a few weeks left it devastated, totally occupied, and utterly helpless.

Brecht bore no poetic witness to its plight until three years later, when—from the comfort and safety of Santa Monica, California—he wrote the ballad called *Children's Crusade 1939* (*CP* 824–36), which tells a story of fifty-five boys and girls wandering through a devastated Poland, seeking "escape" from "all the nightmare" of battles and yearning for "a country / Where there'd be no more war" (st. 6). Though these "children of every race and clime" (st. 43) bridge ethnic divisions and prove almost miraculously altruistic in the face of desolation and desperation, they never find refuge, and the poem radiates so much sympathy for children victimized by war that it has been resoundingly canonized.[1] But if we try to link the misery of Poland in the fall of 1939 to the most important work Brecht produced during that time, we face a much harder question: does *Mother Courage and Her Children* express anything like sympathy—or even empathy—for Poland?

To answer this question, we must first recognize that in the fall of 1939, Brecht was nearly obsessed with the geo-politics of war. After leaving Svendborg in April, he traveled to Stockholm on a visa furnished by the Swedish Social-Democratic Committee in return for a lecture at the Stockholm Student Theater. By mid-July he had settled nearby on the island of Lidingö in what he called an "ideal" residence: half-surrounded by firs, it housed a study big enough to hold "many tables" (*Journals* 31). From this supremely comfortable perch—yet another island refuge—he wrote again and again about the two nations that by secret agreement were brutally invading Poland from west and east: Germany and the Soviet Union.

If Brecht wrote any letters during the first four months of the war, none has survived. But his "work journal" (*Arbeitsjournal*), as it is commonly called (though not by Brecht himself), is packed with commentary that says far less about his literary labors than about the stages of the brand new war. After noting on November 7 that he has finished a radio play called *The Trial of Lucullus*, he quickly turns back to the "epic character" of the war (*Journals* 37–38). On December 7, he ruminates at length on narrative elements in *Lucullus* and on the style of his novel-in-progress, *The Business Affairs of Herr Julius Caesar*, but on December 24, just after telling himself to avoid treating Caesar "from the retrospective angle," he takes an example from the planning behind Hitler's pact with Stalin, which he then considers at length with no more reference to the novel.

Yet the most remarkable thing about this would-be journal of Brecht's literary work in the fall of 1939 is the absence of any comment on the play for which he is now best known: *Mother Courage and Her Children*. Though he started writing it in late September and finished it by early December, he mentions it just once—among several other manuscripts cited in a long list of everything he owned on December 7, ranging from three Japanese masks to an old round table.[2] Were it not for the spasm of bourgeois pride in his possessions that suddenly gripped the resolute Marxist on that December day, his fall 1939 journals would tell us nothing whatever about a play that is not just wholly consumed by war but written at the very outset of World War II.

The absence of any comment on *Mother Courage* in Brecht's journals for the fall of 1939 is hardly more startling than the absence of any reference to the plight of the Poles. On September 5, Brecht notes Hitler's "war of annihilation against poland," but his only other comment is that "poland is not fighting at all" (*Journals* 33). This was hardly true, as we have seen in Chapter 4. But knowing almost nothing of what the Poles were actually doing and suffering in their own land, Brecht was fascinated by three things: the "spook[iness]" of a "war which isn't being fought" (*Journals* Sept. 5, 1939, p. 33); "the neutrality pact" between Germany and the USSR (*Journals* Sept. 1, 1939, p. 32); and above all "the soviet invasion of poland" (*Journals* Sept. 18, 1939, p. 36). By the first phrase he meant that France and Britain were so far waging nothing but a leaflet war on western Germany (*Journals* Sept. 5, 1939, p. 33). By the second he meant the Non-Aggression Pact between Germany and the Soviet Union signed in Moscow on August 23. And by the third he meant the Soviet invasion of Poland on September 17—something secretly authorized by the pact but generally foreseen by no one, least of all Brecht, who spent days trying to explain it to himself.[3]

The chief problem, as Heinrich Olschowsky has observed, "was the widely propagated idea that anti-fascism and anti-Stalinism were incompatible" (Olschowsky 71). Though Brecht satirizes Stalin as an all-consuming ox in the *Svendborg Poems*, he still believed—even after learning on September 1 of the "neutrality pact"—that the Soviet Union might one day liberate the proletariat of the world. To that end, he thought, the Soviets were steering clear of "a war between imperialist states," a war between the "aggressive capitalism" of Germany and the "defensive capitalism" of the "western powers," with "enough barbarism to maintain a barbaric situation" (*Journals* Sept. 7, 1939, p. 34). Brecht thus echoes Stalin in practically equating the attacker and the attacked (Olschowsky 73). Yet if the USSR should ever enter the war, Brecht writes, it could only be "on the western side." Alternatively, with slogans from both Britain and

Germany voicing popular resistance to their respective leaders, Brecht speculates that the USSR might "wait until peoples come along with whom they can enter into alliances, instead of just governments" (*Journals* Sept. 7, 1939, p. 34).

Whatever the plausibility of this prospect, the beginning of the German siege of Warsaw on September 8—with still no intervention by the Western powers—led Brecht to rethink his analysis of the Russo-German pact.[4] What did it really mean? While "the communists," Brecht wrote, "immediately claimed that it was a contribution to peace by the soviet union . . . war broke out" at once, "and hitler claimed in major appeals that his pact had made it possible for him to lead the country against Poland" (*Journals* Sept. 9, 1939, pp. 34–35). If the West does not intervene, he surmised, it is now

> more than possible that poland will be subjugated without any great war, and poland is in the east and not in the west, *and the [Soviet] union will in the eyes of the proletariat of the world bear the terrible stigma of aiding and abetting fascism,* the wildest element in capitalism and the most hostile to the workers. i don't think more can be said than that the [Soviet] union saved its skin at the cost of leaving the proletariat of the world without solutions, hopes or help. (*Journals* Sept. 9, 1939, p. 35, my emphasis).

It is hard to imagine a more damning critique of Stalin and the Soviet Union from a writer fully committed—at least in theory—to "the proletariat of the world." Yet it is also possible that in gradually coming to see how the USSR may have betrayed this proletariat, Brecht may have begun to doubt his own political acumen, or at least the assumption that great writers (like himself) are also great seers.

On September 11, he skewers a freshly published speech that made just this assumption. In this speech, as I have already noted in Chapter 4, H. G. Wells made what he called "a clear public assertion of the supreme value of the creative mind" (*Travels* 122). To demonstrate the value of such a mind (meaning of course his own), he flays Mussolini for "suppress[ing] the works of Voltaire in Italy" (*Travels* 136) and thrashes Hitler for the indigestible dreck of *Mein Kampf*.[5] "[R]eally," Brecht writes, "what a mountain of a philistine! he views hitler and mussolini simply as writers, and finds them stupid, as if lack of literary talent couldn't prevent the cleverest person from appearing clever in a work of literature" (*Journals* Sept. 11, 1939, p. 35). In assuming that political leaders can be judged purely by literary criteria, Wells's speech is itself a mountain of stupidity. But one wonders if Brecht might have discerned within it a cracked mirror of his own assumptions: that his literary talent gave him the power to judge a war whose outcome he could not foresee—and which might betray his expectations.

Whatever might happen later, he was profoundly shocked on September 18 to learn that the Soviet Union had just invaded Poland. "[E]very ideological veil," he wrote, was now "torn to shreds." Fearful that "the Soviet Union could be stumbling into a war on germany's side," he decried its abandonment of the slogan that it "needs no foot of foreign soil" and "the sensational pravda article" that tried to justify the invasion by appropriating

> fascist hypocrisies about "blood-brotherhood," the liberation of "brothers" (of slav descent), all the terminology of nationalism. This is addressed to the

german fascists, but at the same time to the soviet troops. (*Journals* Sept. 18, 1939, p. 36)

Just as Hitler had justified the invasion of Czechoslovakia by claiming to be liberating ethnic Germans from its would-be tyrannical yoke, *Pravda* reported that the Red Army had been ordered to protect "the lives and property of the population of Western Ukraine and Western White Russia," and thus to rescue "the kindred Ukrainians and White Russians living in Poland ... without any rights ..." ("Soviet Rule" 70).

Brecht knew only too well what this sort of protection and rescue meant for Poles. Yet in spite of his disgust with the USSR's "appropriation of fascist hypocrisies" to justify its invasion, he promptly proceeded to cast the Russian occupation of eastern Poland as a move "Napoleonic" in its sudden, unheralded reclaiming of "two provinces which formerly belonged to the russian empire [*reich*]" (*Journals* Sept. 19, 1939, p. 36). As Olschowsky observes, Brecht presumes "an imperial continuity between czardom and Stalin's Soviet Union," whose *reich*—I might add—he implicitly aligns with Hitler's Third Reich. Brecht says nothing about "the rights of a people" who gained those provinces—West Ukraine and West Belarus—by the Treaty of Riga in 1921.[6] To this extent he reflects the state of German public opinion dating back to the Weimar Republic, when most German parties were united in "an anti-Polish choir" and resented the Poles for claiming—by the Treaty of Versailles—a state of their own made up of territories seized from Germany (Olschowsky 75).

In effect, then, Russia and Germany were each supposedly reclaiming territories stolen—as it were—by nefarious treaties. So in spite of the USSR's "fascist hypocrisies" in a *Pravda* article that sounded to Brecht "as if hitler had edited it" (*Journals* Sept. 19, 1939, p. 36), and in spite of his conclusion that the Bolshevik party had become a dictatorship (*Journals* Sept. 21, 1939, p. 37), Brecht somehow kept his faith in the Soviet Union. "The Marxist intellectuals," Olschowky writes,

> were horrified by the mere possibility that with the Pact, the Soviet Union could join Hitler's Germany in the War—yet Brecht set his hope nonetheless doggedly with the Soviet Union as the only power on the continent who had a chance to stop Hitler's onward march. (Olschowsky 79)

Paradoxically, then, even while hoping that the USSR might stop Hitler, Brecht also hoped—or imagined—that the war might destroy "the english empire" or even, he implies, all empires, as "native populations" arise to "mobilise instantly" (*Journals* Sept. 19, 1939, p. 37). But he has little faith in Stalin's capacity to launch such a war. Stalin, he writes, "finds it impossible to start the war in a revolutionary manner, as a people's war, as a proletarian action, as a mass war. ... (*Journals* Sept. 21, 1939, p. 37). With no faith in "the russian proletariat," Brecht imagines the socialists of the world ultimately joining not the Soviet Union but rather the proletariats of Britain and France:

> the proletariats of the western powers must support their governments against hitler ... the least of all is to be expected from the russian proletariat, the hope of the germans [german people] lies with the british labour party and [Leon] blum's

social democrats [in France]. should the Russians intervene again in g[ermany] at the end of the war against hitler and the western powers, the place for the socialists would be on the side of the western powers. (*Journals* Nov. 13, 1939, p. 38).

Comments like these show how deeply the Russian invasion of Poland shook Brecht's faith in the Soviet Union. After all his calculations, he seems to have realized that he could hardly predict which side it would end up on and was left to imagine that the people of Germany—never mind the Poles!—would be rescued by the "proletariats of the western powers," *not* "the russian proletariat." For Brecht as a Marxist theorist, the war is essentially a problem in international politics. It is anything but a cause for outrage or sympathy on behalf of the Poles—let alone admiration for their bravery.

The absence of any such feeling in Brecht's journal entries for the fall of 1939 is all the more startling when they are compared with the words of leading Polish writers both before and after the outbreak of the war. To exemplify the "spiritual climate" of Poland at this time, Olschowsky cites Wladyslaw Broniewski (1897–1962), a decorated veteran of the Polish Legions who had successfully fought the Bolsheviks in World War I. Not only a poet but also a translator of songs from Brecht's own *Threepenny Opera*, he was just as much a Leftist as Brecht, and in the 1930s he was jailed by the Polish government for consorting with the Polish Communist Party. Yet in a poem called *Bajonett aufgesetzt* (*Bayonet put-on*), written just five months before the German invasion, he urges his countrymen to overcome their political differences and "defines Poland as the collective house of everyone who must be defended against outside attackers" (Olschowsky 78).

Furthermore, given what those outside attackers did to Poland, it is almost heartbreaking to read what a leading Polish writer named Zofia Nalknowska set down in her notebook five months later:

17 sep 39 My God, what has happened in these couple days! Likely there isn't any country any more.... [from] the cities Lemberg, Krakow silence on the radio, no trains traveling there, no telegrams can be sent, and no letters or newspapers emerge. 18 sep 39 Last news from yesterday: the Soviet army pushed into the Polish zone.... After the silencing of the broadcast everyone sat there dead, still, silent—each stranger gripped with the same despair. The Germans, the Bolsheviks and between them a shared border. The nightmare of history, well known from the past and once believed to have been overcome, turns back again. (qtd. Olschowsky 79)

Whether or not this Polish writer was alluding to the nightmare from which Joyce's Stephen Dedalus yearns to awake (*Ulysses* 2.377), what she describes is truly a nightmare. But to set her anguished words beside the detached analyses of Brecht's journals is to wonder what has happened to the author of the *Svendborg Poems*, above all the very last of them—"To those Born After." In that poem, as we have seen, the poet deplores the callousness of the man crossing the street while ignoring his friends in need, lacerates himself for eating and drinking while others starve and thirst, and finally imagines that the coming war may be followed by a time when "man is a helper to humankind." If Brecht truly aimed to make literature a source of healing in a time of global war, how could he have so coolly ignored the desolation of Poland in the fall of 1939?

His only answer is *Mother Courage*—and the theory of drama that stands behind it.

Besides setting the play in the seventeenth century as "A Chronicle of the Thirty Years War," Brecht had long eschewed any kind of drama that sought to rouse the sympathy of the audience, that invited them to embrace dramatic illusion as reality, or to identify themselves with any character portrayed on the stage. Ever since 1928, when his satirical musical *The Threepenny Opera* opened in Berlin, Brecht had been developing what he called "epic theater" by means of the *Verfremdungseffekt*, commonly translated as the "alienation effect" or "A-effect" but more accurately called the "defamiliarization effect" or "*V-effekt*." In his "Short Organum for the Theatre" (1948), Brecht explains that a defamiliarizing representation "allows us to recognize its subject, but at the same time makes it seem unfamiliar."[7] As Robert Gordon explains, the *V-effekt*

> makes the everyday appear surprising in order to enable a spectator to interrogate each dramatic event rather than regard it as part of a "natural" order. By exposing the existing social system with its injustice, inequality and corruption as arbitrary rather than normal, the *V-effekt* demonstrates that it can be changed. . . . By making the spectator conscious of the art of its construction, a performance enables her to participate actively in a dialogical argument about how and why a change in society should be effected. (Gordon, "Brecht")

This sort of dialogue demands an audience willing to exercise its reason, *Ratio*, rather than indulging its feelings, *Gefühl*: precisely what Brecht himself does in his detached *Journal* entries on the double invasion of Poland. In bourgeois theatre, Brecht writes, the audience must be transported from the "contradictory world" we live in to a dreamworld of consistency, and "must be entertained with the anger that is the practical expression of sympathy for the underdog" ("Short Organum," paras. 28, 24). By contrast, the *Journal* entries express neither sympathy nor anger. Struggling throughout with contradiction, they tell us something important about the state of mind in which Brecht wrote *Mother Courage*.

In writing this play, Brecht lunges from the broadcast-news immediacy of a present-day war to the history of war in seventeenth-century Europe. According to Gordon, Brecht used the contrast between past and present "to identify the historical determinants of contemporary life" (Gordon, "Brecht"). Rather than robbing past periods of their social structures, however, rather than "stripping them of everything that makes them different" ("Short Organum" para. 36) or "representing human nature as universal and unchanging" (Gordon, "Brecht"), Brecht planted each of his plays in a particular historical period:

> In *Mother Courage*, for instance, Brecht deliberately engineered a comparison of historical and then present-day circumstances: by setting the play during the Thirty Years War (1618–48)—a different yet comparable historical situation to

1939—he encouraged the spectator to think in historical terms about the material conditions that had precipitated the war which was about to engulf Europe. (Gordon, "Brecht")

In other words, the difference between the new war of 1939 and the Thirty Years War of 1618–48—actually a set of wars—compels us to see the new war in the defamiliarizing light of "historical terms." The key link between those terms and the time-present of Brecht's *Journal* entries, then, is a passage in which he reads the new war as explicitly "epic" in his sense of the word:

the war displays a remarkably epic character, it teaches mankind about itself, as it were, reads a lesson, a text to which the thunder of gunfire and exploding bombs merely provide the accompaniment. it exposes its economic aims blatantly, in that case it has direct recourse to economic means. conquests of markets provoke blockades in response, arms buildups the withdrawal of raw materials, the ideological cover-up has worn so thin that it only serves to throw what is really happening into sharper relief. in contrast to the great war when the classes observed an internal truce in the interests of the national war, national wars now stop for the class struggle. the war is quite literally *"meaningless."* (*Journals* Nov. 13, 1939, p. 38)

Among *Journal* entries that say nothing about *Mother Courage* anywhere else, this one plainly adumbrates its lesson. Just as "epic" theater, according to Brecht, must expose its own devices rather than passing itself off as "natural," this war blatantly "exposes its economic aims," or rather reveals to Brecht's Marxist vision how much this new war is an "ideological cover-up" for the "class struggle." Whether or not professional historians would now accept Brecht's verdict, it deeply informed his way of defamiliarizing the new war. He defamiliarized it not only by treating it as essentially economic but also as if it had been fought three hundred years earlier, in a past meant to check anything like the sympathy or anger that might be provoked by staging the Nazi-Soviet seizure of Poland in Brecht's own time.

Yet it would be wrong to suppose that Brecht thought plays should have no emotive impact. As early as *Difficulties of the Epic Theater* (1927–28), he insisted that it would be "wholly incorrect to want to deny feeling in this kind of theater" (qtd. Williams 62). By 1940, Katherine Williams writes, Brecht had come to realize that epic theatre "could and should" excite the audience:

The spectator undoubtedly should feel emotions in the theatre, but these should be as a social and political reaction to the events onstage rather than an expression of empathy with the characters, as was the convention at the time. (Williams, my emphasis)

Rather than purging his plays of all feeling, then, Brecht stages for his audience a running contest between *Ratio* and *Gefühl,* a dialectical struggle between feeling and detached analysis of the socio-political forces represented on stage. Though this dialectical version of the *Verfremdungseffekt* is seldom applied to his poetry, it is perfectly exemplified by one of the *Svendborg Poems*, "Ballad of the Widows of Ossega" (*Werke* 12: 17–18), which is based on a true story: when a group of Czech women lost all of their husbands in a mining accident, the government stubbornly ignored their pleas for help. Surprisingly enough, Brecht's poem voices neither sympathy for the widows nor rage at their plight. The last words of the poem, in fact, are spoken not by any person but rather by the snow that falls on them one November day after they have spent days and nights squatting in the street and begging for someone to help them:

> And there the snow fell, big, wet flakes.
> *That, said the snow,*
> *That we can do for the widows of Ossega.*
>
> (lines 26–28, my translation)

Like the police who threaten them with rifles and the government that offers them nothing but bloated rhetoric, the snow is utterly heartless. And it is precisely the frigid heartlessness of the authorities—of those who callously ignore the desperate need of these women—that provokes both sympathy for them and rage at the economic system that exploits them.

To feel the power of this ballad, then, is to begin to see how a play by Brecht can move its audience precisely by masking or denying any feelings in the characters on stage. *Mother Courage* heightens this complex effect—a dialectical version of the *V-effekt*, as stated above—by foregrounding Poland in its dramatization of the Thirty Years War.

While any playwright who dramatizes history takes liberties with its facts, the liberties Brecht takes in *Mother Courage* highlight the role of Poland in a war that actually centered on Germany. According to professional historians, "the principal battlefield" for all the conflicts of the Thirty Years War "was the towns and principalities of Germany" (Encyclopedia Britannica). Yet the very first conflict mentioned in *Mother Courage* is the Swedish campaign against Poland:

SPRING 1624. THE SWEDISH COMMANDER IN CHIEF COUNT OXENSTEIRNA IS RAISING TROOPS IN DALECARLIA FOR THE POLISH CAMPAIGN. (Scene 1, p. 1)

There is some historic truth here, for the Swedish Empire actually launched a series of attacks during the years between 1600 and 1629, and the third phase of these attacks included a truce that spanned the spring of 1624, when yet another Polish campaign loomed ahead in the following year. But while Sweden's long-running enemy was the Polish-Lithuanian Commonwealth, Brecht turns this alliance into Poland alone. Also, though the Swedes besieged the fortress of Wallhof in 1626, as the stage directions for Act 2 indicate (p. 11), Wallhof (now Valle Parish, Latvia) was in Lithuania, and from seventeenth-century maps of the region it is not clear why the Swedes would have crossed the Polish part of the Commonwealth to reach it.

Brecht's turning of seventeenth-century Poland into a distant mirror of 1939 Poland hardly stops here. Ironically, he may well have decided that the name of the Swedish King who actually led the attacks on Poland—King Gustav II Adolf (1594–1632)—

reeked too much of Hitler to be used in the play. But Brecht's unnamed king clearly prefigures both the Führer and Stalin. In using the most brutal of methods to "liberate" and "protect" both Poland and Germany from the would-be tyrannical grip of the Holy Roman Emperor, the Swedish king anticipates the arguments made to justify the double invasion of modern Poland. Consider what three characters say about this king—"our king"—in Scene 3 of the play, which is set in Poland:

Mother Courage   Those Poles here in Poland had no business sticking their noses in. Right, our king moved in on them, horse and foot, but did they keep the peace? No, went and stuck their noses into their own affairs, they did, and fell on the king just as he was quietly clearing off. They committed a breach of peace, that's what, so blood's on their own head.

The Chaplain   All our king minded about was freedom. The Emperor had made slaves of them all, Poles and Germans alike. And the king had to liberate them.

The Cook   … [I]t cost the king dear trying to give freedom to Germany, … on top of which he had to have the Germans locked up and drawn and quartered 'cause they wanted to carry on slaving for the emperor. Course the king took a serious view when anybody didn't want to be free. He set out by just trying to protect Poland against bad people, particularly the emperor, then it started to become a habit till he ended up protecting the whole of Germany. (*MC* 23)

In the Swedish campaign of "liberation" and "protection" described here, Germany is not the chief agent of aggression but rather—by an irony Brecht gleefully exploits—a victim of it. But when Mother Courage charges that Poland broke the peace by fighting for itself against the king's invasion, she comes very near to saying what Poland did against the Nazis in 1939. Even though Brecht thought on September 5 that Poland was "not fighting at all" (*Journals* 33), he must have learned—even while writing this play— that modern Poland did indeed fight for itself before being forced to surrender.

In the war(s) of Brecht's play, it is hard to know just which side Mother Courage takes. She calls the Swedish monarch "our king," and the play opens in an historic province of Sweden (Dalecarlia), where Count Oxenstierna, the Swedish Commander in Chief, is "raising troops … for the Polish campaign." Oxenstierna is in fact the name of a Swedish noble family dating back to the Middle Ages. But the family names that tumble out of Mother Courage in the opening lines of the play spring from an imagination run riot in defiance of ethnic cohesion and purity. Her own name (Anna Fierling) is German, and her mute daughter Kattrin is half-German, which would seem to make them targets of the Swedish king's "liberation" project. But she calls him "our king," as just noted, and we know hardly more of Kattrin's father than of the fathers of Anna's two sons. Though her elder son combines a Norwegian first name (Eilif) with the Polish surname of his supposed father ("something" like Nojocki), the father he remembers, says Anna, was actually "a Frenchie with a little beard" (*MC* 4) and later she calls Eilif "a Finnish devil" (*MC* 17). The second son, whom the recruiting sergeant takes for a Chinaman, was—says Anna—"a Swiss, but called Fejos, a name that has nowt to do with his father." Christened thus only because his mother was "with a

Hungarian" when he was born (*MC* 4), "Fejos" is surely Brecht's wink at Paul Fejos (1897–1963), a real-life Hungarian-born film director. Yet Mother Courage calls her second son "Swiss Cheese." Like the heterogeneous kids of Brecht's *Children's Crusade 1939*, Anna's children not only flout all rules of ethnic purity but are also doomed to die as victims—or collateral victims—of war. It is crucial to remember that the full title of Brecht's play—*Mother Courage and Her Children*—makes the children almost as important as the woman who will end up sacrificing each of them to her need for profit, or at least her compulsion to bargain.

The first act, however, subtly reveals that the wheels of her trading cart have not yet crushed her maternal feelings. On one hand, she fakes dismay at the prospect of losing her son to the war. When Eilif pulls out of the sergeant's helmet a slip of paper marked with a cross that seems to seal his fate, she cries out in mock pain:

> Oh, wretched mother that I am, oh pain-racked giver of birth! Shall he die? Ay, in the springtime of life he is doomed. If he becomes a soldier he shall bite the dust, it's plain to see. (*MC* 8)

Mother Courage thus mocks the kind of anguish that illusionistic theater highlights to make its audience cry. While feigning such anguish, she also seizes the chance to sell the sergeant a belt-buckle that is worth "two florins" for the "bargain" price of "half a florin" (*MC* 9), and earlier, when the sergeant demands to know why her healthy, muscular sons are dodging military service, she answers in strictly economic terms: "Nowt doing, sergeant. That's no trade for my kids" (*MC* 5). On the other hand, when the sergeant replies that "there's good money" in fighting (and we later learn that Eilif gets ten florins for joining up), all she can do is disparage the value of her progeny— precisely the opposite of what she does with all her other goods. "He's a chicken," she says of Eilif. "Give him a fierce look, he'll fall over" (*MC* 5). It's a good joke, but as a marketing strategy, it makes no sense.

The ending of the scene perfectly encapsulates the conflict inside the mercantile mother of this play. Rather than staging a separation between mother and child that might wring the hearts of the audience, Brecht sends Eilif off with the recruiting officer—and ten florins bounty—before his mother even knows he's gone. Though Dumb Kattrin sounds the alarm with "hoarse noises," her mother and the officer are both immersed in transactions: just as the officer wins over Eilif with promises of ready sex as well as ready money, Mother Courage closes her sale of the belt-buckle by giving the sergeant a "swig of brandy" as lagniappe (*MC* 9).

But the steel armor of this seasoned trader just perceptibly cracks when she learns that Eilif has gone. On hearing from Swiss Cheese that he "went off with the recruiter" (*MC* 10), she "*stands quite still*"—a moment of silent shock, pain, rage, or whatever else we can imagine her feeling—and then says to her now absent son: "You simpleton" (*MC* 10). Her overt meaning is clear: you've made a stupid bargain, Eilif, by trading your life for ten florins. Yet the sergeant sees her pain even as he pricks her hypocrisy:

> Could do with a swig yourself, ma. Plenty worse things than being a soldier. Want to live off war, but keep yourself and family out of it, eh? (*MC* 10)

Unlike rich capitalists, who profit from war, this poor capitalist has begun to learn that she cannot do so without paying a price. As Brecht himself writes of this scene, "Mother Courage loses her son to the recruiter because she can't resist the temptation to sell a belt buckle" ("Texts" 102). Yet she buries the pain of this knowledge by treating it as no more than a minor inconvenience. Though she cannot afford even a single horse for her cart and has lost one of the two sons who have been pulling it, she readily finds a replacement. "You'll have to help your brother pull now, Kattrin," she says (*MC* 10).

Scene 2 stages a reunion between Mother Courage and Eilif two years after the spring of 1624, when he left her to join the army.[8] But rather than embracing him with anything like tearful rapture, she voices no more than surprise at the sight of him, for she is mainly intent on the business of selling a capon to the surly cook who works for a general but doesn't want to buy it for the general's dinner. Partly because she is proud that Eilif has won the general's admiration for his "deed of heroism" (*MC* 12), she badgers the cook to pay up. At first, her initial demand for "sixty hellers" drops through fifty to forty; but when the cook tries to cut the price to thirty, she claims that "this gifted beast" was so smart it "could count" (*MC* 12). What really makes the cook buy, however, is the general's demand for meat worthy of his guest, who—says Eilif himself—has worked up an appetite "cutting down peasants" (*MC* 13).

Now she can demand far more than the paltry hellers that she and the cook have been wrangling over. Even as the cook finally agrees to pay the "criminal price" of fifty hellers, she demands a florin, which was worth nearly six times as much.[9] "A florin, I said. For my eldest boy, the general's guest, no expense is too great for me" (*MC* 13). Nowhere else are maternal affection and mercantile strategy so cunningly combined. By "no expense is too great for me," she does not mean that she will spend all she has for her eldest boy. Instead, she makes the cook pay *her* for his sake, thereby exploiting his newly gained status as both a hero and "the general's guest."

Likewise, his heroism turns out to be nothing but a word for hard bargaining—or tall tales. To explain how he and his men captured "twenty oxen," Eilif says they were caught in the act, suddenly threatened by a gang of cudgel-bearing peasants who outnumbered them three to one and demanded they surrender. But by pretending to haggle for the oxen (offering fifteen rather than twenty florins a head) and thus doing "business" (*MC* 14), Eilif made the peasants scratch their heads long enough for him to cut them all down with his sword. The story, of course, is as Falstaffian and fabricated as the oxen that he says will arrive in "a day or two at most" (*MC* 13), like Lewis Carroll's "jam tomorrow." Even if true, the story exemplifies for Mother Courage nothing but recklessness. Only stupid kings and generals, she argues, need what the general calls "men of courage" to fight for them; a "decent king or general," she says, can make do with men of "perfectly ordinary, average intelligence, and for all I know cowards" (*MC* 15).

Though Eilif does not yet know that his mother is working in the general's kitchen, he implicitly seconds her point by singing about a soldier who spurns his girl friend's advice to keep away from icy water and bayonets. Just after Anna bangs out the rest of the song from the kitchen (an icy current, we hear, carries the soldier away), Eilif recognizes her voice, goes to the kitchen, and flings his arms around her. But the joy of this long-delayed moment of reunion quickly dissolves when Anna slaps him in the face for his reckless daring: for "not surrendering" when the peasants threatened to "make mincemeat" of him (*MC* 17). It doesn't matter that his supposed hacking of the peasants has won the admiration of the general. Far more than courage, which she despises, and even more than skill in bargaining, which he has obviously inherited from her, she prizes his life. Breaking through all the business transactions of this scene, that is its final and crucial point.

Yet none of Anna's children live long. Though Eilif remains for a time alive, Scene 3 stages the death of Swiss Cheese, who—in the three years since the last scene—has become paymaster of the Second Finnish Regiment.[10] Since Anna and Kattrin have been captured in Poland with elements of that regiment, she briefly sees her second son, whom she furnishes with "woolies" against the coming winter as well as with advice on being honest with the "regimental accounts" (*MC* 19). Yet besides implying—almost in spite of herself—that Swiss Cheese's honesty means he is too "stupid" to run off with the regiment's money, she remains in her own dealings a thoroughly devious bargainer. When an armorer offers to sell her a bag of shot for two florins (his colonel needs money for drink), she declines at first because, she says, she can't take "army property"—especially its ammunition (*MC* 18). But she tellingly adds, "Not at that price," and when she learns that she can make a big profit by selling the shot to the Fourth Regiment's armorer, she grabs the bag and tells Kattrin to "pay him a florin and a half" (*MC* 19).

This transaction occupies her at least as much as the departure of Swiss Cheese, which she barely notices. Like Eilif in the first scene, Swiss Cheese gives her no farewell of any kind when he sets off with the armorer, who likewise offers no farewell to a new character named Yvette. A once-gaudy camp follower now widely avoided because of what she calls "lies" about her probably gonorrheal "complaint" (*MC* 19), she sings her sad story to Mother Courage: five years ago, we learn, the enemy soldier who had become her lover went "marching out of sight" to the beating of drums, and though she followed him, she never found him (*MC* 20–21).

The resolutely skeptical "lesson" Mother Courage draws from Yvette's story of abandonment takes its place with her disbelief in the would-be Divine Justice of the Protestant cause. "To go by what the big shots say," she says,

> they're waging war for almighty God and in the name of everything that's good
> and lovely. But look closer, they ain't so silly, they're waging it for what they can get.
> Else little folk like me wouldn't be in it at all. (*MC* 24)

Mother Courage speaks the language of profit. Though she aligns herself with "little folk," she also takes her cue from the big shots. Instead of being outraged by their hypocrisy, by the gulf between their pretensions to piety and their lust for gelt, she seems to admire them: they're not so dumb, they're out for profit, and that's why the small fry are backing this war too. But according to Brecht, Mother Courage herself remains dumb in a fundamental way. She never learns the chief lesson that Brecht wanted to teach in this play—which is that no ordinary person can profit from the war. "[T]he big business deals that constitute war," he writes, "are not made by the little people" ("Texts" 134).

Brecht wrote at length about his aims in this play and about the failure of his audiences to understand them. He was actually dismayed by reviews of the first production of *Mother Courage* in Zurich in 1940, when "the bourgeois press," he says, acclaimed "the heart-rending vitality of all maternal creatures" ("Texts" 85). So he retouched certain scenes to make his title character sound more mercenary, and to show that she is *not* indestructible. Brecht himself records that in the East Berlin production of 1949, which he co-directed, Helene Weigel played Mother Courage as "a merchant, a strong crafty woman who loses her children to the war one after another and still goes on believing in the profit to be derived from the war" ("Texts" 137). Many people saw that she failed to grasp the folly of this belief, but according to Brecht, they did not understand that her failure to learn anything was "the bitterest and most meaningful lesson of the play." The audience, Brecht writes, "did not see what the playwright was driving at: that war teaches people nothing." Furthermore, he writes, not even those who saw the East Berlin production recognized the crimes of Mother Courage: her participation in war-profiteering; "they saw only her failure," Brecht writes, "her sufferings" ("Texts" 137). In blaming his audience for their failure to see the crimes of Mother Courage, Brecht obviously indicts his own title character and tells us how we should judge her. He thus presses us to adopt what has been called "the intentional fallacy": the notion that we can judge any work of literature by seeing how well it fulfills the author's intention (Wimsatt and Beardsley). More often than not, the problem with this way of judging literature is that we have no independent access to that intention: nothing outside the work itself that tells us what the author aimed to do in writing it. But when a playwright tells us exactly what lesson he wants his play to teach, and exactly how to judge his central character, he challenges us to test his stated aims—his stated intentions—against our own experience of the play.

In his extensive notes on the play and on the productions mounted in his lifetime, Brecht made it absolutely clear that Mother Courage was meant to alienate the audience. Rather than soliciting our empathy by means of her invincible "vitality," she is meant to repel our empathy—or at least forestall "complete empathy"—by her soul-consuming obsession with profit. In Brecht's view, she is finally destroyed by the conflict between her maternal sympathies and her quest for profit. "The merchant-mother," he writes, "became a great living contradiction, and it was this contradiction which utterly disfigured and destroyed her" ("Texts" 136). Yet in spite of Brecht's determination to make Mother Courage repulsively mercenary, *Mother Courage* moves us precisely because it fails to do exactly what Brecht wanted it to do. The sheer complexity of his title character resists any formula that would categorize her as simply or even chiefly mercenary: as little more than a "hyena of the battlefield" feeding off the war (*MC* 60).

That's what she is called by the chaplain in Scene 8, when she mourns the news that peace has broken out.[11] Having just bought more goods for her wagon, she's afraid she'll be stuck with them and financially ruined. "You don't want peace but war" says the chaplain, "because you profit from it" (*MC* 61). She has already exposed her mercantile core when he begs her for linen to bandage the bleeding wounds of a peasant and his family. With all her bandages sold, the only linen she's got in her wagon is officers' shirts, which she won't give away. "I'm giving nowt," she says, "don't want to, got to think of myself" (*MC* 45). The chaplain has to lift her out of the way of the wagon to get his hands on the shirts.

Does she then utterly fail to see how brutal and dehumanizing war can be? If so, how can we explain what she says at the end of Scene 6, where she and the chaplain witness the funeral of Tilly, the field marshal of the Catholic imperial forces. When the chaplain calls the burial "a historic moment" (*MC* 54), Mother Courage ruefully remarks on what *she* calls historic. Having learned that during her brief absence on a buying trip, someone has just struck her mute daughter Kattrin over the eye, she says:

> She's half wrecked already, won't get no husband now. . . . she's only dumb from war, soldier stuffed something in her mouth when she was little. As for Swiss Cheese I'll never see him again and where Eilif is, God alone knows. War be damned. (*MC* 55)

To see that she opens the very next scene by saying that war provides "a better deal" than peace (*MC* 56) is to see how impossibly conflicted she is. But the conflict is most powerfully dramatized earlier, when she tries to ransom Swiss Cheese from the Catholic forces. As the Catholic sergeant takes him off to what shortly becomes the threat of execution, Mother Courage is sure she can ransom him. "Thank the Lord," she says of the Catholic forces,

> they're corruptible. After all, they ain't wolves, just humans out for money. Corruption in humans is same as compassion in God. Corruption's our only hope. Long as we have it there'll be lenient sentences and even an innocent man'll have a chance of being let off. (*MC* 35)

Since Yvette knows the sergeant who captured Swiss Cheese, Mother Courage tells her to offer two hundred florins for his release, which becomes part of an impossibly unwieldy set of transactions. To raise the two hundred florins, Anna will mortgage her cart to Yvette's latest boyfriend, a wealthy colonel, and then repay him with money from the regimental cash box that her son had planned to hide away. Realizing at one point that this elaborate scheme may fail, she agrees to sell the cart outright and tells Yvette, "Hurry up and *don't haggle*. It's life or death" (*MC* 35, my emphasis). But as soon as she learns from Yvette that the cash box is gone—thrown in the river lest Swiss Cheese be caught with it—she reverts to bargaining. Rather than paying the two hundred florins which (as Yvette pantingly reports) the Catholics have just accepted so long as it's paid "quick," she tells Yvette to offer one hundred and twenty.

Here the bargainer in Mother Courage becomes almost indistinguishable from the mother. Since she cannot bear to pay two hundred florins because that will leave her nothing to care for her mute daughter, she insists on having both her children *and* the money she needs. "Swiss Cheese'll be back," she tells Kattrin:

> I'll pay two hundred if it comes to the pinch. You'll get your brother, love. For eighty florins we could fill a pack with goods and start again. (*MC* 36)

This radically incoherent plan disintegrates as soon as Yvette returns with the news that the Catholics won't take her lowball offer. Seconds after sending Yvette racing back with an offer to "pay the two hundred," Anna says, "I reckon I bargained too long" (*MC* 37), and the distant sound of drums confirms her fear.

But the worst is yet to come. Besides returning once again to say that Swiss Cheese has been shot with eleven bullets, Yvette reports that Anna herself is now in danger: suspected of knowing both the executed man and the location of his cash box. To test Anna's claim that she does not know the man, Yvette says, the Catholics will gauge her reaction to the sight of his corpse. Thus warned, Mother Courage steels herself. Knowing that she and her daughter may both be killed if they show the least flicker of grief for her dead son, she must stand impassively—holding her daughter's hand—as the soldiers carry in the sheeted corpse and the sergeant, removing the sheet, asks the women if they recognize him. When Mother Courage shakes her head twice in denial, Brecht suggests that "[t]he actor playing the sergeant can command the spectator's astonishment by looking around at his men in astonishment at such hardness" ("Texts" 113). But does her denial signify hardness alone? Knowing the price that she and her daughter would pay for showing any sign of grief, what can she do but steel herself against it? Instead of weeping, shrieking, or lacerating herself for haggling over the life of her son, she must stoically pretend to feel nothing. Does her would-be "hardness" destroy her humanity and make us despise her addiction to business and profit, or does it subtly lead us into the unspeakable depths of her anguish?

Whatever the answer to that question, Brecht's indictment of Mother Courage tells us far less than the play does, for only in seeing the play can we experience the whole truth of her character. The play shows more than her blindness to her own inhumanity. It shows instead, I think, how she herself becomes a battlefield where the struggle for profit and the need to survive wage endless war with maternal solicitude. Though Brecht complains that his audience consistently fails to see her crimes, her crimes as well as her suffering are revealed by the play itself, and both are essential to its power.

Irreducible to any one message, Brecht's play dramatizes the dehumanizing brutality of war by staging its effect on someone who feels that brutality even as she strives to make her living from it. In spite of his determination to keep our sympathies at bay, Brecht's play draws us right into the riven heart of its title character, making her embody the insoluble contradictions of a mother caught up in a war from which she makes her living even as it takes the lives of all her children.

According to Brecht, as I have already noted, "the bitterest and most meaningful lesson of the play" is "that war teaches people nothing" ("Texts" 137). Yet he also believed that *plays* could teach, and specifically that the "right" production of *Mother Courage* could reveal to the proletariat "the connection between war and commerce," and thus demonstrate that "the proletariat as a class can do away with war by doing away with capitalism" ("Texts" 134). Brecht's inference bristles with irony. Besides the fact that war antedates capitalism by several millennia, could the proletariat overturn capitalism without waging yet another war, or at least launching another violent revolution? Yet however implausible Brecht's expectations for the proletariat might be, *Mother Courage* remains a revelatory play about all modern warfare. Viewing the outbreak of World War II through the lens of a series of seventeenth-century wars, it shows how the "polluted" spring of war from which the title character drinks both death *and* her livelihood leaves her—in Brecht's words—"utterly disfigured and deformed" ("Texts" 136).

Notes

1   To commemorate the fiftieth anniversary of Save the Children, Benjamin Britten set the poem for children's voices and orchestra at a concert held in St. Paul's Cathedral in London on May 19, 1969 (*CP* Notes 1191).

2   *Journals* 40–41. According to John Willett, Brecht "wrote the first complete script between 27 September and 3 November" (Editorial Notes in *Letters* 619).

3   As soon as Hitler's foreign minister Joachim von Ribbentrop reached Moscow, Stalin told him what the Soviet Union wanted from its pact with Germany: the Baltics and half of Poland. If not, said Stalin, Ribbentrop might as well fly back to Berlin at once (Caton II: 547). Once Ribbentrop had gained via telegram Hitler's acceptance of Stalin's terms, he signed the pact (Paillat, *GI* 88).

4   On September 9 Brecht mistakenly wrote that the Germans "occupied Warsaw" (*Journals* Sept. 9, 1939, p. 34), but this did not happen until September 27.

5   Wells called it "an ill-written outpouring of patriotic beer-hall and café chatter. It is made up of chewed newspaper, of stuff wiped off café tables and of political hearsay" (*Travels* 139).

6   Made between Poland and Soviet Russia and signed in Riga, Latvia, on March 18, 1921, the Treaty ended the Polish-Soviet War.

7   "Short Organum" para. 42. My account of epic theater and Brecht's theory of the *V-effekt* is highly condensed. For a detailed account of both topics as well as of the vexed question of translating Brecht's "defamiliarizing" plays, see Williams.

8   The battle of Wallhof, whose fortress is mentioned in the heading of this scene, took place in the spring of 1626, when a Swedish army of nearly 5,000 men under King Gustavus II Adolf ambushed a Polish-Lithuanian force of 2,000 men and killed, wounded, or captured something between 500 and 1,000 of them (Podhorodecki). In Brecht's play, the Swedish ambush is called a siege.

9   According to Francis Turner, a florin was worth 288 hellers in 1632. See https://1632.org/1632-tech/faqs/money-exchange-rates-1632/. Note too that in Scene 1, the sergeant pays "half a florin" for a belt-buckle made, says Mother Courage, with "six solid ounces" of silver (p. 9).

10 It is not clear how closely Brecht's "chronicle" follows history here. The Finnish light cavalry fought for Sweden's King Gustave Adolf in the Thirty Years War, but the first of the several battles they fought in Breitenfeld took place in 1631, two years after the date of this scene (October 1629).

11 In 1632, King Gustavus Adolphus of Sweden was killed at the Battle of Lützen, as the headnote to Scene 8 declares (p. 57). Though the war between the Protestants and the Hapsburg Catholics continued until the Treaty of Westphalia in 1648, Brecht writes of this scene, *"Courage and the chaplain hear a rumor that peace has broken out"* ("Texts" 122), and—in the words of the headnote to Scene 8—"PEACE THREATENS TO RUIN MOTHER COURAGE'S BUSINESS" (*MC* 57). But as Mother Courage herself says in the middle of Scene 8, "war's been on again three days now" (*MC* 65).

The Phony War and Evelyn Waugh's
Put Out More Flags

On September 3, 1939, when the German invasion of Poland prompted Britain and France to declare war on Germany, the declaration launched one of the strangest periods in military history. Whether called *la drôle de guerre*, the *Sitzkrieg*, the phony war, the bore war, or the joke war, it was the cruelest possible joke on Polish expectations.

Almost immediately, its phoniness was epitomized by the Saarbrücken Offensive, "supposedly designed," writes William F. Shirer, "to relieve the German pressure on Poland" (*Collapse* 339–40). Since neither Britain nor France would authorize the bombing of Germany for fear of retaliation against Paris, their only response to the relentless bombing of Poland was a ground operation launched from northeast France on the night of September 7–8 along a fifteen mile front southeast of Saarbrücken and then into the Warndt (or Wendt) Forest just west of that city. But General Maurice Gamelin, who ordered this operation, threw into it far less than the full weight of French forces, as he had promised the Poles. Though his eighty-five divisions could easily have overwhelmed the Germans' twenty-three (especially since all German tanks were off in Poland), he dispatched no more than fifteen divisions—and perhaps as few as nine.[1]

Altogether, the so-called Saar Offensive was nothing but a diffident feint. Though the French Second Army captured twenty deserted villages by September 12 and pushed five miles into Germany, the British never joined the offensive, and on September 21, Gamelin halted his men short of the German Westwall (the Siegfried Line) and turned his offensive into a defensive crouch—all the while telling a purely fictitious story to the Poles.[2] On Gamelin's orders, writes Shirer, the French forces stealthily withdrew "in the dead of night so that the enemy would not know of it," and completed their withdrawal on October 4. "In two days," moreover, "with a handful of infantry troops, the Germans took back what the French had taken two weeks to gain," sweeping out the invaders by October 17. "After six weeks of being at war," Shirer concludes, "the great French Army had been unable—or unwilling—to bring the slightest relief to Poland" (*Collapse*, 340). Recalling this humiliating episode, one French colonel wrote: "After the prologue of the 'phony offensive,' we were ripe for the 'phony war'" (qtd. Shirer, *Collapse*, 340).

For all the inoffensiveness of the Saar Offensive, however, the paralysis of the British and French in this period was perhaps best exemplified by Chamberlain's meeting with

General Gamelin, French prime minister Édouard Daladier, and various other officials on September 12 in the town of Abbeville, which straddles the River Somme—here shrunk to a canal—about twelve miles from the coast of Picardy in northwest France. Chamberlain thought it all went swimmingly. "It was the most satisfactory conference I have ever attended," he wrote shortly afterwards. "There was no point on which there was any disagreement between us and when we parted we felt both of us fresh hope and confidence" (Self, *NCDL* 1: 448). Their hope and confidence, however, sprang from the simple fact that they agreed on every point, and what they agreed upon was to do nothing for Poland.

To be sure, France had just been trying to help Poland by invading the Saar and thus trying to harass Germany on its western front. But so far as the record shows, the Saar Offensive was not even mentioned at Abbeville—perhaps because it had already run out of steam by the time Chamberlain met Daladier. Poland itself was a topic they finessed. Though both men knew very well what German bombs and guns were doing to Poland, and though they had both pledged to support it in case of German attack, they quickly agreed to do nothing. Two days before the conference, Chamberlain had coolly noted that "Poland is being rolled up much faster than our people had anticipated" (*NCDL* 4: 445). Now he simply wrote Poland off. "There's nothing to do from a material point of view," he told Daladier, "to save it. The only way of doing so is to win the war." Daladier feebly suggested that they might open up an eastern front by sending supplies through Romania, and thereby encouraging the Polish resistance. But the only thing actually sent to the Poles at this time was a telegram from Gamelin to Marshall Rydz-Smigly, commander of the Polish army, gamely suggesting that Polish soldiers remaining in the country might wage guerrilla warfare against the Nazi occupation (Paillat, *GI* 198). Having left Warsaw on September 7, however, Rydz-Smigly was already headed to Romania, which would shortly serve not as a conduit for war supplies but rather as a refuge for him and his staff as well as for Polish president Ignacy Mościcki and Colonel Józef Beck, Poland's foreign minister (Kochanski 72, 78–79).

Besides the danger of ruffling public opinion abroad, then, both men worried far more about ruffling the feathers of the German eagle than about doing anything effective on behalf of Poland. In the end, except for savoring the good news that the Allies would soon be able to circumvent America's neutrality laws so as to buy planes, the British and French ministers decided to rest on their hands. "Our interest," said Daladier simply, "is to wait" (qtd. Paillat, *GI* 38).

What, then, could France and England do? Thrusting the short-term fate of Poland brusquely aside, the two prime ministers turned to what must have seemed a much more urgent question: the vulnerability of their own cities. Their strategy, insofar as it could be called that, was simply to avoid provoking their enemies—or potential foes. Italy, they agreed, must be given every reason to stay neutral, and since Germany had so far dropped no bombs on France or England, it must be given no reason to do so— especially because the Luftwaffe could do much more damage to the concentrated factories of France and England than allied bombing could do to the dispersed factories of Germany. Also, Chamberlain said, it would be very awkward to strike civilian structures under the pretext of targeting military sites, "above all with respect to the opinion of the U.S."[3]

Thus began the phony war, normally dated from September 3, 1939 to April 9, 1940, when the Germans invaded Norway. But as Tom Shachtman observes, this period of just over seven months "was hardly a time of nothingness" (Shachtman xi). On September 4, the day after war was declared, a German submarine torpedoed and sank the British passenger steamer *Athenia* 200 miles off the Scottish coast, sending 112 people—including twenty-eight Americans—to their deaths.[4] Though this attack provoked no retaliation from Britain, let alone the United States (FDR was firmly against joining the war at this point), it complicates any attempt to generalize about this period, which included not only the Nazis' brutal subjugation of Poland but also the hard-fought winter war between Soviet Russia and Finland (November 30, 1939 to March 13, 1940), which ended with Finland ceding 11% of its territory to the Soviets.

Curiously, Shachtman fails to mention the Saarbrücken Offensive, which first (I believe) epitomized the phoniness of the war he considers. But his history of that war is remarkably broad. Ranging from America through England, Germany, and France, it includes Charles Lindbergh's fierce opposition to any revision of America's neutrality; FDR's maneuvers around that neutrality; Churchill's robust performance as First Lord of the British Admiralty; his relentless badgering of Chamberlain; Stalin's usurpation of the Baltics; General Franz Halder's repeatedly frustrated efforts to overthrow Hitler in a coup; sharp disagreements between General Gamelin and General Alphonse Georges, his deputy, who rightly foresaw that German tank brigades would breach the would-be "impenetrable" Ardennes forest (Shachtman 140); and the propagandizing voice of the fascistic William Joyce, aka Lord Haw-Haw, who repeatedly predicted—via German radio beamed to England—"that England would lose the war" (Shachtman 147). None of these facts, however, gets into Evelyn Waugh's novel about the phony war. While an historian bent on "covering" any phase of history must be comprehensive and circumspect, a novelist can place the magnifying glass of his art over just one small part of that history, such as this one:

> Over a million and a half children, mothers, and teachers from London and twenty-six other cities had been evacuated to the countryside. Not many country women wanted to take more than a couple of children, and very few of them enjoyed having the mothers and teachers sharing their hearths. Some of the children had head lice or wet their beds. . . . The government had made no attempt to house middle-class children with middle-class families or lower with lower. Upper-class children presented no such problems, for they went where money could send them—frequently abroad. (Shachtman 84)

In Evelyn Waugh's *Put Out More Flags* (1942), the problem of housing evacuated children becomes the centerpiece of a novel about a nation nominally at war but actually in a state of bureaucratic paralysis: the target of Waugh's satire. Like Virginia Woolf's *Between the Acts* (1941), much of the action of Waugh's novel takes place at an English country house, and both novels portray a nation inexorably headed for war. Partly because Woolf's novel is set in the summer of 1939, just before war was officially declared, its tone is nostalgic and ominous: strikingly different from that of Waugh's novel. Yet the questions that *Between the Acts* raises about the survival of England anticipate some of the most disturbing questions lurking beneath the satire of *Put Out More Flags.*

Published in 1941, soon after Woolf took her own life, *Between the Acts* adumbrates the war to come even as it looks far backward. It is chiefly the story of a pageant about the history of England—a pageant played out on the ample grounds of a fine old English country house in June of 1939. While telling how the villagers enact scenes from English comedies of successive royal eras (Elizabeth I, Anne, and Victoria) up to the present day, and telling also what they do before, between, and after the acts of this pageant, the novel by its very title situates itself between the two great military acts of the twentieth century. It also previews the imminence of the second one, which—in the form of low-flying fighter planes—quite literally overshadows the otherwise idyllic proceedings. Even before the pageant begins, Giles Oliver (whose family owns the country house) grumbles at its irrelevance to a Europe on the brink of war, "bristling with guns, poised with planes" (Woolf 37). At the end of the pageant, planes zoom overhead, interrupting the stale speech of a dim-witted clergyman—"a piece of traditional church furniture" (Woolf 129). First, he feebly tries to gloss the "meaning, or message" of the pageant as an expression of unity down through the ages: "We act different parts, but are the same," he says. Then, after seeming to listen for "some distant music," he makes his pitch for contributions to "the illumination of our own dear church." Though the pageant has raised £36.6.8 for this cause, he says, a deficit of £175 has given everyone the

> "opp …" The word [opportunity] was cut in two. A zoom severed it. Twelve aeroplanes in perfect formation like a flight of wild duck came overhead. *That* was the music. The audience gaped. The audience gazed. Then zoom became drone. The planes had passed. (Woolf 131)

The imminence of war prompts disturbing questions. "In holding their annual pageant," one critic asks, "is the community then in denial? Or are they defending the way of life that war most threatens, forcing us to consider what, out of the destruction, not only could but should survive?" (Cuddy-Keane xxxv). In *Put Out More Flags,* which one military historian has called "the greatest English novel of the Second World War" (John Keegan, qtd. Rossi, *EW:NM* 296), Waugh treats a much narrower set of questions: how shall the men and women of England meet the threat of a new world war, and more particularly, how shall it be met by Basil Seal, Waugh's ne'er-do-well protagonist?

The second question is promptly answered by Basil's sister Barbara, who lives with her husband Freddy at Malfrey, the family's country estate. Her first response to the prime minister's declaration of war, heard on the radio, is to sense the conflict foreshadowed just as potently as it is in *Between the* Acts:

> [S]he felt personally challenged and threatened, as though, already, the mild, autumnal sky were thick with circling enemy and their shadows were trespassing on the sunlit lawn. (*POMF* 4)

Woolf likewise describes planes flying over a country estate, but the word "trespassing" exemplifies the tonal difference between her novel and Waugh's. While the sound and sight of fighter planes in *Between the Acts* are truly menacing, the shadows of aircraft in this passage—even enemy aircraft—are simply annoying. Seen from Barbara's point of view, they are hardly more disturbing than the spectacle of tramps crossing the edge of her property. And Barbara herself is shaped by a narrator who views with Olympian detachment a whole cast of characters comically unready for another war, comically incapable of facing—let alone promptly repelling—its devastating brutality.

Consider Barbara's second thought, which is about her brother Basil. Too young to have done anything in the first war and now "thirty-five or thirty-six" (*POMF* 22), he has been "from his earliest days … a source of embarrassment and reproach" to his family (10). So when his sister Barbara hears the prime minister's declaration over the radio, she seizes it as the key to Basil's redemption. "I believe," she says to her husband Freddy, "it's what he's been waiting for all these years … Basil *needed* a war. He's not meant for peace" (12). She already sees him as the re-incarnation of Rupert Brooke or Siegfried Sassoon (13).

Each of those names delivers its own ironic charge. Rupert Brooke, a breathtakingly handsome young poet who wrote a series of sonnets in 1914, had hailed the outbreak of the first Great War as if it were a crystal stream coursing through a London slum. "Now, God be thanked," he wrote, that England's youth can "turn, as swimmers into cleanness leaping, / Glad from a world grown old and cold and weary." But since Brooke might, after all, be leaping into something mortally foul, he also foresaw that his "dust" might end up buried in "some corner of a foreign field / That is for ever England."[5] In the mercilessly satirical world of Waugh's novel, the young man ready to live on as immortal (if exported) English dust is replaced by a young man primed to become a target. Basil's fashionable friends in London include a man whose almost total lack of military experience cannot check his eagerness to do something in the war. Alastair Trumpington, we are told,

> had always held it as axiomatic that, should anything as preposterous and antiquated as a large-scale war occur, he would take a modest but vigorous part. He had no illusions about his abilities, but believed, justly, that he would make as good a target as anyone else for the King's enemies to shoot at. (*POMF* 50)

Waugh's own satiric targets include not just Barbara's veneration of Rupert Brooke but also her admiration of another noted English poet of the first World War. Barbara saw her brother Basil, we are told,

> as Siegfried Sassoon, an infantry subaltern in a mud-bogged trench standing to at dawn, his eyes on his wrist watch, waiting for the zero hour. (*POMF* 13)

Unlike Brooke, who never lived to fight (let alone die) in a battle of any kind, Sassoon knew the miseries of trench warfare. But as his poetry reveals, he found life in the trenches anything but heroic. In "Counter-Attack," the title poem in his 1918 collection, *Counter-Attack and Other Poems*, he re-creates a sickening defeat. As "dawn broke like a face with blinking eyes," the speaker of the poem sees bodies sprawled "in the sucking mud" of a trench. When an officer commands "Stand to" for a "counter-attack!" against

German shells and machine-gun bullets, the fate of a mortally wounded young soldier exemplifies the fate of the attack itself: "he sank and drowned, / Bleeding to death. The counter-attack had failed."

Knowing poetry such as this, schooled in the miseries of war by all he knew of World War I, which had lasted into his fifteenth year, Waugh entered World War II with no illusions—or rather with a cavalier indifference to the prospect of getting killed. In late December 1939, shortly after joining the Royal Marines as a second lieutenant, he told Lady Diana Cooper that "[w]e are to be used for what are called 'combined operations' & given posthumous medals." And so far from trembling at the thought of German bombs, he was afraid the convent school that had rented his country house for six months (to be out of London) would not renew the lease "unless we get some decent raids early in the new year" (*L* 131). He could also be seriously fatalistic. In mid-September 1940, just before first seeing action as an intelligence officer in the Battle of Dakar, West Africa, he told his wife Laura what to do "[i]n the event of my not coming back" (*L* 140). On September 26, right after the British failed to overthrow the Vichy French colonial government of Dakar and replace it with De Gaulle, he sounds at once relieved and chagrinned: "Bloodshed," he told Laura, "has been avoided at the cost of honour" (*L* 141).

Was it shameful to pay that price? Waugh's own experience of war ultimately led him to wonder how much blood "honour" was worth. Among all the writers we have considered so far, he alone not only joined the armed forces of his country but also took part in more than one battle. But his direct experience of combat simply confirmed his suspicions of its pointlessness. By the time he wrote *Put Out More Flags* in the summer of 1941, during a long voyage back from the humiliating rout known as the Battle of Crete (May 28–June 1), he had concluded that there was precious little honor to be seen on a battlefield or gained from it.[6] Given all the mismanagement, dereliction, and sheer desperation that he found among the officers and men on Crete and that he exhaustively describes in his diary, it is no wonder he ended up "abominat[ing] military life," as he writes on June 2, just after escaping from the island (*L* 153). His diary of this grueling evacuation—so unlike the miraculous evacuation of Dunkirk just one year earlier—includes word pictures of starving men shrunk to ghostly reptiles and stirring only at night to elude daytime bombs: "As night fell stragglers emerged from the ditches, like ghosts from their graves, and began silently crawling towards the coast. . . . They had all thrown away their packs, had beards and the lassitude of hunger and extreme exhaustion: a pitiful spectacle" (*D* 505).

Many years later, Waugh mined this material for his trilogy of war novels, *Sword of Honour* (1952–1961), and in particular for the second one, *Officers and Gentlemen* (1955). In mid-July of 1941, however, comfortably settled in his own cabin aboard *The Duchess of Richmond* after the "tedious & futile & fatiguing" ordeal of Crete (*L* 153), he sought relief—satiric relief—in composing what he later called "the only book I have written purely for pleasure" (Preface to *POMF*, n.p.). This novel includes some accounts of military training and—near the end—an episode of combat, but its essentially puckish aim is to expose the folly of war: "just as confused and purposeless" as training exercises, in the words Waugh wrote after leaving Crete (*L* 153).[7] His feelings at this time significantly differed from those that followed the promptly aborted British attack on Dakar in September of 1940. While surviving that attack made him feel not just relieved but also slightly chagrinned at the loss of "honour," he felt nothing but relief at surviving the Battle of Crete. Besides spending several grueling days on the ground, he had also resigned himself at one point to being captured (*D* 509). So rather than lamenting any lost honor, this devout Roman Catholic (he had converted in 1930) felt "profoundly grateful to God & his saints for my preservation," for having been "delivered from countless perils to life & liberty" (*L* 153).

By the middle of July 1941, the 38-year-old Evelyn Waugh was singularly equipped to write a novel about war. Starting with *Decline and Fall* (1928), his highly auspicious debut, he had already published five novels plus three other books. After he began his military service, he told a friend "[t]here is no possibility of my doing any writing at all in present circumstances" (*L* 137). But his letters—written chiefly to Laura—sparkle with captivating anecdotes, often about superiors such as the brigadier whose only complaint about the war "is that he misses his hockey" (*L* 138). While writing whenever he could in this way, Waugh learned how to fight, and after nine months' training with the Royal Marines, he served as an intelligence officer in three operations. Given all he had seen of the folly of fighting as well as of training exercises, the fresh follies of the "joke war"—especially as it involved England—gave him just the material he needed for a novel of satire.

As applied to *Put Out More Flags*, however, the word "satire" needs some clarification. By almost universal consensus, Waugh was a satirist: in 1962, Gore Vidal called him "the first satirist of our time" (Vidal). But two decades earlier, Edmund Wilson had called him a "comic genius" (qtd. "Evelyn Waugh"), and in 1999, the author of a highly praised literary life of Waugh declared that *Put Out More Flags* was the final act of "his comic fiction" (Wykes 134). Does this mean that "comic" and "satiric" are interchangeable terms? I think not. Though sometimes overlapping, they differ sharply in terms of how they judge their objects.

Satire and comedy both make us laugh at human behavior, but comedy is indulgent. While comedy exposes the irrationality or inconsistency of human behavior, actions or speeches that qualify as comic are typically products of human frailty that most of us could readily forgive with a chuckle. In Byron's *Don Juan*, a satiric epic with comic interludes, the title character is sexually initiated by a beautiful young married woman who is overcome not by his seductive powers (he's a shy, teenage virgin) but by her own desires. As they sit together in a lovely bower on a warm June evening, here is what happens right after she silently swears to be chaste:

> A little still she strove, and much repented,
> And whispering "I will ne'er consent"—consented.
>
> (Bryon, *Don Juan* I.117)

To set this charming passage beside Jonathan Swift's "A Modest Proposal" (1729) is to see the difference between comedy—or in this case a comic passage—and satire. In taking a reasonable, sympathetic, deliberate tone to argue that the starving Irish should be fed with infants, Swift's "Proposal" prompts its readers not to laugh indulgently but to recoil in horror, to condemn the cruelty of a British policy whose superficial plausibility was undermined by its ruthlessness.

Swift thus exemplifies Vidal's definition of the satirist as "a man profoundly revolted by the society in which he lives" and a man whose "rage takes the form of wit, ridicule, mockery." But this definition does not quite fit the author of *Put Out More Flags*, for Waugh's protagonist—Basil Seal—is not so much a villain as an irrepressible rogue. In *Black Mischief* (1932), Waugh's third novel, Basil steals his mother's emeralds. In the words of David Wykes, he thus proves himself "an undeniably awful man whose monstrous misdeeds represented the world of style, panache, and *elan* that grey modernity would smother" (Wykes 134). So far from being "profoundly revolted" by Seal, Waugh revived him years later. In the story called "Basil Seal Rides Again" (1962), the sixty-year-old rake recovers his youthful outrageousness after his "deviation into rectitude" ("Basil Seal" 503, Milthorpe).

Seal in his prime, then, is anything but a target of vilifying ridicule. Retrospectively viewed by a writer who had already seen for himself the horrors of an actual war, he perfectly embodies what came just before it: the irresponsibility of the joke war. Instead of raging at this irresponsibility, as a battle-hardened veteran might, Waugh celebrates it—in what might be called a *winking* satire. In *Put Out More Flags*, Seal becomes the weapon of ridicule that Waugh fires at a nation of dimwits. Though the novel weaves a story of men and women chiefly occupied in making themselves comfortable, not to mention staying out of the trenches, it does so by means of a language steeped in Waugh's knowledge of war and its weapons.[8]

Consider first the special kind of hand grenade deployed by Basil Seal. In Chapter 6, I noted that "The Workers [who] cry out for Bread" in Bertolt Brecht's poem of that title are wholly occupied with making weapons, specifically *Granaten*, "hand grenades." Bulbous as a pomegranate, which the French call *une grenade*, this compact iron ball with a high explosive core was small enough to be thrown by hand after its very short fuse was lit, and fierce enough to shatter even fortified positions—not to mention human beings. Since the grenade was commonly used by all forces in World War II, Waugh knew exactly how to use it, and he packs this knowledge into what can only be called an epic metaphor.

First the context. Since vast numbers of children had been evacuated from English cities to the countryside, as explained in Shachtman's history of the phony war, Waugh makes Basil's sister Barbara a billeting officer charged with finding homes in her rural neighborhood for city children threatened by bombs. Given that bombs *may* strike England at any time (a joke threat?), she has to cope with stray waifs of all sorts. Worst of all are a disgusting trio from Birmingham called the Connollies, who keep returning to Barbara because no one else can endure them for more than a few days.[9] Having thrown away all chances of a commission in the armed forces, Basil is now staying with her at Malfrey, and he decides to serve his country by taking over her job. Seeking a place for the obnoxious kids, he finds in the local newspaper an advertisement that reads:

> *Paying guests accepted in lovely modernized fifteenth-century mill. Ideal surroundings for elderly or artistic people wishing to avoid war worries ... 6 gns weekly, Highest references given and expected. (POMF 109)*

Though Barbara cannot imagine placing the Connollies in such a house, Basil decides at once to take them there, and thus to serve his country in time of war. "D'you know," he says, "this is the first piece of serious war work I've done so far?" (109).

Leaving the children in the car and thus out of sight, Basil calls on the middle-aged couple who own the Old Mill House and live quietly by themselves. After he says that he seeks housing for "evacuees," which the couple takes to mean "[t]ownsfolk in search of sanctuary," the homeowner explains at length why all the amenities of "this beautiful old house" are worth "six guineas" a week (*POMF* 116)—about £360 or $470 in today's currency. Then Basil activates his weapon:

> This was the time for the grenade he had been nursing ever since he opened the little, wrought-iron gate and put his hand on the wrought-iron bell-pull. "We pay eight shillings and sixpence a week," he said. That was the safety pin; the lever flew up, the spring struck home; within the serrated metal shell the primer spat and, invisibly, flame crept up the finger's length of fuse. Count seven slowly, then throw. One, two, three, four . . .
>
> "Eight shillings and sixpence?" said Mr. Harkness. "I'm afraid there's been some misunderstanding."
>
> Five, six, *seven*. Here it comes. Bang! "Perhaps I should have told you at once. I am the billeting officer. I've three children for you in the car outside." (*POMF* 117)

Like an epic simile, the metaphor is packed with all the technical facts about activating a hand grenade that Waugh had acquired in his military training. And like a soldier hardened by war, Basil steels himself against the couple's desperate pleading. Earlier in the novel, Basil declares that he wants "to be to be one of those people one heard about in 1919; the hard-faced men who did well out of the war" (52).[10] Basil does very well indeed out of this one. Besides impersonating a billeting officer and then sticking the hapless couple with three insufferable kids for what turns out to be eight days (a huge snowfall keeps them all in), Basil soon discovers that he can gather bribes by taking the children back from the houses he targets—starting with the Old Mill.

Besides a metaphorical hand grenade, the novel includes real bombs. None fall on London or any other British city for the duration of this novel, whose three seasonal parts (Autumn, Winter, Spring) stretch from early September 1939 to the German occupation of France in June 1940. But by the summer of 1941, Waugh knew full well that starting on September 7, 1940 in the real world, London had been relentlessly bombed by the Luftwaffe for fifty-six days and nights. So early in the novel, we know how to take the words of Sir Joseph Mainwaring when the "old booby" assures Basil's mother Cynthia that London will never be attacked from the air, that "[t]he Germans will never attempt the Maginot Line," and that "[t]he French will hold on forever" (20).[11]

But as if to prefigure the shattering of these predictions, Basil himself encounters real bombs. While stalking the corridors of the Ministry of Information in quest of a job, he meets "a small, scrubby man carrying a suitcase" containing—he says—bombs (*POMF* 80). Later on, while about to enter the War Office in yet another quest for a job, he meets the same little man, who complains this time that no one will pay any attention to him. After getting both of them past the guards by simply identifying himself as "M.I.13" (Military Intelligence 13), Basil sends the suitcase man to the Chaplain General and promptly gains the ear of a colonel in Internal Security by telling him of "a lunatic loose in the War Office … [with] a suitcase full of bombs" (186). When the bombs explode, non-fatally injuring the Deputy Assistant Chaplain General, news of the bombing "shocks the conscience of the civilized world" and German radio calls it "Churchill's attempt to make a second *Athenia* by bombing the military bishop" (191, 189). What amounts to a practical (if also slightly bloody) joke engineered by Basil, therefore, assumes the enormity of a major war crime like the German torpedoing of the *Athenia*.

Allusions of this kind periodically remind us that in this novel as well as in the real world outside it, even the joke war includes some deadly serious things such as the total defeat of Poland, which is noted in the opening sentence of "Winter" (89). However many war games Basil plays, the threat of war is real, and like Waugh himself, most of the men whom Basil knows have enlisted. They include the aforementioned Alastair Trumpington, who has declined a commission and joined the ranks. When he spends a weekend off-base with his wife Sonia, we are told:

> This was February 1940, in that strangely cozy interlude between peace and war, when there was leave every weekend and plenty to eat and drink and plenty to smoke, when France stood firm on the Maginot Line and the Finns stood firm in Finland …" (*POMF* 135)

But setting aside the would-be firmness of France, Finland was then faltering in its Winter War with the Soviet Union, which had invaded it on November 30 (as also noted in the opening of "Winter," though without the date) and would seal its conquest with a peace treaty on March 13. Also, though Alistair survives both the shambles of a training exercise and the sheer folly of defending the Irish coast against an imaginary attack, a darker end comes to Cedric Lyne, the estranged husband of Basil's mistress Angela. Dispatched to what is probably Norway, which the Germans invaded on April 9 (sometimes considered the end of the phony war), the newly commissioned Cedric struggles in the middle of the night to get his men aboard a ship that has already been mistakenly occupied by Highlanders, with the result that "Everyone said, 'Lyne made a nonsense of the embarkation'" (239). Later on, while needlessly crossing a battlefield alone to deliver an order already anticipated by the company it was meant for, he is instantly killed by an enemy bullet (269–70).

Cedric's very last thought about his risky crossing is not so much that he is "rather brave" as that "the whole thing is so damned silly" (*POMF* 270). The same could be said of the chaotic embarkation to Norway and of the "prolonged shambles" that results from the training exercise in which Alastair is ordered to "put down smoke" so as to cover the movement of his company (*POMF* 166). Is it a joke or the prelude to later disasters on real battlefields? Early in the book, while still wholly idle, Basil tells his sister that both his mistress and his mother seem to have decided that "I ought to be killed" (93). One answer to this murderous absurdity is to leave the country, as Auden and Isherwood actually did when they sailed to America in January of 1939 (see Chapter 4). But in Waugh's novel they are thinly disguised—or rather grossly caricatured—as a pair of pansy-poets named Parsnip and Pimpernel.

Waugh himself was not always anti-gay. During his Oxford years (1921–24), he was dazzled by a set of young bohemians known as the Aesthetes, and the objects of his love—or at least of his homoerotic desire—included Alistair Graham, whom he later re-created as Sebastian Flyte in *Brideshead Revisited* (1945). But while *Brideshead* treats Flyte with considerable sympathy, *Put Out More Flags* has none for any of its gay characters. Besides derisively tracking news of the would-be cowardly pair of fugitives from wartime England, the novel directly pillories a homosexual dilettante who has stayed in London but not enlisted. Like Waugh himself, who unsuccessfully sought a job in the public relations department of the British War Office before joining the Royal Marines (*L* 125), Ambrose Silk is a published writer, and Waugh makes him talk like an Oxford Aesthete. But insofar as Silk evokes Waugh's younger self, it's a self whose epicene affectations are now repressed and scorned by the happily married man of thirty-eight who is also a battle-hardened officer in the Royal Marines.

A self-styled "cosmopolitan Jewish pansy" (*POMF* 87), Silk is also somewhat dim-witted. At a party in the South Kensington studio of a rising young artist named Poppet Green, Silk patronizingly commends her for putting a moustache on the head of Aphrodite in one of her paintings. "[I]t shows," he says, that "you . . . feel strong enough to be facetious. Like those wonderfully dramatic old *chestnuts* in Parsnip's *Guernica Revisited*. You're growing up Poppet, my dear" (36). But actually the moustache has been added by Basil, not Poppet (33), and in any case is just a copycat version of what Marcel Duchamp did to the *Mona Lisa* in his famously Dadaist *LHOOQ* (1919).[12] Furthermore, the phrase "Parsnip's *Guernica Revisited*" alludes to W. H. Auden's *Spain*, a 1937 poem about the Spanish Civil War, and shortly afterwards, Silk links *Guernica Revisited* to the *Christopher Sequence* (42), which alludes to Christopher Isherwood, Auden's lover. The aesthete of the novel is thus clearly linked with a pair of gay poets who have fled abroad.

For all his flaunting of sophistication, however, Silk is both sentimental and credulous, and thus becomes an easy target for Basil's manipulation. Early on in the novel, we learn that Silk has been secretly mourning the fate of a German named Hans whom he had met in Munich around 1930, while living in a workmen's quarter. Though Hans was a Brown Shirt, which is to say a Nazi Storm Trooper, the Nazis' discovery of his "half-Jewish" identity has doomed him to "the unknown horrors of a concentration camp" or just as likely death in "the firing line" (*POMF* 36, 45–48). Silk, then, could have been sympathetically portrayed as one more indirect victim of Nazi persecution. Instead, he becomes a risible victim of Basil, who—after getting his own job at the Ministry of Information—thoroughly exploits Silk's pride in his "art."

Thanks to Silk's publisher, who has been charged with supervising "men of letters" at the Ministry of Information (i.e. Propaganda), Silk lands a job there. First, as "sole representative of Atheism in the religious department," he tries to make the Nazis look bad by reporting such things as "Storm Troopers . . . attend[ing] a requiem mass in Salzburg" (*POMF* 136, 140). Then, inspired by tales of Chinese scholars who cared everything for flowers and nothing for war, he decides to launch a literary review called

Ivory Tower. When Basil realizes that these Chinese scholars "didn't care if their empire was invaded," and that Silk's new paper will "encourage this sort of scholarship" (226), he sees the potential for mischief, and the potential materializes when Basil finds on Silk's desk one day the proofs of a fifty-page story called "Monument to a Spartan," which Silk had written two years before and now plans to publish in his new review. The Spartan of this plainly autobiographical story is Hans, a young Nazi sent to a concentration camp because of his friendship with Ambrose, a Jew. After reading the story, Basil assures Ambrose that the first part is "a first-class work of art." But since the ending plainly exemplifies the ruthless antisemitism of the Nazis, Basil complains that the story "degenerates into mere propaganda" (243). So why not, he asks, end the story "with Hans still full of illusions, marching into Poland?" (244).

When the story appears in print with this patently pro-Nazi ending, Basil promptly reports it to his own supervisor—Colonel Plum—along with "passages in the preceding articles which cast particular ridicule upon the army and the War Cabinet and which urged on the artist the duty of non-resistance to violence" (*POMF* 245). Waugh's fictional poet thus echoes—no doubt inadvertently—what the American novelist Henry Miller wrote in the spring of 1939: "I refuse to go to war, whether for a just or unjust cause.... I believe that the most sane and practicable solution to the present impasse would be to scrap all forms of defense and expose ourselves absolutely to every risk" (*Partisan Review* 51).

The gulf between British and American writers in this period is perhaps nowhere better illustrated than by this startling echo. Writing for an American journal in the spring of 1939, Miller could safely proclaim his absolute refusal to fight in full confidence that at least some of his fellow American writers and intellectuals felt largely the same way. But in the eyes of Waugh, who felt bound to join the Royal Marines even though he came to loathe the folly of war, the idea that an "artist" should simply bow to violence becomes nothing but a target of satire. Along with his story's tribute to Nazi aggression, then, Silk's outspoken pacifism makes him a traitor ripe for exposure by Basil, who proudly tells the colonel that he has found in Silk's new journal "[d]ocumentary evidence" of "[a] fifth column nest" (245)—a clutch of writers working for the enemy, or more precisely, it turns out, a clutch of pseudonyms all adopted by Silk himself—and all vainly pursued by the police.

Having thus betrayed Silk to Colonel Plum, Basil pretends to save him. Visiting his flat one evening, he not only warns Silk of his imminent arrest but also insists that to forestall it, he must leave at once for Ireland disguised as a priest ("Father Flanagan") and carrying nothing but a suitcase. As a result, Silk ends up at a remote country inn without even a pen to write with while Basil takes over his well-furnished flat. Besides gaining credit for exposing a traitor, therefore, Basil also gains the perfect lair in which to entertain Susie, Plum's lovely assistant, for whom he has long lusted.

John Rossi argues that in the second half of this novel, Waugh's characters "all atone for their shallow pasts" (Rossi, *EW:SS*). But what atonement do they make? Even after joining the army, they are not so much heroic as ridiculous or at best pitiable. Cedric dies a pointless death, as we have seen, and as "[t]he war enters a new and more glorious phase" in the summer of 1940, Alastair's unit ends up "destroying local amenities" just to defend seven miles of perfectly unthreatened Irish coastline (276). Then, while proposing to volunteer for a commando unit that will "go to France and creep up behind Germans and cut their throats in the dark," Alastair tells his wife how "exciting" it will be. "They have special knives and Tommy-guns and knuckle dusters," he says, and "carry rope ladders round their waists." To which she coolly replies, "No, darling, I couldn't keep you from the rope ladder" (278).

Sonia thus plays the indulgent mother to Alastair's intrepid boy scout. But their parting exchange is merely a prelude to the much more disquieting one between Basil and Angela after she learns of Cedric's death. Rather than mourning Cedric, she tells Basil that she wants to marry him because "[n]either of us could ever marry anyone else, you know" (278). Since Basil declines her, and thus declines at least temporarily the hand of a woman who is rich as well as beautiful, one might infer that he is not just selflessly indifferent to the prospect of wealth—"I'm not acquisitive, you know"—but heroically committed to fight for his country above all else: "this is no time to be thinking of marrying," he says (279). But is Basil now truly redeemed by a rush of patriotic fervor? Will he "atone" for his life of shameless irresponsibility and mischief-making by risking or even sacrificing himself on the battlefield? Not at all. War is simply "a new racket" offered just in time to amuse a man bored with his old tricks. "There's only one serious occupation for a chap now," he tells Angela, "that's killing Germans. I have an idea I shall rather enjoy it" (283).

In the final joke of the novel, the would-be redemptive heroism of defending one's country becomes a titillating blood sport, which is what makes the joke turn just as dark as the joke war itself. In all his enchantment with this new racket, Basil chillingly anticipates a man of our own time: U.S. Navy Seal Chief Petty Officer Edward Gallagher, who stabbed to death an already captured 17-year-old Islamic State fighter outside the Iraqi city of Mosul on May 6, 2017. Months beforehand, he had told his superior officer that he and his men would go anywhere for the sake of "action," adding "We just want to kill as many people as possible" (Phillips, Baker, Haberman, and Cooper 25).

Killing as many people as possible is of course the antithesis of Alastair's ambition to make himself "as good a target as anyone else for the King's enemies to shoot at." In this novel, it seems, the only alternative to sheer idleness, pointless desk jobs, muddled training exercises, and hopelessly confused military operations is just one of two things: becoming a target or becoming a killer. *Put Out More Flags* thus demolishes whatever is left of the idealism with which young men such as Rupert Brooke entered the first Great War. At the very end of the novel, the benighted Sir Joseph Mainwaring learns from Basil's mother that he has joined "a special corps d'elite" and no longer needs the old man's help. As a result, Sir Joseph is delighted. "There's a new spirit abroad," he says. "I see it on every side" (284). According to the Chinese sage from whom Waugh takes his title, "a drunk military man should order gallons and put out more flags to increase his military splendor" (qtd. Waugh, front matter). Mildly inebriated, so to speak, on what he takes to be the "new spirit abroad," Sir Joseph puts out a smile in place of flags, as if blindly blessing the orgy of killing and dying that has now begun. He sees only what he wants to see "on every side," and only in this sense, as the final sentence tells us, is the "poor booby ... bang right" (284).

Notes

1   Austra, Kochanski 66. Austra writes that the Nazis had thirty-four divisions "along the entire German border," but twenty-three of those were reserve units, and in any case they remained far below the number of French divisions. On the other hand, Brian Bond argues that the German forces could have withstood a French attack. "In purely numerical terms," he writes, "the French preponderance was inadequate to secure a breakthrough…." (Bond 62).

2   About September 13, when he had already decided to withdraw his forces, Gamelin sent a message to Polish Marshall Edward Rydz-Smigly saying that half of his divisions were grappling with the enemy and that French gains had forced Germany to pull at least six divisions from Poland. On transmitting this message to Rydz-Smigly, General Stanislaw Burhardt-Bukacki—Polish military envoy to France—told him, "Please don't believe a single word in the dispatch" ("Western Betrayal," Wikipedia, note 22).

3   Paillat, *GI* 198. To be fair, both the British and French may have been re-assessing the strength of their respective air forces in light of what the Luftwaffe was doing in Poland. On August 23, the French air minister Guy la Chambre had assured Daladier that there was no need to worry about French aviation. But after learning that the Luftwaffe had destroyed 90% of the Polish Air Force in just a few hours, la Chambre not only recognized the comparative impotence of French fighter planes but also the unpreparedness of the RAF (Paillat, *GI* 201).

4   Since Hitler had ordered the submarine fleet *not* to provoke the Allies and thus give them an excuse for waging war, Shachtman infers that this particular sub disobeyed his order (Shachtman 57).

5   "Peace" and "The Soldier." Shortly after turning twenty-seven, Brooke joined the Royal Naval Volunteer Reserve as a temporary sub-lieutenant. On April 23, 1915, enroute to what turned out to be the disastrous battle of Gallopoli, he died of an infected mosquito bite and is buried on the Greek island of Skyros.

6   Though the Royal Navy rescued 18,000 British, Australian, and New Zealand troops from an island suddenly occupied by German paratroopers and hammered by German bombs, almost 4,000 of the Allies were killed and over 11,000 captured.

7   On the night of April 19–20, nearly three months before the evacuation of Crete, Waugh took part in an operation much smaller but equally disorganized, as his diary explains in detail: the commando raid on Bardia, on the east coast of Libya (*D* 495–96).

8   Though his haughty manner rankled the men who served under him, he prided himself on his knowledge of the technicalities of war. Writing to Laura from a training camp on February 25, 1940, he says: "My stock is high. I gave a twenty-minute lecture on reconnaissance patrols which was greeted with universal acclaim" (*L* 137).

9   John Rossi suggests that in naming the loathsome children "Connollies," Waugh was needling his old friend and fellow writer Cyril Connolly (Rossi, *EW:SS*). Yet with a little stretching of dates, he might also have imagined the trio as somehow spawned by James Connolly, the Irish revolutionary who helped to lead the Easter Rising of 1916 and was executed shortly thereafter.

10   By contrast, Guy Crouchback, protagonist of Waugh's *Men at Arms* (1952), aims to become "one of the *soft-faced* men who did well out of the war" (*Men at Arms* 26, my emphasis).

11 Just as ignorantly, Basil himself tells his fashionable friends that "the [German] army, like all armies, was intensely pacifist; as soon as it became clear that Hitler was heading for war, he would be shot" (*POMF* 30).
12 When pronounced letter by letter, *LHOOQ* sounds like "elle a chaud au cul," meaning "she has a hot ass." Ironically enough, the slur fits Aphrodite—goddess of love—far better than Leonardo's lady.

Exodus and Occupation in Irène Némirovsky's *Suite Française*

If the ending of Evelyn Waugh's *Put Out More Flags* marks the end of the joke war, Irène Némirovsky's *Storm in June*—the first of the two novels of her *Suite Française*—re-creates not so much the real war as its immediate aftermath: the Exodus of eight to ten million refugees put to flight by the German invasion of France in the late spring of 1940. The second novel, *Dolce*, which treats the German occupation of a French town called Bussy, ranges from the spring of 1941 to the first of the following July, when the occupying soldiers leave to serve on the Eastern front right after the German invasion of the Soviet Union.[1] Némirovsky conceived these two novels as part of a pentad that would include three more: *Captivity* and two others tentatively titled *Battles?* and *Peace?* (*SF_T* Appendix 349). But she was arrested before she could write more than the first two novels. Concentrating on those two, therefore, I begin by comparing *Storm in June* to Hanna Diamond's comprehensive history of the Exodus, *Fleeing Hitler* (2007).

Diamond's book is hardly the first study of its subject. Besides trailing many other studies of the Exodus, especially in French, it appeared a full fifty years after what she herself calls "the most complete and most authoritative book on the topic": Jean Vidalenc's *L'Exode de mai–juin 1940* (1957).[2] Even in English-language histories such as Julian Jackson's *The Fall of France* (2003), the Exodus gets four and a half pages (including two photographs). "No account of the Fall of France," Jackson writes, "can avoid asking what the Exodus reveals about the state of mind of the French people in 1940" (J. Jackson 174).

Yet if Diamond overlooks Jackson's pages on the Exodus, which she does not mention, her own book goes a long way toward answering his question. Possibly the best record of the Exodus now available (at least in English), her historical narrative lets us see more clearly than ever—by contrast—how Némirovsky fictionalized it.[3] Beginning with the French government's shambolic abandonment of Paris just before the Germans entered it on June 14, Diamond meticulously documents the chaos of the Exodus. Even as the French prime minister Paul Reynaud ordered most of the government to leave the city on the night of June 8–9, working-class Parisians were "given the strictest orders to stay where they [were]" (Alex Werth, qtd. Diamond 44). With no clear instructions, French troops thought they should somehow defend the city, and most Parisians "still believed [it] would be defended" even though "all men from 18 to 50" were ordered to depart (Diamond 48–49). Not until June 13 was Paris officially declared an "open city" by a military government that asked its people "to abstain from all hostile acts" (qtd. Diamond 50). By this time many people had already left. But according to Diamond, many who did so "would probably have remained at home" if they had known it would be declared "open," and at least one old man opted to stay because he "would not know where to go" (Diamond 50). The crucial point she makes is that Parisians were simply left to fend for themselves. "As Parisians flooded out of the city on 11 June," Diamond writes, "no officials remained to oversee evacuation or organize the departure of the population" (Diamond 49).

It is this chaotic Exodus that Némirovsky's *Storm in June* re-creates. In the spring of 1941, when she started work on her novel, she was a 38-year old novelist of Ukrainian extraction whose previous books had already won her high acclaim. Yet even though she was a thoroughly assimilated Jew who had lived in France since 1918, she was never granted French citizenship, and she was eventually caught in the net of antisemitism cast by the collaborationist government of Marshall Philippe Pétain. In July 1942, after spending two years with her husband and daughters in the French village of Issy-l'Évêque in Saône-et-Loire, just inside the occupied zone, she was arrested and soon dispatched to Auschwitz, where she died of typhus on August 17, 1942, at the age of thirty-nine.

For almost sixty years, the minutely handwritten words of *Suite Française* lay entombed in a large leatherbound notebook carefully preserved but never examined by Némirovsky's two daughters—Denise and Elizabeth—until the mid-1990s, when they finally decided to entrust it to a French institute "dedicated to documenting memories of the war." Though Elizabeth died before reading the notebook, Denise laboriously typed it out, and after discovering that it was the manuscript of a two-volume novel, she sent it to Éditions Denoël, which published the French original in 2004. Two years later it appeared in English (Anissimov 394–95).

Suite Française is unquestionably historical. Straddling the line between fiction and history, it shows how the German invasion and occupation of France suddenly transformed—or deformed—French society. Nevertheless, this set of novels differs from historical narratives of these events in two important ways. First, like every other literary work examined in this book, it was written by an author who had no way of knowing how the war would end, more precisely how or even if she and her compatriots would see the end of being occupied. Second and more remarkably, *Suite Française* radically inverts the way all narrative histories and even most historical novels represent major historical events. In *Fall of France*, for example, Julian Jackson highlights generals, prime ministers, and major events such as the Panzer advance through the Ardennes forest on May 10-12, which led to the Germans' fateful crossing of the River Meuse on May 13 (J. Jackson 39–47). Events such as these and the historical figures who shaped them likewise inform Tolstoy's *War and Peace*, which Némirovsky took as her model for *Suite Française*.[4] Both Napoleon and his Russian adversary, General Mikhail Kutuzov, play leading roles in the novel, and the real-life Battle of Borodino is narrated in detail.

But *Suite Française* narrates no battles of any consequence, and while Pétain is mentioned twice in *Dolce* (*SF_T* 227, 241), neither he nor any other general or politician is anywhere portrayed—not even in fictional disguise. Also, though the characters of

Storm in June range from aristocrats and bourgeois professionals to working-class figures, the novel portrays a mass of people not only defeated by an invading army but also abandoned by their leaders and left to find their own way to safety. The only politician mentioned in *Storm in June* is Jules Blanc, a leading French Communist who is fancifully described as having been "twice Prime Minister [and] four times Minister of War" but who has left for Portugal by the time we learn of him.[5]

So far as I know, no one has faulted the absence of historical figures in *Suite Française*—the near-total omission of any reference to an actual military or political leader. But its omission of any reference to Jews has revived a charge first made in the 1930s against Némirovsky's earlier fiction, which was read as a betrayal of her own people. Ruth Franklin, for instance, has called her "the very definition of a self-hating Jew" because her earlier novels, especially *David Golder* (1929), trafficked "in the most sordid anti-Semitic stereotypes" (Franklin). This charge has been meticulously critiqued by Susan Suleiman, who faults it chiefly for its oversimplification.[6] Also, whether or not Némirovsky's early novels can be justly called antisemitic, Suleiman shows that her later short story "Fraternité" (1937) subtly reveals the kinship between two men who seem quite different: an immigrant Jew and an assimilated French-born Jew repelled by this "wretched creature" (qtd. Suleiman 27) whom he briefly encounters while waiting for a train. Though Franklin claims that this antisemitic revulsion is shared by Némirovsky herself, the story as a whole demonstrates the "inassimilability" of all Jews (qtd. Suleiman 29). In other words, it aims to show that Jews can never escape their Jewishness, no matter how assimilated or "Christian" they become. (Némirovsky's assimilated Jew is named "Christian," and Némirovsky herself was baptized in Paris on February 2, 1939.) Since Némirovsky died at Auschwitz precisely because she was a Jew, her story is both probing and prescient.

Setting aside all her other fiction, however, *Suite Française* has been faulted for including no Jewish characters of any kind even though Jews were stigmatized as "enemies of France" by Pétain's Vichy regime.[7] Long before starting work on her novel in May 1941, Némirovsky knew very well what the Vichy law of October 4, 1940 decreed: that "foreign residents of Jewish descent may be interned in special camps by decision of the *Préfet* of the department where they reside" (*SF_T* Appendix 362). Even before this decree, which she copied out as just quoted on the day it was issued, she could see it coming. Having learned by September 13 that the Vichy government "had decided to take measures against stateless persons," she appealed directly to Marshall Pétain. Admitting that she and her husband had been "born in Russia" but not mentioning their Jewishness, she appealed to him on two grounds. Besides having lived in France with her husband "for twenty years," she had been contributing "for many years" to *La Revue des Deux Mondes*, a prestigiously conservative periodical directed by André Chaumeix, whom she cites as a reference. "He could attest to my character," writes Némirovsky, "since he was recently willing to support my application for naturalization, a procedure that was probably interrupted due to the war" (qtd. Weiss 113–14). After also pointing out that she is "personally known to the family of Monsieur René Doumic"—the previous director of the *Revue*—as well as to the widow of Henri de Régnier, the French symbolist poet, she states that she has "never concerned herself with politics," that she has "written only literary works," and that she has "tried [her] best to make France well-known and well-liked." Given her status as a woman of letters, she

> cannot believe, Sir, that no distinction is made between the undesirable and the honorable foreigners, those who have done everything possible to deserve the royal welcome France has given them. I ask therefore your kindness in including me and my family in the latter category of people, so that we can reside freely in France and so that I may continue to exercise my profession as a novelist. (qtd. Weiss 114)

Read in light of the novel she would go on to write, this letter bristles with unintended irony. To enhance her appeal, Némirovsky dons a string of pearly names starting with that of André Chaumeix, who was not just a director of the *Revue* but a strong supporter of Pétain's collaborationism as well as a frequent visitor to his residence in Vichy's Hotel du Parc. But neither Pétain nor Chaumeix ever lifted a finger on Némirovsky's behalf. On the contrary, her biographers argue that Chaumeix is the original behind the fictional character of Gabriel Corte (Philipponnat and Lienhardt 361), a writer so infatuated with his own prestige that he cares for almost nothing and no one else.

If this is true, Némirovsky's portrayal of Corte could well be read as a covert critique of her own earlier self: of her sense of entitlement, of her assumption that literary distinction placed her not just outside the world of politics but above "the undesirable": the sort of people that Corte despises when he sees them on the road. And let us remember what happens to the only character in *Storm in June* who entertains an antisemitic thought. Not long after Charlie Langelet tells himself "with a scornful smile" that he can safely stay in France during the Occupation because "he was neither Jewish nor a Mason, thank God" (*SF* 168), he is fatally struck by a car.

There is one more glance at antisemitism in *Dolce*. In Chapter 2, one of the first things done by the occupying German forces is to put up posters that "used drawings or caricatures to illustrate world domination by the English and the detestable tyranny of the Jews" (*SF_T* 198). But can two passing references to antisemitism make up for the total absence of Jews in a novel about a time and place in which many thousands of them—including Némirovsky herself—were threatened with the cruelest of prospects?

We might answer this question indirectly—by considering how a French historian of both Jewish descent and exceptional distinction treats Jews in *Strange Defeat*, the poignant study of the fall of France that he drafted immediately afterwards. It is the work of an altogether remarkable man. Besides having gained a Sorbonne professorship for his landmark studies of medieval kings and French rural life, the 53-year-old Marc Bloch was a decorated veteran of World War I who volunteered for service in World War II. Since he had been personally "jolted" by the return of antisemitism in the 1930s (Fink 34–35), long after the exoneration of Dreyfus, he states at the outset of *Strange Defeat* that he was born a Jew, but "never professed any creed, whether Hebrew or Christian" (Bloch, *SD* 3), and his only other reference to Jews ties them to the reactionary *bourgeoisie* of the 1930s.[8] The absence of any other reference to Jews could be explained by chronology, for Bloch finished his book in September 1940, just before the Vichy government passed the first of its anti-Jewish laws. But by July of 1942, when Bloch added several notes to his text, arrests and deportations of Jews in France were well underway.[9] Does the absence of any reference to these alarming events in *Strange Defeat* make its author a self-hating Jew? I believe the answer is no. And just as Bloch professed his Jewish origin only in the face of antisemitism, Némirovksy hated flaunting her Jewishness as much as denying it, and having to justify herself made her seethe (Philipponnat and Lienhardt, 269). If a Jewish historian working in the early 1940s can write about the fall of France without making Jews a substantive part of his account, cannot a Jewish novelist working in the same period do the same? Surely the answer is yes—and not least because *Captivity*, the novel she planned to write but never even started before her arrest, was meant to include the plight of Jews in a concentration camp (*SF_T* Appendix 349).

Nevertheless, to compare *Storm in June* with Hanna Diamond's history of the Exodus is to see that besides excluding Jews as well as all figures of political or military consequence in France at this time, the novel barely touches on facts that Diamond reconstructs by means of eyewitness testimony from actual refugees. Though Némirovsky lived through the fall of France, she never took to the road after June 1940 (when she and her husband Michel settled in Issy-l'Évêque), let alone reported on the Exodus as Ernest Hemingway had reported on the Spanish Civil War before writing *For Whom the Bell Tolls* and Martha Gellhorn had reported on refugees in Czechoslovakia before writing *A Stricken Field*. At best, Némirovsky's knowledge of the Exodus and Occupation was fragmentary. She kept abreast of international war news (such as the German invasion of the USSR in June of 1941); she doubtless listened to BBC radio, as her characters do on two occasions (*Dolce* 210, 239); and she carefully read the *Journal officiel de la République française*—the official record of all acts taken by the French government, especially as related to the status of Jews (*SF* Appendix 342). But she obviously did not have what she told herself she needed while writing *Storm in June*: "[an] extremely detailed map of France or Michelin Guide" and "[t]he complete collection of several French and foreign newspapers between 1 June and 1 July [1940]" (*SF* Appendix 347). Lacking a detailed map, she scrambles French geography. Besides mislocating the town of Paray-le-Monial, as Sandra Smith notes (*SF* ix), she puts the Sabaries family farm in Bussy (*Dolce* passim) after first placing it near Vendôme (*SF_T* 58), which is over 100 miles northwest of Bussy. Furthermore, the letters she wrote from July 1940 to July 1942 (when she was arrested) say not a word about refugees.[10] At one point she calls herself "completely isolated from society" and not even up on "all the recently adopted directives toward the press." To some extent, she fed on rumors—such as the "persistent" but misleading reports that Issy might become part of the Vichy "Free Zone" (*SF* Appendix 361).[11]

By contrast, Diamond offers recorded facts. Mining sources such as the diary of a journalist named Georges Sadoul and the *Journal* of Georges Adrey, a Parisian metalworker who left the city on foot, she finds the French even more riven by lawlessness, selfishness, and heartlessness than Némirovsky's novel does. According to Jean Dupaquier's introduction to Adrey's *Journal*, the sense of solidarity generated by the common suffering of rich and poor soon gave way to egotism (Diamond 74). And to pillaging. While just a few things—a basket of food, a tank full of gas—are stolen in *Storm in June*, Sadoul reports that hungry refugees "at every moment" took empty bags into people's houses and walked out with full ones while "not a soul trie[d] to stop this shameful behavior" (Sadoul, qtd. Diamond 76). Charity was scarce. Though local authorities sometimes furnished food and drink to those on the road, some farmers demanded money for a jug of water, some restaurants grossly overcharged refugees, and in Limoges and Poitiers, "the first floods of Parisians" were simply turned away "with closed faces" as the refugees cursed the villagers with "famine, bombing, and all the calamities they now feel they endure" (Alfred Fabre-Luce, qtd. Diamond 75). Acts of theft could be not just inconvenient, as in the novel, but downright ruinous. One woman came on foot from Paris with a lady "who had shared all her tribulations" but also stole her whole fortune of 6,000 francs (Jean Moulin, qtd. Diamond 76–77). Worse still was what befell a family who left Paris with an aged aunt in their car. When she died on the way, they put her body on the roof, spent the night in a barn, and then discovered the next morning that both the car and the body had been stolen—leaving them no way to get a death certificate and claim their inheritance.[12] *Storm in June* has no thefts on this scale, and it also has nothing to say about what French soldiers did to fleeing women who joined them for protection: if they did not reciprocate with sexual favors, they were typically raped (Diamond 77).

Set beside Diamond's history of the Exodus, then, *Storm in June* paints a picture much less brutal and more circumscribed, but also fully reflecting the warts on the face of its subject. En route to her mother's house, for instance, Charlotte Péricand shares her food with others sitting around her at a café and urges her children to do the same with their sweets. But as soon as she learns that there is no more food of any kind to be had in the town, she scolds the children for giving away those sweets. In what might be faulted as an overstatement of the obvious, we are told that "Christian charity ... fell from her like useless ornaments, revealing her bare, arid soul" (*SF_ T* 48). More broadly, the novel portrays the whole of French society in such a way as to show how the Exodus brought out the worst of its failings as well as—in just a few cases—the best of its instincts.

Its characters, first of all, exemplify every level of French society from the aristocracy to the working class. As Nathan Bracher observes, Némirovsky "continuously filters history through the deforming lenses of her characters," and both novels—*Storm in June* and *Dolce*—highlight their "reaction to the maelstrom of history" (Bracher 26–27). Yet according to Bracher, the key to *Storm in June* lies in what the young priest Philippe Péricand tells the thirty mostly orphaned poor boys—the Penitent Children of the 16th arrondissement—just before he trucks them from Paris to the safety of the country. "[P]ublic misfortunes consist of a multitude of private misfortunes" (*SF_T* 23), he says, and "we are conscious of the solidarity that binds us, we members of a body that is one and the same."[13] Plainly alluding to the doctrine that all Christians participate in the mystical body of Christ, especially when taking the sacrament of Communion, Philippe urges his charges to think of themselves as all parts of one suffering body. Likewise, Bracher asks us to read the whole novel in this light—as a story of characters bound together by the "solidarity" of suffering (Bracher 81–82). But this commonality is no stronger in the novel than it was among actual refugees of different classes. Since Philippe's poor boys are chiefly united, if at all, by their murderous hatred of him and his class, his invocation of solidarity is just one of the many ironies exposed as such by the bitter divisions that atomize nearly all the characters in *Storm in June*.[14]

What then does the novel tell us about what Julian Jackson calls "the state of mind of the French people in 1940"? Whether or not all of them ever inhabited any *one* mental state, part of the answer lies in the rhetorical question posed in the midst of Chapter 6, where we are told of Parisians "overwhelmed by anxiety and fear" (*SF_T* 29): fear of losing not just their houses but their very lives. "Qui pensait aux malheurs de la Patrie?" (*SF* 56), asks the narrator. "Who was thinking about the misfortunes of the Nation?" One answer appears in Chapter 15, where a working-class woman named Hortense weeps upon learning that "the Germans marched into Paris this morning" (*SF_T* 67)—evidently the morning of June 14, 1940:

> Her tears were rare and burning, the tears of a hard woman who had not often pitied either herself or others. A feeling of rage, of sorrow and shame invaded her, so violent that she felt a physical pain, throbbing and acute, in the region of her heart. Finally she said:
>
> "You know that I love my husband ... Poor Louis, it's just us two and he works, he doesn't drink, he doesn't run around, in short we love each other, I have only him, but suppose they told me: you will see him no more, he just died, but we have victory ... Well then, I would like that better, ah! I assure you, this is no joke, I would like that better." (*SF* 98, my translation)

Convulsed by rage, sorrow, and shame, Hortense not only thinks about the misfortunes of France but also weeps for its defeat. For the sake of victory, she says, she would have been willing to give up even her loving, hard-working husband—all she's got. Yet aside from this burst of dismay at the fall of France, Hortense cares for no one outside her tight family group. Just as Gabriel Corte is repelled by the "vulgarity" of the bloodstained bandages swaddling Hortense's own head (*SF_T* 61), she herself despises Gabriel, whom she once saw with his mistress Florence at the house of a countess who employed her. When Jules's wife Aline objects to his theft of Gabriel's food, Hortense insists he was right to take it: "Those two," she says of Gabriel and Florence, "they don't deserve to live, they don't, I'm telling you!" (*SF_T* 65). At the end of the chapter, after dining on Corte's "excellent" edibles, Hortense and her companions judge him "less harshly," but the stories she tells about the self-absorption of academics and writers like Corte "made them laugh to the point of tears" (*SF* 98–99, my translation): tears quite different from those that Hortense has just shed for the fall of France.

This sudden shift to laughter—this lurch from rage and shame at the defeat of her country, for whose victory she would have traded even her husband—perfectly exemplifies Némirovsky's way of fictionalizing the Exodus. She aimed, first of all, to play up contrasts—such as the contrast between misery and prosperity (*SF_T* Appendix 343) or as above between shame and derision. Since playing up contrasts meant highlighting human feelings, she also clearly distinguished her aims from those of the historian. While planning her set of novels in the summer of 1940, she wrote:

The most important and interesting thing is the following: historic facts, revolutions, etc. must be touched upon, whereas what will be developed is daily lives, human feelings, etc.—*especially the human comedy.* (Notebook, qtd. Weiss 133, my emphasis)

*The Human Comedy—La Comédie humaine—*is the omnibus title given by Honoré de Balzac to all the novels and novellas that he published between 1829 and 1847. In his 1842 Introduction to the series, he explained that he had set out to explore in his fiction precisely what historians had neglected:

As we read the dry and discouraging list of events called History, who can have failed to note that the writers of all periods, in Egypt, Persia, Greece, and Rome, have forgotten to give us a history of manners? (Balzac)

As Balzac conceives them, manners express the radical—even zoological—differences between one person and another. Just as a sheep differs from a lion, a businessman differs from "a student, a statesman, a merchant, a sailor, a poet, a beggar, a priest … Thus," he writes, "social species have always existed, and will always exist, just as there are zoological species." But for Balzac, society is more freakish than Nature. While animals simply "rend each other," human beings fight with the aid of mental tools. "Men, too, rend each other; but their greater or less intelligence makes the struggle far more complicated" (Balzac).

To set this caustic assessment of human nature beside *Suite Française* is to see that while Némirovsky's two novels may be Tolstoyan in theme and scope, their *dianoia—*their sociological core—is Balzacian. In *Dolce,* the first thought that strikes the German Lieutenant Bruno von Falk on seeing the large, over-furnished house of Madame Angellier is that "One of Balzac's characters might live here" (*SF_T* 235). Later on, Madame Angellier is harshly compared with Madame de Montmort, the grandest lady of Bussy. "[A]s an aristocrat," we are told, Madame de Montmort "was more attached to spiritual values than the bitter, materialistic middle classes (to whom Madame Angellier belonged)" (*SF_T* 253). But if the class differences exemplified by these two women are just as important for Némirovsky as they were for Balzac, the "spiritual values" of the aristocrat in this pairing turn out to be superficial and officious. While Madame Angellier habitually suspects her tenants of stealing from her whenever they buy any food, Madame de Montmort wants to know such things as whether or not the women of the town go to Mass. Her "spiritual values" thus amount to petty tyranny and help to explain why she is the most repellant character in *Dolce.* "Of the two families who owned all the land in the region," we are told, "—the Montmorts and the Angelliers—the Montmorts were the most hated" (*SF_T* 253).

Ultimately, then, the comparison of the two families hardly favors the so-called aristocrats. If Balzac's human beings put a freakish twist on Nature, Némirovsky puts her own twist on Balzac's conviction that the French social system of his time was chiefly threatened by "the bourgeois values of material acquisitiveness and gain," which "were steadily replacing what he viewed as the more stable moral values of the old-time aristocracy" (Encyclopaedia Britannica). In *Storm in June,* the aristocratic Péricands do all they can to dissuade their young son from fighting the German invaders.[15] In *Dolce*, Madame de Montmort and her husband the Viscount not only collaborate cravenly with the Germans but also do absolutely nothing to help the farmers and villagers of Bussy—not even selling them, let alone giving them, vegetables from their garden. On the contrary, after catching a farmer named Benoît Sabarie in the act of trying to steal vegetables from her garden one evening, Madame de Montmort vainly scolds him for doing so even as he calls her "heartless and stingy" for not sharing her plants (*SF_T* 291), and runs off. She then mentally damns him in explicitly Balzacian terms. Hearing "the sound of German footsteps getting closer," she says to herself, "Oh, I really hope they caught him. I really hope they killed him. . . . What a man! *What a species*! What vile people!" (*ST_T* 292, my emphasis).

Enraged by the insolence of a man whose species seems so different from her own, she demands that her husband denounce him to the Germans for having "a gun at home," which she thinks he must have because he "bragged about hunting in [our] grounds all winter" (*SF_T* 203). Since the Viscount knows that openly denouncing Benoît would infuriate the townspeople, he offers to tell the Germans to look for a gun at the Sabaries' farm but will also ask them "to keep the matter quiet" and he will "make the Germans promise not to punish him too severely" (*SF_T* 293). Fat chance. Nothing could better illustrate the fatuity as well as the deviousness of this would-be aristocrat. Whatever the Germans might promise, what he tells them could readily lead to the execution of a man whose welfare he is obliged by his very rank—*noblesse oblige*—to protect.

Inverting Balzac's formula, wherein the values of the bourgeoisie threaten those of the aristocracy, it is Madame Angellier—exemplar of "the materialistic middle classes"—who finally proves courageous. At first she repels us by despising her daughter-in-law Lucile, the altogether sympathetic heroine of *Dolce*. She loathes Lucile for three things: not caring enough about her husband, Madame Angellier's son, who has been captured by the Germans; not hating the German officer as much as she does; and worst of all, treating this German "guest" so politely that she seems ready to "fall into [his] arms" (*SF_T* 238, 309–10). Yet Madame Angellier's hatred of the Germans has a rare value in a world where her compatriots spend much of their energy hating each other even while marveling at the politeness of their occupiers.

The latter reaction was actually widespread among the French. In his comprehensive book on the Occupation, Ian Ousby records that besides paying for "even the food and drink which they could just as easily have plundered" (Ousby 54), the Germans struck the French as ubiquitously well-mannered. "[T]he favourite words that the French found for praising their conquerers," Ousby writes, "became the catchphrase of the day. *Ils sont correct*: they behave properly" (Ousby 55). In *Dolce,* where the shopkeepers of Bussy soon learn that the Germans would "buy anything" and could even be readily fleeced (*SF_T* 199), they win the admiration of Madame de Montmort, who finds them "cultured" and even judges them by "the way they hold their knife and fork" (*SF_T* 291). Likewise, the Viscount de Montmort tells his wife, "The Germans are behaving politely to everyone. They salute the women, they stroke the children. They pay cash" (*SF_T* 294). By such means they buy the would-be aristocrats of the town. As Madame Angellier ruefully reflects, the Montmorts even "entertained the Germans in their own home" (*SF_T* 308).

In terms of the actual history of the Occupation, then, Madame Angellier becomes a *résistant*. In confining herself to her room and thus cutting off all contact with the German officer billeted in her house, she is performing what was implicitly defined as resistance in July 1940, right after the Occupation began, when a journalist named Jean Texcier published a pamphlet called "Conseils à l'occupé" / "Advice to the Occupied." Shun the German, Texcier advised. "Do not listen to him, do not talk to him, ignore him. . . ." (qtd. Ousby 151). In February 1942, when Némirovsky was composing *Dolce*, a writer named Jean Bruller (pseudonym Vercors) launched his underground press, Les Editions de Minuit, with what Ousby has called "the first literary expression of resistance": a story about a man and his niece who refuse to speak to the German officer billeted in their home even though he is exceptionally polite, speaks French fluently, and loves French literature (Ousby 151–52).

Whether or not Némirovsky ever saw the pamphlet or read the story, Madame Angellier exemplifies the kind of resistance they both endorse. Alone in her room, she comes "to feel that she [is] a race apart—staunch, as implacable as a fortress" (*SF_T* 308). Furthermore, in offering to hide Benoît in her own room even as the Germans are hunting him down for shooting one of their officers, she is unequivocally courageous. Though the Germans threaten to execute by firing squad anyone caught sheltering Benoît, Madame Angellier tells Lucile that she will do so: "some would treat [him] as a criminal and others as a hero," she says. "And what about me? I've already chosen . . . in spite of myself" (*SF_T* 312).[16] And when Lucile says, "we could be denounced" for hiding Benoît, she proudly declares, "Frenchmen don't denounce one another" (*SF_T* 313).

Since we already know that Montmort has told the Germans about Benoît's gun, she evidently means that "*true* Frenchmen don't denounce each other." In September 1940, a poet named Robert Desnos published an article in *Aujourd'hui*—a new and "independent" Paris newspaper—urging people in the name of "dignity" to stop denouncing each other. But they didn't. By 1942, letters of denunciation that were often anonymous and mostly antisemitic were rumored to be inundating the Paris Kommandantur at the rate of 1,500 a day (Ousby 146). In *Dolce* likewise, Madame Angellier's claim that Frenchmen don't denounce each other reminds Lucile of what Lieutenant Bruno once told her in confidence: that on the day he arrived in Bussy, "there was a package of anonymous letters" in which people accused each other of various deeds including "being spies" (*SF_T* 313). In having all the letters burned, however, Bruno does something very like what German authorities actually did when they "outlawed such communication" (Ousby 147).

In *Dolce*, Madame Angellier never writes such a letter, and so far from denouncing Benoît herself, she is clearly among those who would treat him as a hero. She thus personifies what Lucile says to herself about the impact of war on the "multifaceted" complexity of human nature: "only" those who have "observed men and women in times like this, she thought, can be said to know them. And to know themselves" (*SF_T* 335). By doing all she can to aid Benoît, Madame Angellier reveals the courageous core of a woman we first know only as a tyrannical mother-in-law. By contrast, the spineless Viscount blames ex-soldiers such as Benoît for the fall of France: "[I]n the end," he thought, "it was the soldiers' lack of discipline, their lack of patriotism, their 'bad attitude' that had been responsible for the defeat" (*SF_T* 231). But Benoît is the only Frenchman in *Suite Française* who attacks a German soldier, and he thus reminds us of the only other character who tries—however recklessly—to fight the Germans.

At the outset of *Storm in June*, the 17-year-old Boy Scout named Hubert Péricand desperately yearns to form with his friends a volunteer group of sharpshooters to "fight all night long" and "save their bombed-out, burning Paris" (*SF* 11). As the second son of a rich Parisian family, Hubert is one of those "younger boys" whose raw courage Marc Bloch says could have been harnessed in defense of the country—if only his training had started months before (Bloch, *SD* 133), if only the authorities had called up "every man between sixteen and sixty," as Hubert himself says (*SF_T* 8). Instead, as the family decides to leave the besieged city, Hubert's desperate plea to be allowed to stay behind and fight beside his friends elicits only his father's pity: "My poor boy." And when Hubert realizes "to his horror" that the war is lost, "he felt himself burst into tears" (*SF_T* 13).

Already resigned to defeat, the father nearly castrates the boy's instinctive eagerness to fight. But the rift between them is just one of the cracks in this extended family. Another emerges when the family's servants are allowed into the drawing room to hear the latest war news on the radio. While Hubert has not been called to serve and his older brother Philippe (now a priest) has been exempted for weak lungs, the widowed nanny in charge of Hubert's younger brothers has given three sons to the war. So even while taking the hand of the eight-year-old Bernard, who is crying because Hubert has just kicked at his toys, this grey-haired lady is herself "crying for … sons whom she imagined already dead, all of them" (*SF* 8). Her sacrifice dwarfs that of her employer, Madame Charlotte Péricand, who simply has to take her father-in-law and her four younger children to the presumed safety of her mother's house in Burgundy early in the morning.

But the Péricand household is riven by more than the Balzacian gap between family and servants. The family itself is split, as just noted, by the conflict between the parents' sense of total resignation and Hubert's desperate urge to fight. When he suddenly imagines that "we" can let the Germans advance so that (he implies) "we" can ambush them, his mother tells him to wash his hands and comb his unruly hair. In response he thinks, "How I hate this family" (*SF_T* 8) and kicks Bernard's toys. This is no mere spurt of adolescent pique at a nagging mother. Facing the imminent threat of catastrophic defeat, Hubert is the only member of this family who yearns to fight for his country, no matter how futile this yearning may seem to his elders. And it is impossible, I think, to overstate the importance of the fact that what he hates is not the enemy, not the menacing invaders, but the suffocating passivity of his own elders.

His rage erupts still more fiercely nearly two months later in the city of Nîmes, where he turns up grinning and pink-cheeked, in glowing health, just in time for his own funeral. His mother, grandmother, and younger siblings are about to leave for a funeral mass being held for him as well as for his paternal grandfather and his brother Philippe, who—as already noted—has been murdered by the boys he led out of Paris. Reports of Hubert's death were somewhat exaggerated. Though his mother was told that he had been killed at the Battle of Moulins, Hubert had simply stood behind an inflamed barricade at one end of a bridge while French soldiers vainly fired their machine guns at German tanks advancing at lightning speed (*SF_T* 82). Weaponless and despairing, he had witnessed the battle after slipping away on his bicycle one night from the house where the family was briefly staying, and though he momentarily felt the urge "to rush the bridge, lead the soldiers, throw himself on the enemy tanks and die shouting '*Vive la France!*'"(*SF_T* 84), he had dropped from sheer exhaustion, then found his way to a country hotel where he was not just fortuitously fed and billeted by a dancer with lovely legs but also given his first taste of sex.

This trial by fire and sex—a combination we shall see again in Henry Green's *Caught*—leaves Hubert ready to scorn any impulse to idealize him or anyone else. Mourned as a hero so long as he is thought to be dead (his mother tells her friends that "he has given his life for the honour of France" [*SF_T* 137]), he is filled with something very like "la rage"/ "the rage" that Marc Bloch said would be roused in the young by "l'ombre du grand désastre de 1940" (Bloch, *ED* 109)—"the shadow of the great disaster of 1940." Just as Bloch resolves to tell the shocking truth about generals who are called "*great*" even after leading their men into disaster (*SD* 26), and just as Bloch deplores the none too rare "stories ... of headlong flight with the commander's car outstripping the rest of the field" (*SD* 105), Hubert is revolted by the "conspiracy of lies" that will be told about the utterly humiliating defeat of France:

> The people around him, his family, his friends, aroused a feeling of shame and rage within him. He had seen them on the road, them and people like them; he recalled the cars full of officers running away with their beautiful yellow trunks and their painted women ... And to think that no one will know. ... We'll do everything we can to find acts of devotion and heroism for the official records. Good God! To see what I've seen! ... [E]verywhere you look, chaos, cowardice, vanity and ignorance! What a wonderful race we are!" (*SF_T* 142–43)

This rush of thoughts plainly reveals the mind of a shatteringly disillusioned teenager who is something less than a model of probity: though he bitterly recalls the sight of officers running away with their painted women, he has just savored in bed the charms of a lovely dancer. Nevertheless, more than any other passage in the novel, Hubert's passionate outburst encapsulates its import. Just as Marc Bloch arraigns the old men of France for failing to wage a modern war and thereby betraying its youth, Hubert nails what has vitiated French society. It is not just riddled with cowardice and riven by class division but atomized by a selfishness that goads nearly every character we meet into hatred, distrust, resentment, contempt, or exploitation of others, leaving no room for patriotic fervor or even animus against the enemy. "More and more," wrote Némirovsky to herself in 1942, "the world is becoming divided into the haves and the have nots. The first don't want to give anything up and the second want to take everything. Who will win out?" (*SF* Appendix 345).

In *Storm in June*, the prime example of those who don't want to give anything up is Gabriel Corte, who is implicitly linked with the arch-collaborationist Marshall Pétain.[17] Since Pétain appears nowhere in the novel, not even in fictional disguise, it is only indirectly that Némirovsky exposes the hypocrisy of his claim to sympathize with refugees. In taking command of the nation on June 17, Pétain declared by radio: "I offer myself to France in order to ease her suffering. In this painful hour, my thoughts go out to the refugees in their misery, who are travelling along our roads in utter destitution. I extend to them my compassion and my solicitude."[18] In actuality, most of the French people who heard this broadcast were overwhelmed with relief because they thought the war was over. But in the days immediately following the broadcast and before the armistice was signed, many people were bombed or machine-gunned to death in the Loire Valley (Diamond 113–14). Without even alluding to this disaster or to Pétain's empty words of compassion, Némirovsky reveals that the "members of the government" and "celebrities" who are luxuriously housed in the Grand Hotel of the "Queen of French spas" (*SF_T* 145, 147)—clearly Vichy—care nothing for refugees dead or alive, for people desperately seeking a place to stay.[19]

Nevertheless, Corte is made to feel something of their desperation when a basket of food is stolen right out of his arms just after he buys it during a stop on his trip south. Finding no way to get his dinner back, he and Florence wander about in search of their car and soon fall into fighting each other, "driven mad by hunger, fear, and exhaustion" (*SF_T* 76). Yet after spending the night on a bench, they somehow cross a bridge even as German trucks and guns come toward them, and while pushing Florence's head down under his coat, Gabriel has a rare spasm of altruistic courage: "a passionate, urgent desire to save Florence" (*SF_T* 79). As if in reward, they are both re-united with their car, which also means that Gabriel recovers his manuscripts and "his life":

> He would no longer be an ordinary man, suffering, starving, both courageous and cowardly at the same time, but instead a privileged creature, protected from all evil. He would be Gabriel Corte! (*SF_T* 80)

Ironically, he finds nothing extraordinary in his own fleetingly heroic impulse to save Florence. Though "courageous and cowardly at the same time," this paradoxical mix is part of what he considers "ordinary" —being "an ordinary man." What makes him extraordinary, he thinks, is his *exemption* from suffering, which is precisely why he could never write a novel such as this one. For being Gabriel Corte—recovering his public identity—means forgetting all the miseries of being a refugee. After reaching the Grand Hotel at seven o'clock in the morning and "collapsing with exhaustion," Gabriel and Florence "felt they had been reborn" because "[t]hey were recognized and surrounded" (*SF_T* 145).

By contrast with Gabriel and Florence, with the cowardly Count de Furières, with the pseudo-aristocratic Péricands, and with Corbin the bank manager, Maurice and Jeanne Michaud seem to embody an integrity evident nowhere else in *Storm in June*. In a note to herself as she started work on the novel, Némirovsky wrote: "Stress the Michauds. People who always pay the price and the only ones who are truly noble" (*SF_T* Appendix 342). Even after Maurice's fifteen years as a bank accountant, this middle-aged couple earn together just enough to pay their bills. They keep afloat only because of Jeanne's temporary secretarial job, and they are intensely anxious about their only son, Jean-Marie, who has been called up to serve in the army and whose last letter was dated June 2. Furthermore, they are betrayed by Corbin. Though he orders them to meet him at the bank's branch in Tours (about 145 miles southwest of Paris), he breaks his promise to give them a ride; since he takes instead his mistress Arlette Corail (the same dancer who ends up in bed with Hubert), the Michauds must travel on foot. Realizing after three days that they will never reach Tours, they return to Paris, and in late July they finally manage to get a letter to Corbin asking for instructions and some pay. Pouncing on what he takes to be their effrontery, he replies that by failing to reach Tours at the appointed time as well as failing to contact him, they have effectively resigned and are therefore entitled to no "compensation whatsoever" (*SF_T* 162).

The Michauds are saved from destitution by the Count de Furières, who responds to Jeanne's entreaties by granting six months' salary to each of them. But we can clearly see how brutally Corbin mistreats them, and how much his heartless egotism underscores by contrast their kindness, their honest effort to do their jobs, and their devotion to each other and their son. While Corbin hypocritically complains to the Count that "everyone [was] thinking only of himself" in the chaos of flight, and that none of his staff could meet him in Tours (*SF_T* 160), the Michauds not only do all they can to reach it but also—in the course of their arduous journey amidst a fleeing crowd—take part in "that active and attentive sympathy that working people normally preserve for their own families or the poor" (*SF_T* 49).

For all their compassion, however, not even the Michauds are exempt from murderous wishes under the most harrowing conditions. Consider what Jeanne thinks and feels right after she and Maurice survive a machine-gun attack that leaves three shredded bodies on the ground. Realizing that Tours has been bombed, she says to herself:

> Did the bank even exist any more? Was Monsieur Corbin buried beneath the rubble with his files? With his valuables? With his dancer? And his wife's jewellery! But that would be too good to be true, Jeanne thought with sudden ferociousnesss. (*SF_T* 53)

This thrill of vengeance is soon felt by the dancer herself after she finds her way to the comfort of a country hotel. Still resenting Corbin for having made such a fuss about taking her in his car after hers was damaged, she scornfully relishes the remembered sight of his terrified face when they reached Tours just in time to be bombed. She is also tickled by a further thought: while he lost both his personal effects and the bank's documents, she has lost nothing at all—not even a single handkerchief or make-up box (*SF_T* 89).

Different as they are, both Jeanne Michaud and Arlette Corail thus indulge in *schadenfreude*, and elsewhere in the novel, bombs elicit something comparable from the people they miss. In *Strange Defeat*, Marc Bloch declares that the prospect of being struck by this new weapon of war filled him with "la vraie peur" (Bloch, *ED* 38)—"true dread." But the bombs of *Storm in June* provoke quite different feelings. In the city of Orléans, where Corte and Florence spend the night of June 11 after leaving Paris that morning, a silent crowd gazing up at a gradually disappearing plane could sometimes

> hear a distant explosion. "It didn't hit us," they would think, *sighing with happiness.* "It didn't hit us. It's aimed at someone else. We're so lucky!" (*SF_T* 42, my emphasis)

As already noted, Gabriel is lucky enough to reach the Grand Hotel as well as to avoid getting bombed or machine-gunned. Yet even though he finds himself both recognized and cosseted at the hotel, one thing cracks the shell of his egotism. While bathing in his suite, he suddenly realizes that his time as a writer has ended. Just as Bloch found the old generals of France shackled to the past, Gabriel suddenly realizes that his work in progress—the manuscript he has "rescued" from fire and bombs—will have nothing to say to the future, to whatever new world may arise from the ashes of defeat:

> The passions he described, his feelings, his scruples, the history of a generation, his generation—they were all old, useless, obsolete. "Obsolete!" he repeated in despair. (*SF_T* 149)

Though only fifty, then, Gabriel takes his place with a more pathetic example of obsolescence: old Monsieur Péricand, father-in-law of Charlotte Péricand and grandfather of Hubert. At the funeral service for the old man, Hubert shocks his mother by saying, "I don't mind and neither do you. He was old and ill. What would he have done in all this chaos?" (*SF_T* 141). The only thing the old man does before dying, apart from requiring constant nursing care and thus impeding the flight of the younger Péricands, is to dictate his will to a notary summoned just after midnight to his bedside in the nursing home of a rural village. (After a panic-stricken Charlotte forgets him while escaping with her children from a burning house, he is taken in by nuns.)

The length and precision of the old man's will—especially from someone who has so far spoken scarcely one syllable—are about as plausible as the soaring notes of the nearly six-minute aria sung by the dying Violetta at the end of Verdi's *La Traviata*.[20] Like the last notes of Violetta, the last words of the old man demand a maximum suspension of disbelief, but they reward us with a succession of ironic twists on the practice of charity.

Among other things, the old man leaves five million francs to the institution he "founded, known as the Penitent Children of the 16th Arrondissement" (*SF_T* 116). This would-be charitable bequest—worth about $100,000 in 1940, when the franc was valued at 2 cents—can give no pleasure to Charlotte, who has clearly suffered pain every time she heard her father-in-law say that he planned to make it (*SF_T* 10). In acting on his plan, the old man also turns the institute into a monument to himself, since he decrees that its front hall will display either a sculpted bust or a life-size portrait of him on his deathbed (*SF_T* 117).

Having thus made his charity a means of self-aggrandizement, he tries to make amends for having long since antagonized his sister, for having taken—apparently— everything left by their mother, Henriette Maltête, whose very surname connotes the pain of a headache ("mal a la tête"). This reparational bequest, however, is virtually nullified by what the Germans have just done to it. In leaving his sister "the property I own in Dunquerque" (*SF_T* 117), the old man fails to realize that Dunquerque, aka Dunkirk, has been bombed to rubble. His last two bequests compound this ignorance. In declaring that his "château in Bléoville" (the evidently fictional town of "Wheatville") should become "a home for former soldiers severely wounded in the war," he is thinking of the first World War, which means that most if not all of those who might benefit from this bequest are now probably dead. And in leaving to his "faithful valet an annual income of one thousand francs for the rest of his life" (*SF_T* 118), he evidently fails to realize that this amounts to about twenty dollars a year.[21]

Soon after Monsieur Péricand breathes his last, we learn just how well his "venerable institution" has managed to achieve its goal—"instill[ing] morals in delinquent minors" (*SF_T* 10). On the very day that Charlotte Péricand leaves Paris with four of her children and her father-in-law, her son Philippe is asked to drive thirty of the institution's boys from Paris south to the presumed safety of a large country estate. Since Philippe has just returned to visit briefly with his family, he knows none of the boys, and when he first sees these "unfortunate children" ranging in age from eleven to eighteen, he feels something like fear (*SF_T* 22). It springs in part from physiognomic stereotyping, for in some of the older ones he sees "the low brow, the thick hands of killers." But in none of them—including the "small . . . and scrawny" younger ones, with lowered eyes and "tightly clenched" lips—can he find "a single glimmer of love." To Philippe they seem "children of Satan" beyond reclaiming or redeeming (*SF_T* 22).

In murdering Philippe soon after, while they are all spending the night on the grounds of a château, the boys confirm his worst fears—almost too melodramatically. Némirovsky herself calls his death "melo" or "schmaltzy," in Sandra Smith's translation (*SF* Appendix 347), and Hanna Diamond claims that the murder "does not ring true" to what she knows of the actual Exodus (Diamond 216). Yet two things make it at least plausible. In the long shadow of French history, the boys' killing of the priest re-enacts the anti-clerical violence of the Reign of Terror, when revolutionary authorities killed hundreds of priests as well as exiling some 30,000 others (Collins and Price 176–177). Just as important, the murder of Philippe reminds us that these boys had never been called to fight for their country, trained to pitch their aggressions at its enemy rather than at one of their own elders. If the authorities had called up "younger boys," as Marc Bloch says they should have (quoted above), they could readily have found work for the hands—however thick—of the older boys who attack Philippe. Instead, the boys embody the most extreme version of what we find in many other characters: hatred. We have already seen that even after being raised in comfort and affection far exceeding what the institute offers to its boys, Hubert hates his own family.

His priestly older brother yearns to feel something quite different: to "overcome . . . at all costs" his visceral aversion to his charges (*SF_T* 22). Paradoxically, what breaks both his heart and his resolve is not their recalcitrance or unruliness but their mechanical docility, their unresponsiveness to any of his friendly overtures, their refusal to show any feeling, their impenetrable deadness. "[T]heir souls," he perceives, "were shut off, walled up, secret and silent." As a result, he finds it "almost impossible to feel" any love for them, as the "Grace of God within him" normally ensures. Instead, as he tramps along with the boys, "[h]e wanted only one thing: to be rid of them as soon as possible" (*SF_T* 126). In spite of his claim that he and they all share in the "solidarity" of Christ's mystical body, as noted earlier, their "species" differs from his own quite as much as the species of Benoît differs from that of Madame de Montmort, who wants him killed. Likewise, just as Philippe wants only to be rid of the boys as soon as possible, they want only to be rid of him. Whether or not French boys ever actually killed a priest during the Exodus, the murder of Philippe rings all too true to the Balzacian vision of *Suite Française.*

Furthermore, whatever sympathy we may feel for the well-meaning Philippe, *Storm in June* checks our sympathy for almost everyone else. Consider for instance what happens one night to Charles Langelet. After driving south with the aid of gas stolen from a pair of newlyweds, this wealthy, dilettantish bachelor returns in autumn to his Parisian apartment. Delighted to be "reunited with all his wonderful possessions" (*SF_T* 167), relieved that he still has plenty of money, he is also pleased to encounter a group of friends at a bar in the early evening: so pleased that he suggests they all meet for dinner later on at a restaurant near his apartment. But given the shortage of electricity in the newly occupied city, it is "pitch black" (*SF_T* 170), and though Charlie thinks he knows "every step of the way" (*SF_T* 174) to the restaurant on this rainy night, he fails to see a speeding car while crossing a road and takes "a terrible blow to his head" that shatters his skull. The driver is Arlette Corail, the dancer, who recognizes Charlie's battered face because she was part of the group at the bar that he had planned to meet for dinner. But aside from thinking "poor guy!" she mentally blames him for not "paying attention," and mainly laments her own "rotten luck" (*SF_T* 174). Like nearly everyone else in this novel, she cares most of all for herself.

In the later 1930s, the weekly magazine *L'Illustration*—the French version of the American magazine *Life*, for those old enough to remember it—repeatedly warned in both pictures and words against the threat posed by Germany's ever-growing military might. Near the end of a long editorial on this threat in April 1936, a journalist named Ludovic Naudeau compared French politicians to little boys fighting blindly over a lump of sugar in the middle of the road while a car speeding furiously toward them— aka Nazi Germany—is about to crush them all (Naudeau 389). Walking through a pitch dark city to meet old friends for dinner in one of his favorite restaurants, Charlie personifies the blindness deplored not only by Naudeau but also by Marc Bloch, who clearly perceived how many French people—civilians and soldiers alike—were unable or unwilling to see how radically the advent of a second war had changed their world.

Charlie's death is punctuated by an incident that crystallizes this disruption. Before leaving his apartment for dinner, he had carefully removed from its packing case one of his most beloved possessions—a Sèvres statuette of *Venus at the Looking Glass*—and placed it on a polished Chippendale table where no one but he is allowed to touch it (*SF_T* 171, 173). Earlier in the day, he had not only asked Madame Logre, the concierge of his building, to clean his apartment; to save money (he had always been stingy), he had also insisted she do so in six hours even though the dust had been gathering for so long that she felt—as she told him—that she could not finish that day. Her suppressed fury at his insistence finds a perfect outlet just before she finally leaves his apartment. After accidentally knocking the statuette of Venus to the floor and thus smashing its head to bits, she blames Charlie for leaving it "at the edge of the table" and finally concludes, "I don't care what he says. He can go to hell for all I care!" (*SF_T* 175). Having just been killed, Charlie is thus damned as well—by one more woman who blames him instead of herself, and who almost certainly hates him more than she hates any invader.[22]

Rather than ending on this note, however, the novel ends with the homecoming of Jean-Marie, long-awaited son of the Michauds, as well as with the promise of new life, however unpredictable its future might be. At the end of his own painful meditation on the fall of France, Marc Bloch writes that "France of the new springtime must be the creation of the young" (Bloch, *SD* 175). *Storm in June* concludes with the returns—in September 1940—of two young men who have so far survived the war. Just as Jean-Marie returns to his parents in Paris, the long-absent Benoît escapes from German captivity, returns to the Sabarie family, and marries Madeline, who by the winter of 1940–41 has conceived their first child. Aptly enough, the novel ends with the birth of a new season:

> the first rain of spring began to fall, still cold, but torrential and urgent, carrying its way down to the smallest roots of the trees, down to the very heart of the deep, black earth. (*SF_T* 189)

To some extent, the rejuvenating tone of these last words of *Storm in June* is echoed by the ending of *Dolce*, when the Germans leave Bussy just after Lucile succeeds in driving Benoît to Paris and thus thwarting his capture.[23] But measured against the actual history of the Occupation, the ending of *Dolce* requires a major suspension of disbelief. Given the kind of retaliation that German authorities took for anything done against their forces, Lieutenant Bruno's response to Benoît's shooting of Bonnet, the other German lieutenant, is pure fantasy.

To be sure, the novel nods to historical fact by featuring an announcement that anyone caught sheltering Benoît will be immediately executed (*SF_T* 306), and in the 2015 film version of the novel, the Viscount is taken hostage for the shooting of Bonnet and then executed when Benoît is not found. This event is perfectly consistent with what the Germans actually did while Némirovsky was writing her novels.[24] But even in the film version of the novel, Bruno takes no action against Benoît for shooting the two guards who have found him in Lucile's car at a checkpoint. Instead, since Benoît has been wounded in the shoulder, Bruno helps Lucile to lift him into the car and thus allows them to escape—as Lucile smiles her thanks to the German lieutenant.

Though we can hardly blame Némirovsky for this melodramatic ending of a film scripted by others, her own ending is just as historically implausible. Besides never searching Madame Angellier's house, let alone her own room (where she hides Benoît), Némirovsky's Germans take no hostages for the shooting of the officer, let alone executing anyone. Also, when Lucile asks Bruno for a travel pass and petrol coupon so that she can drive "one of [her] farmers" to Paris to visit his "seriously ill" daughter (her cover story for taking Benoît there), her request is instantly granted (*SF_T* 335). Finally, when the departing Bruno gives Lucile the address of an uncle who works for "the Commandant in greater Paris" and whom Bruno has asked to help her "as much as he can," she tells Bruno that his life is "precious" to her (*SF_T* 337). In this would-be "sweet" ending of *Dolce*, *Suite Française* becomes a bilingual pun as well as a title signifying both literature and music: a set of novels about France *and* the set of six "French suites" that Johann Sebastian Bach wrote for the clavier between 1722 and 1725. In playing these suites while staying with the Angelliers, Bruno may seek to remind them that Germany can produce great music as well as brutal wars.

Lucile's last words to Bruno also evoke the paradisal moment when they experience their love at sunset in the Angellier garden: a place "where there is no war, no death, where wild animals and deer live together in peace" (*SF_T* 321). Yet this, too, is a fantasy. Just as soon as Bruno tries to take her, to rape her—"tearing at her clothes, crushing her breasts"—she recoils at his otherness: "Foreigner! Foreigner! Enemy, in spite of everything. Forever he would be the enemy. . . ." (*SF_T* 321). A love that yearns to transcend all differences is suddenly ruptured by the Balzacian consciousness of absolute difference, the unbridgeable gulf made by war as well as by his lust to vandalize her love.

Lucile's deep ambivalence toward Bruno was something felt by Némirovsky herself. Just as Bruno's departure to fight on the Eastern Front stirs Lucile to "pity and a profound, almost maternal tenderness" (*SF_T* 337), Némirovsky imagined Bruno dying heroically in Russia as a parallel to the heroic death of Jean-Marie—"the two full of sorrowful nobility." But just "how," she asked herself, would Jean-Marie die? "And what is heroism these days?" (*SF_T* Appendix 350). Is it any more possible or plausible, we might ask, than a love that transcends both war and national enmity? Grappling with a war whose ending she could not foresee, Némirovsky could not answer either question definitively. But in her pair of novels, the impact of war reveals like nothing else how "complicated, multifaceted, contradictory, [and] surprising" human beings can be (*SF_T* 335). Measured against the recorded facts of the Exodus and the Occupation, *Suite Française* is demonstrably fictitious. Yet it may justly claim to have told at least one set of truths about human nature in time of war.

Notes

1   Operation Barbarossa—code name for the German attack on the Soviet Union— started on Sunday, June 22, 1941.

2   Diamond 242. This is just one of the French studies of the Exodus that she herself cites (241–42).

3   In *After the Fall* (2010), Nathan Bracher treats both *Fleeing Hitler* and *Suite Française*, but so far as I know they are compared nowhere else. To this day, the Exodus still fascinates novelists as well as historians. In *Le Miroir de Nos Peines* (2020), which fictionally revives the months of April to June 1940, Pierre Lemaitre mercilessly portrays "the mismanagement, stupidity, and poltroonery" of the French army high command as well as the misdeeds of refugees themselves: their "violence, brutality, and callous disregard for the desperation of others" (Edward Bradley, email to the author of September 30, 2021).

4   In a series of notes made on June 2, 1942, Némirovsky not only tells herself to "[r]eread Tolstoy" but also writes that she has tried to do in *Storm* just what he did in *War and Peace*: depict "the historical scenes . . . from the perspective of the characters" (*SF* 351, 354). At one point early in *Storm in June*, Gabriel Corte tells his mistress how "remarkabl[y]" Tolstoy's novel portrays minor characters (*SF* 16). For a detailed comparison of Tolstoy's novel and *Suite Française*, see Cenedese.

5   *SF_T* 149–50. Jules Blanc (1881–1960), a leading Communist, never served as either prime minister or minister of war. Also, since Gabriel Corte is an ardent collaborationist and therefore a staunch enemy of all Communists, the idea that he has enjoyed and exploited the patronage of Jules Blanc must be an in-joke.

6   "Irène Némirovsky" 13. See also her book-length study, *The Némirovsky Question*.

7   According to Jackson, the "National Revolution" launched by the Vichy regime branded "Jews, Communists, and Freemasons" as "enemies of France" who must be punished and persecuted (J. Jackson 233).

8   In the face of the Popular Front, he says, the Synagogue "trembled even more violently than the Church" (Bloch, *SD* 165).

9   On August 20–23, 1941, over 4,200 Jewish men, including 1,500 Frenchmen, were arrested and taken to the new Drancy camp, in the suburbs (Fontaine Thomas). On July 13, 1942, Némirovksy herself was arrested and taken to Pithiviers concentration camp (*SF* Appendix 366). Three days later (on July 16), police arrested 12,762 people in Paris, and the total arrested there and elsewhere in France included nearly 6,000 women and over 4,000 children under the age of sixteen (Ousby 189).

10 On August 9, 1940 she mentions a brief announcement about "foreigners" in "a small local newspaper" and on August 8, 1941 she copies another announcement from *Le Progrès de l'Allier*—a "Republican" newspaper published in the occupied city of Moulins and clearly controlled by the Germans (*SF* Appendix 361, 364).

11 Like Issy, Bussy was just inside the occupied zone—sixteen miles southeast of Bourges and seventy-three miles west of Issy.

12 Diamond, 77. While the Péricand family of the novel loses track of its patriarch, who dies among strangers, they eventually recover both his body and his will.

13 Here the translation is mine, for the sake of accuracy. The French original reads: "nous avons conscience de la solidarité qui nous lie, nous members d'un même corps" (*SF* 49). Elsewhere I cite Smith's translation as *SF_T*.

14 In a further irony, the word "solidarité" is later used in *Dolce* to signify a conspiracy to hide a murderer. When the Germans cannot find the man who has killed one of their officers, they suspect that everyone in the village "must be helping him, hiding him, feeding him." More than by the crime itself, the Germans are vexed by "the solidarity [solidarité], the complicity they could sense all around them" (*SF_T* 307 / *SF* 357).

15 In her plans for volume 3 of her pentad, *Captivity*, Némirovsky planned to present them as "total collaborators" (*SF_T* Appendix 350).

16 In the 2015 film version of the novel, Benoît is hidden not in Madame Angellier's room but in the attic of her house—and only with reluctance does she let Lucile hide him there. Besides thus obscuring her courage, the film radically changes the ending of the novel—as noted below.

17 In his very first radio broadcast as the new prime minister on June 17, 1940, Pétain declared: "It is in a spirit of honour and in order to preserve the unity of France … within the New European Order which is being built, that I today embark on the path of collaboration" (qtd. Ousby 86).

18 Qtd. Bracher, 77. Julian Jackson quotes part of Petain's speech (p. 143) but not this part—even in his section on the Exodus.

19 To be fair, however, the government did not move to Vichy until early July 1940 (Diamond 110). In Bordeaux, where the cabinet met on June 15, ministers found no accommodations and parliamentarians were angrily denounced by refugees (Diamond 97).

20 Némirovsky herself thought the will "too long" (*SF_T* 347).

21 In 1940, the French franc was worth about 2 cents. See https://newworldeconomics.
    com/foreign-exchange-rates-1913-1941-2-the-currency-upheavals-of-the-interwar-
    period/. Later on, Charlie Langelet takes comfort from the fact that his fortune is "in
    America" because "[t]he franc would remain low for a long time" (*SF_T* 168).
22 In a note on the manuscript, Némirovsky says that Charlie's death symbolizes "the end
    of the liberal bourgeoisie" (qtd. Philipponnat and Lienhardt, 361, my translation).
23 In Némirovsky's plan for her third novel, *Captivity*, Benoît not only keeps eluding the
    Germans but also helps both Hubert and Jean-Marie escape from a German prison
    (*SF* Appendix 350).
24 On September 16, 1941, for instance, General Field Marshall William Keitel ordered
    that the killing of one German soldier would be punished by the execution of 50–100
    Communists, and on October 22, 1941, two days after the German military
    commander of Nantes was shot, German authorities executed forty-eight hostages at
    the Châteaubriant camp (Fontaine Thomas).

9

War, Fire, and Sex: The London Blitz in Henry Green's *Caught*

The dawn of World War II might be considered a sliding signifier. Strictly speaking, it designates September 1, 1939, when—at precisely 5am—the German army launched its brutal invasion of Poland. Yet French troops had no substantial contact with the German army until May 10, 1940, when its Panzer tanks penetrated the would-be "impenetrable" Ardennes forest. So we might consider May 10 the dawn of combat for the French. Together with the Exodus precipitated by the German invasion, the first months of the Occupation might then be viewed as an extended dawn, or a black morning, which is why I have just considered how Irène Némirovsky fictionalizes both. The crucial point here is that both events mark for the French the real beginning of a war whose end Némirovsky could not foresee.

For Britain, I would argue, the black morning advanced in three major phases: first, along with the French army, the British Expeditionary Forces sent to France were defeated by the Germans and evacuated from Dunkirk between May 27 and June 4, 1940; second, from July 10 to October 31, 1940, the Royal Air Force beat back the German Luftwaffe in what was largely a battle of the skies; and third, starting on September 7, 1940, the Luftwaffe systematically bombed London almost every night until mid-November. The Luftwaffe also bombed many other British cities in raids lasting altogether until May 11, 1941, but what concerns me here is the autumn 1940 phase of the London Blitz, for that is a vital part of what Henry Green fictionalizes in the novel titled *Caught*.

Let me then consider first what is probably the most authoritative historical narrative of what London suffered in the autumn of 1940: Juliet Gardiner's *The Blitz: The British Under Attack* (2011). Just as Hanna Diamond mines a wealth of journals and diaries for her history of the French Exodus of 1940, Juliet Gardiner plumbs a great variety of sources to construct her narrative of the blitz—starting from its very first day. For instance, after quoting Herman Göring's September 7 radio announcement that "German squadrons . . . now, for the first time, are driving towards the heart of the enemy in full daylight," she notes that "over a hundred and fifty planes" were seen that afternoon from the garden of Meresworth Castle in Kent, forty miles from London, by a visiting American journalist named Virginia Cowles (qtd. Gardiner 7–8). Then, to show how the planes appeared as they flew into London, Gardiner quotes from a televised interview with a man who witnessed them from the roof of Sainsbury's, where he then worked as a 17-year-old porter: "they were heading straight for London, and it was going to be the docks that were going to get it" (qtd. Gardiner 9).

Indeed they were. According to Gardiner, some "three hundred German planes" first bombed the Ford Motor Works at Dagenham, about thirteen miles northeast of central London, and then headed for Silvertown, "a jumble of docks, warehouses" and workers' houses on the river's north bank just eight miles from the city (Gardiner 9). Minutes after the bombers rained down "high explosives and fire bombs," Gardiner writes,

> the huge factories and warehouses lining the river on both sides from North Woolwich to Tower Bridge were on fire. Two hundred acres of timber stacks, recently arrived from North America and the Baltic, burned out of control along the Surrey Commercial Docks, the main timber importing centre in Britain: within twenty-four hours only about a fifth of the two and a half million tons was left. (Gardiner 10)

To Station Officer Gerry Knight, it seemed as if "the whole bloody world's on fire" (qtd. Gardiner 10).

Besides describing the mayhem wrought by the first night's bombing raid, Gardiner explains the Auxiliary Fire Service (AFS), which Henry Green joined in October 1938, right after the Munich Agreement. Instead of manning fire engines, the auxiliaries used vans and taxi cabs to haul their trailer pumps, and they vastly outnumbered the regulars. "[F]or every regular fireman," Gardiner writes, "there were fifteen auxiliaries," and—quoting Cyril Damarne, one of their instructors—"it was quite a big job getting them all trained" (Gardiner 10). They were hardly prepared for the blitz. Never having "been called to a major fire before," they were so overwhelmed by this one—an "inferno burning out of control, impossible to put out"—that they had to be withdrawn before "being trapped by the sheets of flame" (Gardiner 11).

In Chapter 2, I noted that Anthony Beevor's authoritative history of the Spanish Civil War treats Hemingway's *For Whom the Bell Tolls* as part of the cultural historiography of the war. Near the end of her history of the blitz, Gardiner does something comparable with Henry Green's *Caught*. She commends it in particular for "powerfully portray[ing]" the split between regular firemen and AFS members, who were "were paid less, often inadequately trained, poorly equipped and housed in distinctly substandard accommodation."[1] Yet she fails to note how vividly Green portrays a feature of the blitz that Gardiner barely touches. She mentions it just once— in quoting the words of a psychoanalyst named George Franklin: "Sexual desire, especially in women, was much intensified during the blitz" (qtd. Gardiner 184).

In *Caught*, this point is exemplified by the thought that one night pulses through the mind of a character named Prudence: "War, she thought, was sex" (114). The idea that war is sex—that war is an aphrodisiac—is one of many things that separate Green's novel about the blitz from Gardiner's history of it. But many other differences spring from the simple fact that Green thoroughly exploits the freedom licensed by fictional form. While Gardiner narrates the sequence of bombing raids that followed the horrific first one and shows how the British contrived to endure them, Green puts the first raid into his final chapter. Though set in November 1940, "after nine weeks of air raids on London" (*Caught* 168), this chapter highlights the process by which Richard Roe struggles to explain to his wife the sublimity as well as the horror of the first night of the blitz.[2] Even while speaking, he can hardly articulate what he so vividly recalls: the Turnerian magnificence of "the mile-high pandemonium of flame reflected in the quaking sky" (*Caught* 172). Besides thus commemorating the aesthetic impact of fire, which historians seldom chronicle but which surely plays its part in the wartime intensification of sexual desire, Green moves backward and forward in time, plunging not only into Roe's family life but also into the darkest memories of a regular fireman named Albert Pye, who is haunted and finally driven to suicide by the realization that he once raped his own sister—and thereby drove her insane.

Based on Green's own experience as an auxiliary fireman in London from October 1938 to Christmas of 1940, *Caught* tracks the opening year of the war right up through the blitz of autumn 1940, and as just noted, it includes vivid descriptions of what incendiary bombs did to the London docks on the fateful night of September 7. But unlike Gardiner's history of this period, *Caught* highlights the cravings of the libido.[3] Crossing class lines, desire drives the well-to-do businessman Richard Roe, the married protagonist of the novel, almost as much as it drives Albert Pye, who—even though better paid as a regular fireman than the auxiliaries—can barely afford to buy cocktails for Prudence in a Soho nightclub.

In *The Heat of the Day* (1948), whose very title is subtly erotic, Elizabeth Bowen likewise recalls the cocktail-fueled mood of sexual susceptibility that aroused upper-class Londoners in September 1940, when the unpredictability of what the blitz might do prompted everyone to seize not just the day or the night, but each other:

> The very temper of pleasures lay in their chanciness, in the canvaslike impermanence of their settings, in their being off-time—to and fro between bars and grills, clubs and each other's places moved the little shoal through the noisy nights. Faces came and went. There was a diffused gallantry in the atmosphere, an unmarriedness: it came to be rumoured about the country, among the self-banished, the uneasy, the put-upon and the safe, that everybody in London was in love—which was true, if not in the sense the country meant. There was plenty of everything in London—attention, drink, time, taxis, most of all space. (Bowen 81)

In this early 1940s mecca for restless singles, or for anyone on the libidinous prowl, Bowen's chief characters are a pair of upper-class lovers who run afoul of a counterspy seeking to bed the woman in return for shielding the treasonous behavior of the man.[4] In *Caught*, Henry Green likewise foregrounds the role of sex in blitz-struck London, but he is equally preoccupied with the relation between his upper-class protagonist and the working-class members of the Auxiliary Fire Service.

Green himself, whose given name was Henry Yorke, had been crossing class lines since reaching his manhood. As grandson of a baron, son of a wealthy Birmingham industrialist, and heir to a stately home in Gloucestershire, Green was a child of privilege, "born a mouthbreather with a silver spoon," as he wrote in his interim autobiography, *Pack My Bag* (1940). Socially he outranked Evelyn Waugh, whom he came to know at Oxford in 1924, during Waugh's last year and Green's first. But whatever Green's aristocratic lineage might have predicted, he soon grew fascinated with characters quite different from himself. By the time he finished his preparatory years at Eton, he had drafted most of his first novel, *Blindness*, which appeared in 1926, when he was just twenty-one. In the same year he decided to complete his education by making an extraordinary move. Leaving Oxford without taking a degree, he went to work on the floor of H. Pontifex and Sons, his family's manufacturing firm in Birmingham, and eventually became managing director. More important, he thus gained material for his second novel, *Living* (1929), which is set in and around a Birmingham factory. Marginalizing the owners and foregrounding instead the lives of the workers, *Living* richly displays what Green had learned about the figurative potency of working-class speech.[5]

Turning back to his own class, Green's third novel, *Party Going* (1939), portrays a crowd of the idle rich trapped by fog in a London train station hotel while en route to a party in the south of France, which they never reach. Though it "brilliantly illustrates money's power to insulate the few from the hardships of the many," as Stephen Wall observes, and says nothing explicit about the outbreak of war, *Party Going* could be construed as an allegory of Britain's paralysis in the face of war's imminence, especially its failure to do anything effective on behalf of France. But war soon trumped all other topics in Green's mind. By the late 1930s, he felt bound to write his autobiography because of "the war which seems to be coming upon us now and that is a reason to put down what comes to mind before one is killed" (*Pack My Bag* 1). Fittingly, *Pack My Bag* includes vivid portraits of the shell-shocked soldiers who were billeted at Green's family home during World War I, when he was a child. Together with these memories of the first war, the imminence of the second one, and specifically of an air attack on London that could suddenly take his life, charged his writing with an urgency unknown to leading American writers in this period. As shown above in Chapter 1, urgency is nowhere audible in the statements they made for the *Partisan Review* in the spring of 1939. Safely distanced by the Atlantic from the coming war, they could calmly calibrate their responses to it or even—like Allen Tate—dismiss it altogether as irrelevant to their literary lives. Meanwhile, British writers such as Green and Waugh felt compelled not just to defend their country but to risk their lives in doing so.

In October 1938, the 33-year-old Green joined the Auxiliary Fire Service, a volunteer force that had just been formed to help the fire brigade fight the fires sparked by incendiary bombs that were soon expected to fall on London. And fall they did. Starting on September 7, 1940, the Luftwaffe bombed the capital for fifty-six nights, killing eight hundred auxiliary firemen along with nearly twenty thousand others (Wood in Green, *Caught* vii). Green was lucky. While serving as a fireman right up to Christmas of 1940, he not only survived the blitz but also mined his experience for *Caught*, which he started writing in June of 1940 and finished by Christmas of 1942.

Most of the novel charts the same stretch of time covered in Waugh's *Put Out More Flags*: the months of the so-called "joke war," when Britain and France did little more than wait for the arrival of German bombs, guns, and tanks. But *Caught* blazes its own trail through this era. While Waugh's novel satirizes the fecklessness of upper-class characters hardly burdened with children and faced with a war they scarcely know how to fight, Green's upper-class protagonist, Richard Roe, reckons deeply with both the complexities of family life and the working-class travails of men and women in the AFS. Torn between his wife and child in the country and his unattached life in London, which includes an affair with a gossipy dispatch driver named Hilly, Richard spends so much time with his working-class mates that he comes to sympathize with them deeply, and particularly with Albert Pye, who is driven to suicide by a series of conflicts revolving around sex.

Chronologically, the novel moves from the declaration of war on September 3, 1939 through the evacuation of Dunkirk in the late spring of 1940 to the beginning of the blitz in the following September. Like Waugh's *Put Out More Flags*, it marks such notable events as the Soviet war with Finland in the winter of 1939–40 and the German invasion of Norway starting on April 9, 1940. But since none of Green's characters leaves England, *Caught* merely glances at these foreign events, and it also scrambles chronology. Instead of beginning with the September 1939 declaration of war, which comes only in the middle of chapter five (*Caught* 44), the story starts several months later, in the winter of 1939–40, with the first of three short leaves that Richard takes from his fire service duties in London.[6] After traveling by train to his parents' country house, where his wife Dy and his five-year-old son Christopher are waiting out the war, Richard spends a few days with them each time.

During each leave Richard relives the anguish of his first departure, when he was called up "three days before the outbreak" of war, meaning September 1, 1939.[7] At that point Richard felt the imminence of death just as keenly as Henry Green had in rushing to write his autobiography before he was killed. For Richard too, the outbreak of war means the end for him as well as for London:

> [C]ertain of death in the immediate raid he expected to raze London to the ground, he was soon saying farewell to his family away out in the country whenever he was alone, losing them because he loved himself so well that he was afraid. In his self pity he might have been sighing goodbye to adored unreality. All that was real to him then was his death in a matter of days.[8]

In the ensuing months, the absence of raids brings him no genuine relief but only the sense that he has gained a stay of execution. "On his first leave," we learn,

> he was still terrified of dying, perhaps because his son was older, also because his wife was miserable in the country, but almost entirely because, now that he had been parted from them, he could not bear to leave for ever, never to share life with them again just when he discovered how it had been shared. (*Caught* 27)

In starting with the first of Richard's brief returns to his wife and child, Green's novel makes it clear that his condition as a husband and father will be inseparably part of what he brings to the sexual temptations as well as mortal terrors of life in the London Fire Service. The opening chapters of the novel also explore something just briefly portrayed in Waugh's *Put Out More Flags*: the impact of war on the relation between a father and his son.

In a narrative that is otherwise barbed with satire, Waugh's account of Cedric Lyne's trip with his eight-year-old son Nigel before embarking for Norway, where he will die in combat, sounds perhaps the one note of poignancy. Though Nigel's admiration for his father as "a man-at-arms and a hero" (Waugh, *POMF* 213) is just one more target of that satire, the boy's parting words to his father at the end of their two days together are almost heartbreaking. After taking Nigel out of school for an overnight at the family's country house, speeding him to London, presenting him to his self-absorbed mother Angela (who promptly dismisses him), fielding his eager questions about guns and fighter planes, buying him a model bomber, feeding him lunch, and taking him to see *The Lion Has Wings* (a propaganda war film about RAF bombing raids), Cedric puts Nigel on the train that will take him back to school. When Nigel says, "It's been absolutely ripping, Daddy," Cedric asks, "Has it really?" To which Nigel answers: "The rippingest two days I ever spent" (*POMF* 220).

No such moment arrives in *Caught*. Instead of exchanging anything like this spark of pure affection, Richard and his son never quite manage to communicate. On the first morning Richard spends with Christopher during the first of his leaves, the boy can barely bring himself to say which sweet shop he likes best, and when they take a walk alone together—a walk that Richard feels "might be his last" before the bombs arrived (*Caught* 5)—he also feels estranged "from his young son … by the years that are between" (7). He tries to bridge the gulf by telling the boy of a "secret" place where hobgoblins live, but after insisting that "everybody knows" this secret, Christopher says he disbelieves it. Though Richard then agrees with the boy that a coughing deer—one of a herd they see—is going to die, the cough joins the drone of an overhead warplane to sound a note of separation: "the separation that war had forced into their lives" (8). Richard cannot even bear to get too close to Christopher as he takes his leave that night in the hall:

> Standing there, awkwardly shaking hands, he wished, and wished too late, that he had never made a point of not kissing Christopher. He was upset, at that moment no contact with his son could have been too close. But he did not dare, for he was afraid, if he took Christopher in his arms, that he would break into tears, and then the boy might be frightened. (8)

His fear of frightening the boy and his deep ambivalence toward intimacy are further complicated by an incident that took place sometime before the declaration of war, when Richard still worked as a company executive in London and his wife and son were still living there with him.[9] While visiting a toy store with his nanny, Christopher was abducted by a woman who lured him to her flat, where his "astounding screech of hate and fright" at his predicament (14) soon led to his being rescued by the police and returned to his parents. But that is just the beginning of another story. Though the woman is sent to a mental asylum, she turns out to be the sister of Albert Pye, the regular fireman in charge of the substation to which Richard is posted just before the war breaks out. As a result, the relations between the two men are severely strained. Instead of apologizing for what his sister Amy did to Richard's family, Pye tells Richard that he resents what has been done to his sister. Since Richard concludes "that he could never make this man realise what had passed," he decides to tell Pye that "whatever happened before the war was best forgotten" (37).

But we gradually learn that what happened before the war—specifically what Pye may have done to his own sister during their adolescence—cannot be forgotten. At the end of the "chaotic day" on which the auxiliaries are mobilized, Pye himself remembers fighting in France during the first war, and the memory of its earth—variously "cold, wet" or "cracked and dry"—leads him "back to the first girl he had known" (38). In a moonlit grass lane near the village where he spent his childhood, he took her while she panted "through her nose," repelling him with "true, roughened hands" and murmuring tearfully, "Will it hurt?" (39). In linking this memory of rape with the imminence of another war that "physically excited him" (38), Pye seems to experience war itself as erotic.[10] But the memory of what was evidently his first sexual experience is shadowed by the memory of what he saw on the way home: "his own sister, out whoring maybe as he had been, up now from off her back no doubt, out of a low shadow cast by the moon" (40).

Months later, this memory returns "with a shock." When the psychiatrist treating Pye's sister asks him to explain what childhood experience might have left her mentally impaired and unwilling to marry, Pye suddenly realizes that the girl he took in the grassy lane was *not* "Mrs. Lane's little girl," whom he took soon after on a riverbank for what must have been the first time. "[I]n the blind moonlight," he now sees, "eyes warped by his need, *he must have forced his own sister*" (134, my emphasis).

But rather than confessing any of this to "the rotten-gutted bastard of a doctor" (136), Pye simply offers to "think it over," and on the bus back to the substation he soon diverts himself by ogling a girl whose blue eyes were "hedged with long lashes that might have been scythes to mow his upstanding corn" (136). Though springtime has just drawn the Nazis into Norway, Pye thinks only of sex:

> Elated at his release from the asylum, he asked himself what he would not give to have this puss mouth jam off his cheek by a river bank on such an evening as the weather today seemed to promise after the first long winter of war . . . . (136)

Pye's libido never sleeps. During the first weeks of training for the fire service, Richard finds that the sight of "a girl of any kind" would strike Pye "dumb" in the midst of conducting a ladder drill. He "followed her with his eyes until she was gone," we are told, "and only then was able to pick up the lecture he had learned by heart, where her legs had scissored it off his tongue" (27). Knowing Pye's addiction to sex, Richard soon learns how to feed it. One day in September 1939, two sexy young women seek his advice about a wall of sandbags piled outside the window of their flat. Accosted as "Fireman" by the foreign, "expensive" Ilse on his way back to the substation from posting a letter to his wife, Richard is taken by elevator to her flat, introduced to her flatmate Prudence, invited to bathe there anytime, and offered a tall glass of Cointreau with water and ice. Though this could obviously be the prelude to a dalliance, Richard declines a bath and tells the girls he will send up his "officer in charge"—namely Pye— to advise them (28). He might thereby "do himself a bit of good with the skipper," he thinks, even though he expects the girls to despise the man (48).

But since they don't, Pye soon launches an affair with Prudence. Though "tolerably miserable" about a pilot who had "gone away in August" and "was now said to be marrying someone else," she lets Pye take her regularly to an expensive nightclub, where he titillates her with stories of "such excitements as had come his way on peacetime fires" (114). If hardly smitten, Prudence is nonetheless available, like one of those "pretty creatures" Richard thinks about earlier: girls "left behind alone as train after train went out loaded with men to fight" but then "hungrily seeking . . . yet another man with whom they could spend last hours . . ." (61). Sitting next to Pye, who "always" looks at her with eyes "begging" for bed, Prudence sees his lust as a force driving everyone at this time. "War, she thought, was sex" (114). But for Pye, it's a costly habit. He resents having "to pay six shillings for a jug of washy lager, less than two pints," plus the nightclub entrance fee and an average of three "white ladies" for Prudence at four shillings and sixpence each—altogether an "exorbitant expense" for Pye (114).

Meanwhile, Richard too is gradually drawn into the vortex of wartime sex. As balm for his homesickness, as confidant and surrogate for his far-off wife, he turns to Hilly. He still loves Dy, or more accurately still desires her, for during his first short leave we are told that he "could not keep his hands off her" (31). But back at the substation, Richard realizes that the outbreak of war has shattered "the architecture" of his peacetime life and family relations (90), and the threat of death, he tells Hilly, makes daily duties such as "cleaning and dusting pretty silly" (90).

Given the imminence of death, all that seems to matter is desire. On his first night out with Hilly at a Soho nightclub, when Richard asks her if she thinks "anything is possible between people now," she answers, "But, Richard, of course. This war's been a tremendous release for most" (95). Though he promptly says, "Not for me," he has already been imagining "a great deal going on all round between girls and men" and feeling haunted by "[w]hat he might be missing" (96). Without at first offering to fill the gap herself, she fills him in on substation gossip. Pye, she says, thinks Richard has been "squeak[ing]" on him to District Officer Trant—has been telling Trant that Pye has gone "adrift" to visit his sister in her asylum. But the real squeaker, Hilly says, is an old soldier named Arthur Piper, who "got a job redecorating Trant's quarters up at Number Fifteen"; having somehow learned that Pye "was going off early," she says, he "repeats everything" (99). Unwittingly, she thus prompts Richard to tell her about the abduction of Christopher, which—he says—explains Pye's campaign against him. "And now that man," says Richard, "is trying to set the station against me, because his sister walked off with my child. As if that was my fault. Saying that I tipped Trant off about him" (100).

Denying this charge, Hilly says Pye is taking full advantage of the war. Regular firemen like him, she says, are making "about twice as much money as they've ever had," and "this war is Peewee's great chance. . . . [A] man of his age and his experience may end up anywhere, quite high up, honestly, if the war lasts long enough" (103). On top of which, she adds, Pye has been taking Prudence to this very nightclub "every single night" when he was supposed to be on duty. This revelation makes Richard feel so "excited and jealous" that when all the lights go out except for a blue spotlight on a famous black lady singer, he leans over to kiss Hilly "on the mouth" (106–7).[11] As Richard strokes the soft inside of her right arm while listening to the singer in the dark, "[t]here was no trace of Dy left," and when Hilly answers "Of course" to his question about whether Pye has slept with Prudence, Richard is "suddenly sure this must mean that Hilly . . . would go to bed with him that night" (108).

Ironically enough, then, Richard takes his sexual cue from the very man he considers his enemy. But as Richard eventually learns, Pye is not his enemy, and as we soon learn, Pye is caught—the title word—in a series of ever-tightening binds. Newly appointed to run the substation without ever having given orders before, "[h]e knew now, for the first time, the sense of *impotence* which goes with authority, the feeling that those he commanded did not care" (80, my emphasis). Those who command him are no kinder. Early one day, his auxiliaries are called to their first fire. After one man faints "in excitement" and the rest race to it in taxis, which "in those early days . . . drew the pumps" (as also reported in Gardiner's history of the blitz), they enter the wrong house while the fire next door is put out by one old lady on her own. As a result, Pye is witheringly scolded by Trant and "was never the same since" (77–78).

Furthermore, besides getting "cover[ed]" for extra leave when he is summoned to visit his sister at the asylum (82), Pye has to cope with the misery of the visit itself. To a man already "wrought up by the outbreak of war" (85), the visit proves "more horrible than he had dreamed" (84). After seeing Amy in a green padded room furnished with just two armchairs bolted to the floor, and hearing this childless woman asking "when he was going to bring her child" (84), Pye cries on the return bus ride. As soon as he gets home and learns that Trant has repeatedly tried to reach him the day before, he wrongly infers—as noted above—that Richard "had given him away," reported his unauthorized absence to Trant and thus caused him to be posted "adrift," absent without leave (85).

Pye digs himself out of this hole only by covering it with layers of lies. After having himself "booked out on leave" at the proper time of ten (85), when it was actually much earlier, Pye tells Hilly to say that during those early hours she was taking him around to inspect fire hydrants (87). He fabricates compulsively, not just to cover his absences from the substation but also to titillate Prudence as a prelude to sex. As if channeling Othello, who won the heart of Desdemona by describing "the dangers [he] had passed" (*Othello* I.i.169), Pye tells Prudence over their nightclub drinks that he once saved another fireman who had fallen head first through the collapsed floors of a burning building into the flooded basement below. "He knew that she knew he had lied," we are told, but he also felt "this was the sort of story she wanted for afterwards, when, the third 'white lady' finished, they were to go up to her flat" (116).

Superficially, this working-class character seems quite distinct from the upper-class Richard Roe. But I have already noted that in launching his affair with Hilly, Roe takes his cue from Pye. Likewise, with startling effect, Green's restlessly roving narrative technique sometimes aligns Richard with his social inferiors. Like a movie camera, one chapter starts with Mary Howell's trip to see her irresponsible son-in-law Ted (109), turns to Pye's nightclub storytelling, and then cuts from one to the other by way of a brief glance at Richard in *flagrante delicto*, growing "hot" with Hilly's naked body in his arms (114).[12] Also, after a long passage about Pye's impatient designs on Prudence, Hilly and Richard re-appear "on a sofa, naked" just before we are told that "at that instant," Mary's daughter Brid has been crying over the absence of her "feckless" husband (115). With Richard's feelings already linked to Pye's lust, the sudden shift to Hilly wriggling into the "gondola" of Richard's body (115) prompts us to recall that

Richard's wife Dy is "miserable" off in the country away from him (27) and to realize that, like Brid's husband Ted (as Mary imagines him), Richard has forsaken or at least forgotten his wife and child to savor the sweets of "another dish" (113).

This is not to say that wartime lust levels all class barriers. Given the salary paid by his company on top of his modest pay as an auxiliary fireman, Richard can readily afford the nightclub drinks that men such as Pye and Ted can barely pay for, if at all. Nevertheless, all three are shown exploiting—or accused of exploiting—the sexual opportunities that war provides.

Along with such opportunities, the war of waiting that suddenly became the London Blitz of late 1940 also brought fire-breathing bombs. Though this phase of the war is mostly confined to the final chapters of the novel, Richard's first conversation with Hilly in the middle of the book—in November 1939—is once again cinematically intercut with a vivid preview of the blitz. Their exchange is contrapuntal. Hilly claims that the London Fire Brigade surpasses "any other," and even though Richard reminds her that Pye and Chopper, the other regular fireman, "had no idea what they were doing" when they entered the wrong house, Hilly assures him that "they'll be all right when raids start, when the time comes, if it ever does" (91). To show that she "was wrong about Chopper," the narrative leaps forward to a night almost a year later, when Richard and Chopper and the rest of their crew are called to a site where "two heavy bombs had fallen within a hundred years of each other" (91).

With Pye now dead (we later learn how), quietly taking cover "in his coffin, eaten by worms six feet underground" (94), the crew is led by Chopper, with Richard in charge of a pump crew. From a bronze equestrian statue in the middle of a square they can see that gas mains up ahead on two sharply converging streets are spewing thirty-foot-high fans of flame.[13] Richard and his men help to lay out hose along one of the streets, but even as every pump starts roaring, the firemen are menaced by a slowly descending chandelier flare as well as by two bombers drawn by the lighted mains. As machine guns fire at the bombers, Richard enters a nearby surface shelter in search of regular firemen but finds only a soldier in the near corner clutching and ravenously kissing a girl who stands between his legs.

"[A]bashed" by this fresh evidence that war spawns lust rather than heroism, Richard steps outside to find that Chopper, though "second in command at this incident," had "packed it in," stopped doing anything at all. (Earlier, thinking the bombers had seen them, Chopper had thrown himself to the ground.) When Chopper reluctantly looks into the shelter after Richard shoutingly asks him to do so, he comes out not to complain of the soldier's malingering but instead to shout back, "almost with reverence, 'More power to his elbow mate, more power to it'" (94). But the power of heroism is nowhere to be found. After the passing of three pathetic figures—a "twisted creature" on a stretcher coughing blood (94), a battered looter dragged along by the police, and an old lady with a handkerchief held to her mouth and her eyes on the ground—the soldier totters drunkenly out of the shelter and shoutingly begs Richard for a shilling to buy another drink. When Chopper learns from Richard what the man said, he vomits.

Within a chapter chiefly focused on November 1939, this whole episode is framed by a conversation in which Richard finally admits that "[r]aids may not be anywhere near as bad as we imagine," and Hilly—who gets the last word—assures him that "those men you think so hopeless now will be wonderful, honestly wonderful, you'll see" (94). The chapter thus compels us to view the early, raidless months of the joke war through the flames of the real war that broke out less than one year later, when we see just how "wonderful" these firemen turn out to be.

But well before the raids begin, Pye is targeted by Trant, the District Officer, when Trant learns from Piper that Pye is "never in" at night, "duty or not" (118). (His men know very well that he spends every night "with a tart" [120].) At one point, Trant lacerates Pye for a slew of failings: the messiness of his office, the filthiness of the buttons on his tunic, the insubordination of his men.

Thus goaded to crack down hard on the substation, Pye obliquely charges the cooks with giving extra portions to Piper and thereby so infuriates one of them—Eileen—that she quits. Fearful that he will be blamed for losing the "rarity" of a good cook, Pye is further shaken by Trant's official caution that he must "change his ways" (131) as well as by a second summons to the asylum, where the doctor who is treating his sister delivers "a shock that [takes] all his breath" (134). Merely by asking Pye why his sister never married, as we have seen, the doctor leads him to realize or at least suspect that her deranged condition may be due to his having unwittingly raped her in the dark: "forced his sister that night long ago" (138).

Pye never divulges this memory to the doctor, but he never escapes it. Besides haunting him, "always at night" (118), it remains tethered to his sister's abduction of Christopher, which he is never allowed to forget. Soon after returning from his second visit to the asylum, he comes to the substation just as Richard is showing his wife and son around. Though Richard has invited them only because he expects Pye to be out on his leave day and because Christopher longs to see the fire engines, Pye nevertheless shows up, and even though Richard awkwardly introduces him to Dy and the boy, nothing Pye does to entertain Christopher—such as letting him ring the firebell and wear a regular fireman's helmet—can stanch Dy's unexpressed loathing of him or, just as significantly, his own unstated resentment of her as a "crafty whore" (143). Earlier, as we have seen, Pye projected the memory of his incestuous lust onto the twisted recollection of seeing "his own sister, out whoring maybe as he had been, up now from off her back no doubt" (40). Now the guilt he cannot escape makes him silently inflict it on Richard's wife.

But as if to sharpen the blade of guilt lodged in Pye's mind, Piper starts to circulate the story of the abduction, which is soon reframed as a story of how Pye himself took the boy from the cloakroom of a nightclub while his parents drank champagne inside. Whether or not this version gets back to Pye himself (we aren't told), he tells Prudence over the phone that he feels "terrible" because he's been threatened with a writ if he doesn't pay something for the care of his sister (147–48). And since Prudence doesn't care and won't see him, he feels compelled to confide in Richard: to share over drinks not only his awareness that Dy "switched 'erself away" from him when they met but also (once more) his resentment at the "lock[ing] away of his sister" and even—by stages— his fear that he might have mistaken the identity of "the first [girl] I 'ad, see" (155). Without, of course, revealing that she might have been his sister, he admits that the memory of this episode cuts into his sleep. Also, since "the invasion of the Low

Countries" is said to have begun (150), it is evidently late May of 1940, when some 338,000 British soldiers—along with French and Belgian troops—were surrounded by Germans at Dunkirk. Besides thinking that "we've lost the entire British army" because of the "lunatics" who run it (151–52), Pye seems to share at least some of the discomfort felt by his men, who "had nothing whatever to do at such a time but scrub floors and polish brass," and were sometimes jeeringly asked, "Why don't you go and fight?" (150).

As if to answer this question, Pye tells Richard that he—that is, Pye himself—"could join as an officer gunner in the RAF" (157). When the astounded Richard asks if he isn't "really" too old for this job, Pye says he's "thirty-five," only "two years" over age. But since we already know that Pye fought in the first war (38), which ended in 1918, he cannot be younger than thirty-eight and is probably forty or more.[14] Even at thirty-five, Richard thinks, Pye must be "years over age" and "insane" to think he could fight (157).

Later, half drunk and wandering in "the vast, moonlit night" after closing time at the substation (158), Pye is driven nearly insane by rage, guilt, and lust: rage at Prudence's refusal to see him, guilt over the ineradicable "memory of his sister's moon draggled crawl" (158), and "lust" for any woman he can find (163). War too vexes him. Knowing that "the evacuation of Dunkirk was on," and "brothers were dying fast" across the channel, he fears that in a week "it might be anybody's turn" and doubts that "his men would be of much use in the great fires they had to expect if Hitler did come over" (161). Meanwhile, groping in a dark doorway for what he thinks is a girl, he seizes instead a runny-nosed boy of eight— "[r]ising nine"—who says he is "lost" (164). Though Pye takes him back to his own room for the night and to breakfast the next morning, the whole episode reminds him of the abduction of Christopher. Worse still, he learns from Chopper that Trant has "caught him adrift" again, out of the substation and unavailable when Trant arrived "[t]o give them a drill" (159). Thus the full meaning of the title of the novel clicks into place. Threatened with discharge because he has been *caught* shirking his responsibilities, Pye is now "in dread" (167).

Only on the final page of the novel do we learn that well before the bombing raids begin, Pye commits suicide by putting his head into a gas oven. Richard himself pulls him out of the oven, as he tells Dy near the end of the final chapter, set in November 1940, "after nine weeks of air raids on London." By this time, after a bomb has knocked him out and left him with "nervous debility" (168), Richard has been sent home. Here he tells his story. Though one of the night raids has already been impersonally narrated in a flash forward, as noted above, the second account of a night raid—the "first night" of the raids (172), September 7, 1940—is largely narrated by Richard, who repeatedly struggles to re-create the experience for Dy. While she aims only "to keep his mind vacant so that he should have complete rest" (170), he strives to make her see "the whole thing" even while admitting that "about a blitz . . . there's always something you can't describe" (175). More than anywhere else, it is here that the novel itself sets out to rival even the eyewitness accounts that would later populate historical narratives such as Juliet Gardiner's *The Blitz*.

Essentially, Richard's account reinforces the previously told story of a night raid in which the firemen proved to be something less than—in Hilly's words—"wonderful." During the blitz, Richard admits, they have been transformed in the eyes of the public: once chided for not serving "in the army," they have since become "absolute heroes . . .

to everyone" (170–71). Richard himself salutes the heroism of a fireman named Shiner, who "stood up top of a pile of timber throwing planks off to get down to the seat of the fire."[15] But when Dy says "you were all wonderful," Richard insists "there was nothing wonderful about" their evacuation from a commercial dock where great open sheds of timber had burst into gigantic flames (178).

Richard's "nothing wonderful" nicely exemplifies the critique of "nationalistic rhetoric about soldierly heroism" that Kristine Miller finds in *Caught*.[16] Nevertheless, what proves wonderful in the most literal sense of the word is what Richard and his mates see on his "first night" of fire-fighting:

> They saw the whole fury of that conflagration in which they had to play a part. And they cowered where they sat beneath the immensity. For, against it, warehouses, small towers, puny steeples seemed alive with sparks from the mile-high pandemonium of flame reflected in the quaking sky. This fan, a roaring red gold, pulsed rose at the outside edge, the perimeter round which the heavens, set with stars before falling into utter blackness, were for a space a trembling green. (172)

In this passage, one of several in which the unnamed narrator interrupts the story that Richard tells his wife, the destructiveness of the fire and its defiance of anyone's capacity to fight it are subsumed by its sublimity: a purely aesthetic effect rivalling that of paintings such as J. M. W. Turner's *Burning of the Houses of Lords and Commons*, a title he gave to two paintings first exhibited in 1835. While evoking Turner (whether knowingly or not), Green also anticipates Louis-Ferdinand Céline's *Féerie pour une autre fois* (1952–54), where, as Nil Santiáñez notes, the bombing of Paris "is described as a stunningly beautiful spectacle of colors and sounds not unlike painting and music" (Santiáñez 239). Just over twenty years ago, in early September 2001, this paradox was shockingly re-affirmed. A few days after the World Trade towers of New York City were set aflame, the German composer Karlheinz Stockhausen called the spectacle "the greatest work of art imaginable for the whole cosmos" (qtd. Castle).

Though Stockhausen was almost universally reviled for this statement, it can be read as one more version of the paradox articulated by Green and Céline. Just as war for all its horror can generate "ecstasy" in some soldiers, as Hemingway says, the stunningly chromatic spectacle of conflagration—a "mile high pandemonium of flame"—can overpower, at least momentarily, the horror of its destructiveness. Richard himself tells his wife that as he and his mates crossed Westminster Bridge en route to the burning docks, the sight of the fire was "fantastic" (172), pre-empting the glory of anything that might be done to vanquish it.[17]

Richard's account of the firemen's efforts to do so commemorates not so much heroism as incompetence. After driving through the dock in a taxi that was boiling over from the strain of towing a heavy pump, they did not know if they had the "right wharf"—the one they had been sent to: "there was not one officer to report to, no one to give orders" (174–75). The only order they eventually got—from an officer who stepped out of a surface shelter—was to take cover from the bombs being dropped by what "seemed to be at least five planes overhead" (177). Fortunately, none of the bombs came near Richard, and though Piper was killed because he refused to stay under cover, some of the firemen—"green as [they] were" (177) —did surprisingly well. But Richard was largely occupied in fetching a bucket of drinking water for a subaltern, and by the time he returned with it, incendiary bombs had ignited a line of timber right across the men's escape route. Also, since broken glass from the blasted skylights of the timber shed had cut their hose, they "had to give up," Richard says, and were simply told "to get out as best we could" (181).

Unable to find the rest of his crew or their pump, Richard can do scarcely more than take a taxi that will somehow carry him through the smoke and flying cinders. After finding most of his crew and a collection of pumps on the other side, he decides—as "number one" of the crew (186)—that they should not run away from the fire but rather stay and fight it if they could. Yet on a night when both Piper and Shiner are eventually killed by bombs, his main object is simply surviving. After Shiner saves his life by warning him not to crouch behind a high-voltage distributor box, which he mistakes for a sandbox and which is shortly blown up by a bomb, Richard huddles in a jammed, pitch-black shelter. Then, having emerged and walked back to the dock in quest of "definite orders," he encounters what he calls "the last extraordinary thing in that fantastic night" (188). With "about a dozen Auxiliaries" at the Dock Gate leaning exhausted against a wall in full view of a "terrific" blaze, one of the fire chiefs pulls up, asks Richard where his pump is, points to "a great ocean-going merchantman ablaze … from end to end," and orders Richard to take his pump and "put it out" (188–89). For Green as for Waugh, this is just the kind of order that exemplifies the folly of those in command.

Leaving the ship to burn, Richard and his fellow survivors finally manage to save from the fire just one "untouched" timber yard by late morning (189). But when Dy says, "I wonder what's the meaning of it all?," Richard says nothing more about anything done by the firemen, heroic or not. He says only that Dy has "always been most unfair to Pye" (189). To her astounded face he recites the litany of woes that drove Pye to commit suicide. He "wasn't in the least ready to have men under him"; lust drove him to spend more money than he could afford on Prudence, and so much time that "[h]e was caught out once or twice, absent without leave"; he "could not forgive" the "asylumization" of his sister; he was being threatened with legal action if he did not pay for her keep; and finally, Piper told the District Officer that Pye had kept a boy in his room overnight (190).

Though this might well be construed as an act of kindness toward a little boy who called himself "lost," and Richard is "sure" it "wasn't" sexual, it makes no dent in Dy's hatred of Pye. "I shall always hate him," she says, "and his beastly sister" (191). With these words, the very last she speaks, she goads Richard into shouting, "God damn you … you get on my bloody nerves, all you bloody women with all your talk," and when Christopher "gravely" approaches him, he says simply "Get out" (191).

Besides "pit[ting] men against women," as Miller says, and thus restoring the gender barriers eroded by his own sense of helplessness in fighting fires (Miller 101), Roe's outburst ends the novel by undermining what its superficially rounded structure might have led us to expect. Having begun with a family briefly united during the first of Richard's leaves from the fire service, it ends with his return to his wife and child after the harrowing ordeal of fire-fighting his way through the blitz. But the family is not thereby re-united. Though Richard's status as the victim of "nervous debility" implies that his return will be permanent, his final conversation with Dy shows them wholly divided, powerless to imagine—much less share—each other's feelings. Just as the two stories of fire-fighting largely undermine the assumption that the firemen will be or are "wonderful" and heroic, the final conversation between Richard and Dy nearly sabotages any expectation of their being emotionally re-integrated, or of Richard's overcoming his earlier sense of subtle estrangement from his son. I say "nearly" because, as Miller rightly notes (101), Richard's "Get out" to Christopher is followed by a softening, "Well, anyway, leave me alone till tea, can't you?" (191). To the very last word of the novel, Richard struggles to re-integrate the warring halves of his own psyche.

Nevertheless, this is not just one more example of the gulf between men and women, between faithful wives and adulterous husbands, or between those who have fought fires they can never fully describe and those who have not. While Richard has formed with the other firemen a bond that penetrates class barriers, and while he admires the heroism of Shiner, Pye takes his life before the night raids begin, so that Richard knows him only as a man burdened by a combination of grievances and frustrated desire. Richard does not know the deepest source of Pye's misery, the one thing Pye has never confessed to anyone.

In the end, defying the notion that war makes a "brotherhood" of soldiers or that the terrors of the blitz united all British classes in a "People's War" against it, *Caught* represents war as something that drives individuals apart.[18] Not in the way the British were riven at the end of 1938, when—as Green much later recalled—London became "an angry divided town, families divided against each other, old friends after a few sharp words not speaking to old friends" (*Surviving* 267). Once the blitz had obliterated the case for appeasement, this kind of division ended. But rather than showing how war unites a nation against its attackers, or how the task of fire-fighting draws together men normally divided by class, the novel exposes the gulf between one man and another as well between a man and his wife, with each one caught up in a feeling— whether guilt, resentment, or hatred—that is finally incommunicable.

Paradoxically, however, *Caught* communicates to its readers precisely what its characters cannot communicate to each other, and thus tackles in a particularly potent way the whole question of whether wartime experience can be communicated at all to anyone who has never directly braved the threat of bombs, bullets, artillery, or towering flames. A few years ago, this question was powerfully answered by an American writer named Phil Klay, who—after serving four years as a Marine officer in Iraq—won the National Book Award for *Redeployment* (2014), a collection of stories based on his experience of war. Early in 2014, just as his book appeared, he wrote the following for *The New York Times*:

> [V]eterans need an audience that is both receptive and critical. *Believing war is beyond words is an abrogation of responsibility — it lets civilians off the hook from trying to understand, and veterans off the hook from needing to explain.* You don't honor someone by telling them, "I can never imagine what you've been through." Instead, listen to their story and try to imagine being in it, no matter how hard or uncomfortable that feels.... [I]n the age of an all-volunteer military, it is far too

easy for Americans to send soldiers on deployment after deployment without making a serious effort to imagine what that means. (Klay, "After War," my emphasis)

Six years later, in August of 2020, Klay re-affirmed this point in a Zoomed interview at Dartmouth College with James E. Wright, former president of Dartmouth and himself a Marine veteran as well an historian of twentieth-century wars.[19] After hearing Klay insist again that a soldier's experience *can* be communicated, I sent him a passage in which Marc Bloch—the French historian whom I often cite in Chapter 8—describes his "baptism of fire" (*SD* 55) while serving with the French army during the spring of 1940. Though Bloch did no fighting himself, he knew from his own experience exactly how the "whistling scream" of a dive-bomber could shred the nerves of anyone who heard it (*SD* 54). On May 22, 1940, when Bloch was part of a convoy moving along a road in Flanders, the convoy was bombed after first being machine-gunned from above. The bombing attack terrified him. Though it killed no one, so far as he knew, it left him "profoundly shaken" (*SD* 55)—for reasons he explains with graphic precision.

For one thing, he says, French troops were demoralized to see in the sky over their heads hardly any French fighter pilots (*SD* 55). For another, aerial bombing was something new to them. As a decorated veteran of World War I, Bloch had known both artillery bombardments and machine-gun fire. But unlike those two kinds of attack, which never cracked his self-command even while striking him with "cold-blooded fear" ("une crainte à froid," *ED*), bombing filled him with a "true dread" ("la vraie peur," *ED*) that left him uncontrollably trembling after he crawled out of a ditch. Paradoxically, the terrifying effect of bombing did not spring from its destructiveness. Bombing, Bloch thought, was probably no more dangerous than many other threats to a soldier's life, and the number of losses it reportedly caused was "relatively small" (*SD* 56). Nevertheless, he insists, aerial bombing tortures the nerves. The spectacle of great weight falling from on high makes soldiers feel wholly defenseless, and when the scream of its descending whistle turns into the bursting of the bomb, it

> shakes every bone in one's body. It seems to crush the very air with unparalleled violence, and conjures up pictures of torn flesh which are only too horribly borne out in fact by sights [of terribly mangled bodies].... A man is always scared of dying, but particularly so when to death is added the threat of complete physical disintegration. (*SD* 57)

In his autobiographical *Prelude*, as I noted in the Prologue, Wordsworth once declared that the pages of history could never capture what he and his contemporaries *felt* at the time of the French Revolution. But as both historian and eye-and-ear-witness, Bloch captures precisely what the sight and sound of German bombs in the deadly spring of 1940 made French soldiers feel. After reading Bloch's account for first time, Phil Klay wrote to me, "This is fantastic! . . . Remarkable, the fine distinctions he makes between different threats" (email of 8 August, 2020).

In re-creating just how it felt to be machine-gunned and bombed, Bloch crosses the line between history and autobiography, which qualifies as literature insofar as it either incorporates imagination or re-creates experience so personal that it cannot be documented or verified as a fact. Does this mean that historical narrative is generically unfit to re-create the feelings of a period or event it records? Absolutely not, for Gardiner's history of the blitz includes a plethora of eyewitness reports that often reveal just what the witness felt as well as what he or she heard or saw. Quantitatively, Gardiner also offers much more information about the blitz than Green's novel does. While *Caught* mentions the deaths of just two men on the first night of the blitz (Shiner and Piper), Gardiner tells us that on that same night, "436 people were killed and 1,000 seriously wounded," including "seven firemen" (Gardiner 23).

Yet Gardiner does not furnish anything like the whole lives—including sexual experience, which she mentions in passing only once—of individuals caught up in the blitz. Collectively, her scores of eyewitnesses testify to the horrific destructiveness of the blitz as well as to the bravery and almost incredible stamina of the British people, but none of her witnesses voices anything like what is ultimately felt by Richard Roe: awe and even erotic excitement at the sublimity of fire, guilt over his adultery, pity for the suicidal despair of a man whom his wife loathes, and rage over his conviction that his wife and child would never understand any feelings so alien to their conception of all firemen as heroes. If Gardiner's narrative offers a far greater *quantity* of truth than *Caught* or any other novel could convey about the blitz, Green's novel conveys a richer *quality* of truth: a truth embracing the whole lives—physical, social, familial, emotional, sexual, and psychological—of men and women caught up in the blitz.

Notes

1   Gardiner 364. Gardiner's comment may be read as a corrective to one of Kristine Miller's in a book published earlier. Though Miller argues that *Caught* critiques the ideology of "the People's War," which supposedly bridged class differences (Miller 93), she also states that Arthur Pye—the regular fireman and substation leader in the novel—aims "to create a temporary working arrangement under which professional and volunteer firemen from all walks of life could cooperate to fight the fires of the Blitz" (Miller 86). But as I argue below, Pye's efforts to promote such cooperation are not only frustrated by the differences Gardiner cites but also overwhelmed by inner conflicts that he cannot resolve.

2   Though Kristine Miller describes Richard Roe as a "widower" (Miller 91), his fraught relation to his quite living wife Dy is an essential part of the novel right up through its final chapter, where Richard is explicitly called "her husband" (*Caught* 184). Also, in the Viking Press edition of this novel (1950), the final chapter includes the sentence, "He had forgotten his wife" (178) just before Richard tells her the story of the dock fire on the first night of the blitz. For some reason this sentence does not appear in the New York Review Books edition (2016).

3   This is not a topic wholly ignored by historians, as evidenced by Lynne Olson's discussion of the affairs conducted in London at this time by leading American diplomats such as Averill Harriman (Olson, *Citizens*, passim). But Olson's account of wartime sex does not include the working classes, and while Miller argues that *Caught* shows how "the rhetoric of the soldier hero fails to account for masculinity on the

home front" (Miller, 95), she barely mentions the potency of sexual desire in Green's novel.

4   Less directly, desire and the blitz also intersect in Nancy Mitford's hugely popular novel *The Pursuit of Love* (1945), which sold 200,000 copies in its first year of publication. In the end its protagonist, Linda Radlett, dies in childbirth after decamping from London during the blitz. Having married and left two husbands, she was illegitimately pregnant by a wealthy French duke whom she considers the love of her life, but since their love affair began in Paris and antedates the blitz, this is not a story of what bombs did to their libido.

5   Such as that of the foreman, Mr. Bridges, who says at one point, "Worry. I've 'ad enough of that washing about in my head to drown a dolphin." Kristine Miller notes that like Green, Elizabeth Bowen and Rosamond Lehmann were "upper middle-class" contemporaries who "mingled selectively with the working classes during the war." But unlike Bowen and Lehmann, Green "had experienced these social differences in the workplace long before the war" (Miller 85).

6   Though no specific dates are given, Richard is said to have started his fire service training "nine months" before the declaration of war (*Caught* 26), which would be December 1938, and since the oaks at his parents' country estate are "bare" during his first visit (*Caught* 7) and the garden displays "soiled swans of snow" during the second, which comes "seven weeks" after the first (*Caught* 22, 24), at least two of Richard's leaves come during the winter.

7   *Caught* 26. Since Green himself was mobilized on September 1 (*Surviving* 278), I presume that is the date he intends—though it was actually two days before the declaration of war on September 3.

8   *Caught* 26. In 1960, Green wrote of his own feelings on September 1, 1939: "So I was alone in London on that dreadful morning, forty-eight hours before war was declared, and dressed alone into the still unfamiliar uniform with prickly trousers, alone, frightened, sickened, sure of dying" (*Surviving* 279).

9   Having spent two years working for Pontifex, Inc., his family's engineering firm, Green himself continued to manage its London office by calling in "every third day"—his day off from the fire service—"all through the war," and the company made up the difference between his normal salary and his fireman's wage (Green, *Surviving* 268). On Richard's first date with Hilly, which apparently takes place in December 1939, he tells her that he is still paid a salary and will take sick leave to "help get out the dividend warrants" (96)—presumably something routinely done at the end of each calendar year.

10   "That night, as he crept back, who would have thought that he was in for two wars" (39).

11   Since "she pretended to remember the south, the man who had gone" (107), the song could be "My Man's Gone Now" from George Gershwin's opera *Porgy and Bess* (1935). My thanks to Steve Swayne for this reference.

12   From the time of his student days at Oxford, when he spent "every afternoon at the cinema" (Wall), Green was an avid movie-goer.

13   The square and the equestrian statue are both unnamed. Since the statue is said to be "facing south" with "[t]wo great streets converg[ing] ahead at a sharp angle" (92), it suggests the statue of Charles I, which faces south toward the convergence of Whitehall and the Mall. But Charles's statue stands in the center of a circle.

14   He could be thirty-eight in 1940 after serving in World War I only if he had joined the army at the age of sixteen—in the very last year of the war. Since the British recruited

16-year-olds at the beginning of the war, this is just barely possible. But for Pye to be thirty-five in 1940 after fighting in World War I is impossible.

15   *Caught* 180. Writing of his own experience in the fire service, Green described London's regular firemen as "an extraordinary race of men" who included "heroes, some of them perhaps." But they were also so fearful of losing their "precious pension[s]" that they would never allow any recruit for the Auxiliary Fire Service to fail, no matter how inept he might be (*Surviving* 275).

16   Miller 93. The novel shows, she goes on to say, "that the myth of the fearless fireman in the People's War is no more than a fiction" (Miller 98).

17   Just after telling his wife that the fire was "fantastic," however, Richard silently thinks, "It had not been like that at all" (172). According to Miller, these "parenthetical asides" in his narrative show him "thinking outside the limits of the ideological script," and nursing "the secret fear that he is more helpless than heroic" (Miller 100). But Miller overlooks Richard's unstated wonder at the sublimity of the fire.

18   Before the blitz begins, Richard spouts a vacuous cliché to Chopper: "It brings everyone together, there's that much to a war" (46). But Chopper himself "pack[s] it in" on the first night of bombing, as noted above, and as we have seen in Chapter 2, the notion that soldiers always form a "brotherhood" is also bitterly critiqued in Hemingway's *For Whom the Bell Tolls*.

19   For the interview, see https://montgomery.dartmouth.edu/phil-klay

Epilogue

Even though large tracts of Europe and many old and famous States have fallen or may fall into the grip of the Gestapo and all the odious apparatus of Nazi rule, we shall not flag or fail. We shall go on to the end. We shall fight in France, we shall fight on the seas and oceans, we shall fight with growing confidence and growing strength in the air, we shall defend our island, whatever the cost may be. We shall fight on the beaches, we shall fight on the landing grounds, we shall fight in the fields and in the streets, we shall fight in the hills; we shall never surrender . . .

As the new prime minister of Britain, Winston Churchill spoke these words to the British Parliament in London on June 4, 1940, just after what he called a "miracle of deliverance." In nine days, a hastily assembled fleet of more than eight hundred vessels—ranging from Royal Navy destroyers to fishing boats and pleasure yachts—had just evacuated 338,226 Allied soldiers of Britain, Belgium, and France from the port of Dunkirk on the northwest coast of France, where they had been cut off and surrounded by German troops. Churchill was an electrifying speaker. Renouncing the gospel of Neville Chamberlain, whose tireless efforts to appease Hitler were aptly summarized by the arch maxim, "If at first you can't concede, Fly, Fly, Fly again," the new PM embodied absolute, unyielding defiance: "we shall never surrender."

This kind of defiance is hard to find in the literary works we have considered above. The only one that features a true *jusqu'au boutiste*—a man bent on fighting to the very end—is Hemingway's *For Whom the Bell Tolls*. All alone and clutching his submachine gun at the base of a pine tree in the hills above Segovia, Robert Jordan resolves to kill an enemy lieutenant even though he knows that he will be killed or captured by the lieutenant's men. But the final moment of this novel is heroic only in the most tortured sense of the word. By the time he reaches this moment, Jordan not only knows that his Republican cause has been hopelessly corrupted by Soviet manipulators like Karkov; he also knows that the would-be brotherhood of the revolutionaries is a scorpions' nest of treachery and murder. In this context, Jordan's final act—more precisely his resolution to kill the lieutenant, which the ending of the book leaves yet to happen—is the final stage of a purely personal rush of excitement: the kind of excitement that explains why Hemingway thought war "the best subject of all" for literature even though he also branded it "a crime against humanity."

Can participation in such a crime ever be heroic? In her notes for the third volume of *Suite Française*, which she never lived to write, Irène Némirovsky planned for Jean-

Marie Michaud—the soldier son of the hardworking, good-hearted Michauds—to die "heroically." But how would he die, she asks herself, "[a]nd what is heroism these days?" Her quandary takes its place with the skepticism voiced by nearly all the rest of the literary works we have examined, with their relentless attack on what Wilfred Owen had called "The old Lie" just months before he was killed in action near the end of World War I:

> The old Lie: *Dulce et decorum est*
> *Pro patria mori.*

The ancient notion that it is sweet and fitting to die for one's country, as Horace once declared, found few takers at the outbreak of World War II. Though Evelyn Waugh and Henry Green both risked their lives in different ways to defend their embattled nation, neither one celebrates heroic resistance. On the contrary, after barely surviving the evacuation of Crete in the late spring of 1941, Waugh seized the weeks of leisure afforded by a long sea voyage home to write a satirical novel about an anti-hero: a man who does all he can to avoid serving his country until he finally decides to become a killing machine. Likewise, even after spending more than two years learning how to fight fires and doing so through the first months of the Blitz, Henry Green writes a novel about a fire-fighter who, in the end, cannot accept his wife's insistence that he and the other firemen "were all wonderful." Estranged from both his son and his wife, who cannot fathom his sympathy for a man she loathes, Richard Roe himself never learns just how the unholy alliance of lust and guilt finally drove Albert Pye to suicide: the antithesis of a glorious death on the battlefield or in the midst of fighting an incendiary bomb.

The other works we have examined express a further range of feelings—other ways of resisting heroism itself. In *A Stricken Field*, Martha Gellhorn speaks a language not of defiance but of pity for refugees that her fictional self, Mary Douglas, is finally powerless to save. In "September 1, 1939," Auden not only decries the prospect that he and his contemporaries must suffer "again" all the horrors of another war, but also covertly reveals how much "the knowledge of being loved" has made him want to live rather than sacrifice himself for any cause, no matter how urgent. More affirmatively, as I have noted in passing, Joyce's *Finnegans Wake* confronts the coming war by celebrating the resilience of the human race, its power to survive the horrors of war and defy by derision the univocal tyranny of Hitler's voice: "heal helper! One gob, one gap, one gulp and gorger of all!" (191: 7–8).

Like *Finnegans Wake*, Brecht's *Svendborg Poems* ridicule the speeches of Hitler while also affirming human resilience. Speaking to those "born after" the Nazi era, Brecht chronicles his "dark times" for the sake of future generations, who (he thinks) may live in brighter times, when man becomes "a helper to humankind." Just as important, Brecht's poems deploy all the weapons of literature—especially irony and satire—against every form of oppression including Stalinism. Yet even though this whole collection of poems is intensely political, they sometimes stage a quarrel between political convictions and lyrical impulses that refuse to be crushed. Brecht's defiance thus becomes an act of imagination, flaunting its freedom in and through a language that celebrates beauty even as it eviscerates euphemisms, evasions, and lies.

Yet for all the brilliance of the *Svendborg Poems* and the other works we have considered, the most extraordinary piece of writing prompted by the outbreak of World War II remains the play that Brecht composed in the fall of 1939, right after Soviet troops joined Nazi troops in crushing Poland: *Mother Courage.* Whether or not Brecht was right about the proletariat, whether or not it could ever overturn capitalism without waging yet another war, or at least launching another violent revolution, *Mother Courage* remains a revelatory play about all modern warfare. Viewing the outbreak of World War II through the lens of a series of seventeenth-century wars, it shows how the "polluted" spring of war from which the title character drinks both death *and* her livelihood leaves her—in Brecht's words—"utterly disfigured and deformed."

It may be argued, of course, that Churchill's heroic resolve was in the end rewarded by victory. Yet the history of war in the latter half of the twentieth century and the first two decades of the twenty-first hardly demonstrates that war remains a heroic enterprise. While the Korean War rescued democracy for the southern half of that peninsula, the death toll of the war in Vietnam—altogether nearly three and one half million—cannot possibly be justified by its outcome, which left the country to do precisely what it had aimed to do ever since gaining its independence from France in 1954: govern itself.

In 2021, furthermore, the United States withdrew without a warning from the longest as well as most futile war in its history. In the nearly twenty years stretching from December 2001 to the end of August 2021, the war in Afghanistan not only cost over two trillion dollars (with more bills to come) but also took the lives of 2,448 American service members, 3,846 U.S. contractors, 66,000 Afghan soldiers and police, 47,245 civilians, and 51,191 members of the Taliban and other opposition forces (Knickmeyer). The colossal wastefulness of this whole project, which has left the Taliban back in charge of a nation that never could be wrested from them, was epitomized by the very last known U.S. drone strike of the war. While meant to kill an Islamic State suicide bomber who threatened U.S.-led troops as they were leaving Kabul airport in late August 2021, the missile actually killed ten Afghan civilians, including a longtime worker for a U.S. aid group and seven children (Aikins).[1]

Where does all this leave us? Chiefly because World War II ended in victory for the U.S. and its allies over the unholy alliance of Germany, Italy, and Japan, it is commonly remembered as a "good" war waged by "the greatest generation." Fought and won in just three and a half years, it seems in retrospect to epitomize heroism at its best as well as—one might say—most efficient.[2] But this "good" war ended very badly for the nations of Eastern Europe, and in the more than seven decades since 1945, the armed forces of the United States have compiled a record of slow-motion futility and failure almost unprecedented in the history of war: fourteen years in Vietnam and then—as just noted—twenty years in Afghanistan.

Perhaps the weight of this catastrophic sequence can best be measured by the words of an ancient Roman poet. At the outset of Vergil's *Aeneid,* written just over 2,000 years ago, the titular hero Aeneas and his men are forced by a storm to land at the North African city of Carthage after sailing away from the burning ruins of Troy. While exploring Carthage, Aeneas and his faithful friend Achates discover that the walls of a brand new temple to Juno have just been adorned with paintings of the Trojan War. In the eyes of Aeneas, the paintings stir tears for every Trojan depicted in them. He is moved above all by the painting of his father, King Priam, who is shown reaching out his "weaponless hands" ("manus … inermis" [1.487]) to buy from Achilles the corpse of Priam's son Hector, whom Achilles has killed. Tearfully viewing this painting along with the others, Aeneas says, "Sunt lacrimae rerum, et mentem mortalia tangunt" (1.462). At once untranslatable and unforgettable, this line surely means something like, "These pictures weep for us, and our mortality."[3]

In late August of 2021, televised film of Afghans running after and clinging to U.S. military planes rolling through Kabul airport recalled to many people a well-known photograph taken forty-six years earlier: the picture of South Vietnamese scrambling to board an American helicopter perched on a Saigon rooftop after the city fell to the Viet Cong in April 1975. Between these two pictures stands another indelibly stamped on the memories of all those old enough to remember September 11, 2001: twin towers belching flame and columns of smoke, the flashpoint of an event that not only goaded the U.S. into the Afghan war but that also occurred—by an astounding coincidence— on the very day and at the very time that my wife and I first visited the ruins of Troy. (Having reached Istanbul the day before, we had just begun a long-planned tour of ancient sites in Turkey—starting with Troy.) Like the paintings that brought tears to the eyes of Aeneas, all of these much more recent pictures seem to me to weep for us— and our mortality.

As I reach the end of this book, let me speak as an American just old enough to remember reading—at the age of six in August 1945—a big black newspaper headline announcing the end of World War II, when Japan surrendered after the atomic incineration of Hiroshima and Nagasaki had killed or maimed some 200,000 of its people, most of them civilians. I will not dispute the well-known claim that this very first and (so far) only use of the atomic bomb on human beings may well have saved American lives. Yet given our chronic incapacity to grasp as a nation just what we can and cannot accomplish with our ever more lethally sophisticated weapons, I believe that we can never know too much about the origins of our involvement in the wars of the past. Histories tell us much, and will continue to tell us more, about the origins of World War II as well as about its early years. But the literary works we have examined in this book tell us even more about questions generally slighted or even wholly overlooked in historical narratives of the two World Wars: how modern warfare has revolutionized the whole concept of heroism; how the imminence and outbreak of war felt to ordinary people—whether soldiers, refugees, firemen, or even poets and novelists—who could not foresee its end; how the war informed or deformed their whole lives; and how it shredded their most intimate relationships. To compare any history of the first years of World War II with a work of literature about them, especially a novel, is to see exemplified not just the formal differences between history and literature, as I have explained them in the Prologue, but also the radical difference between recording past events and re-creating the lives of those who lived through them. If we truly seek to understand the past, we can never have enough of either one.

Notes

1   In a review essay titled "The Lie of Nation Building" (2021), Fintan O'Toole shows exactly how the war against the Taliban was not only launched in ignorance but also driven by "deliberate unknowing" (O'Toole 17).
2   On the history of how this "good" war has been sanitized and mythologized, see Samet.
3   Robert Fagles makes two lines of it: "even here, the world is a world of tears, / and the burdens of mortality touch the heart" (*Aeneid* 1.558–59). No English version of the line can be anything more than a translator's best guess.

Bibliography

Aikins, Matthieu. "Times Investigation: In U.S. Drone Strike, Evidence Suggests No ISIS Bomb," *The New York Times*, September 10, 2021. https://www.nytimes.com/2021/09/10/world/asia/us-air-strike-drone-kabul-afghanistan-isis.html [updated November 3, 2021].

Anderson, Benedict. *Imagined Communities: Reflections on the Origin and Spread of Nationalism*, 2nd ed. New York: Verso, 2006.

Andreas-Friedrich, Ruth. *Berlin Underground, 1938–1945*. New York: Holt, 1947.

Anissimov, Myriam. "Preface to the French Edition." Némirovsky 387–95.

Applebaum, Anne. *Red Famine.* New York: Doubleday, 2017.

Auden, W. H. "September 1, 1939," in *Another Time*. New York: Random House, 1940. https://www.poets.org/poetsorg/poem/september-1-1939

Auden, W. H. *Collected Poems* [*CP*], ed. Edward Mendelson. New York: Random House, 1976.

Auden, W. H. *Prose*, vol. 2 [*P2*], ed. Edward Mendelson. Princeton, NJ: Princeton University Press, 2002.

Austra, Kevin R. "Operation Saar: A Lost Opportunity," *HistoryNet*, August 19, 1999. https://www.historynet.com/operation-saar-a-lost-opportunity-september-99-world-war-ii-feature.htm

Avalon Project. "Nazi-Soviet Relations 1939–41," *Documents in Law, History, and Diplomacy*, Yale Law School. https://avalon.law.yale.edu/subject_menus/nazsov.asp

Avalon Project. "Nuremberg Trial Proceedings Vol. 10 [*NTP*]. Ninety-Ninth Day, Wednesday, 4 April 1946," *Documents in Law, History, and Diplomacy*, Yale Law School. https://avalon.law.yale.edu/imt/04-04-46.asp

Avalon Project. "The French Yellow Book" [*FYB*], *Documents in Law, History, and Diplomacy*, Yale Law School. http://avalon.law.yale.edu

Baker, Carlos. *Ernest Hemingway: A Life Story* [*EH:LS*]. New York: Scribner's, 1969.

Baker, Carlos. *Ernest Hemingway: The Writer as Artist* [*EH:WA*], 4th ed. Princeton, NJ: Princeton University Press, 1973.

Balzac, Honoré de. "Author's Introduction to *The Human Comedy*." https://www.gutenberg.org/files/1968/1968-h/1968-h.htm#link2H_4_0012

Beevor, Anthony. *The Battle for Spain: The Spanish Civil War 1936–1939*. London: Weidenfeld & Nicolson, 2006.

Benjamin, Walter. *Understanding Brecht.* London: Verso, 1983.

Benjamin, Walter. *Selected Writings* [*SW*], ed. Michael W. Jennings, trans. Rodney Livingstone and Others. 4 vols. Cambridge, MA: The Belknap Press, 1999.

Bierce, Ambrose. "An Occurrence at Owl Creek Bridge" (1899), in *An Occurrence at Owl Creek Bridge and Other Stories*. North Chelmsford, MA: Courier Corporation, 2012.

Bloch, Marc. *Étrange Défaite* [*ED*]. *Témoignage Écrit en 1940*. Paris: Société des Éditions Franc-tireur, 1946.

Bloch, Marc. *Strange Defeat* [*SD*]: *A Statement of Evidence Written in 1940* (1949), trans. Gerard Hopkins. New York: Norton, 1968.

Boa, Elizabeth. "Poetic Authority and Power in the *Svendborg Poems*." Speirs 153–71.

Bohlen, Charles E. *Witness to History.* New York: Norton, 1973.

Bolloten, Burnett, *The Spanish Revolution: The Left and the Struggle for Power during the Civil War.* Chapel Hill, NC: University of North Carolina Press, 1980.

Bond, Brian. *France and Belgium 1939–1940* (The Politics and Strategy of the Second World War). London: Davis-Poynter, 1975.

Boyd, Gavin. "André Marty and Ernest Hemingway," *Forum for Modern Language Studies* 55.1 (September 2018): 1–19.

Bowen, Elizabeth. *The Heat of the Day.* New York: A.A. Knopf, 1949.

Bracher, Nathan. *After the Fall. War and Occupation in Irène Némirovsky's* Suite Française. Washington, DC: Catholic University of America Press, 2010.

Brecht, Bertolt. *Svendborger Gedichte* [*SG*], *Werke* 12 (1939): 7–87.

Brecht, Bertolt. *Brecht on Theatre: The Development of an Aesthetic,* ed. and trans. John Willett. New York: Hill & Wang, 1966.

Brecht, Bertolt. "Short Organum for the Theatre, A," *Brecht on Theatre,* 179–204.

Brecht, Bertolt. *Svendborger Gedichte* [*SG/B*]. *Mit dem Kommentar von Walter Benjamin: Zu den Svendborger Gedichten* (1939). Frankfurt am Main: Suhrkamp, 1973.

Brecht, Bertolt. *Poems, 1913–1956,* ed. John Willett, Ralph Manheim, and Erich Fried. New York: Routledge, 1979.

Brecht, Bertolt. *Werke. Große kommentierte Berliner und Frankfurter Ausgabe* [*GBA*], 30 vols., ed. Werner Hecht, Jan Knopf, Werner Mittenzwei, and Klaus-Detlef Müller. Frankfurt am Main: Suhrkamp, 1988–2000.

Brecht, Bertolt. *Letters,* ed. John Willett. New York: Routledge, 1990.

Brecht, Bertolt. *Journals 1934–1955* [*J*], ed. John Willett, trans. Hugh Rorrison. New York: Routledge, 1993.

Brecht, Bertolt. *Brecht on Art and Politics* [*A and P*], ed. Tom Kuhn and Steve Giles; Part Five, ed. Stephen Parker, Matthew Philpotts, and Peter Davies, trans. Laura Bradley, Steve Giles, and Tom Kuhn. London: Methuen, 2003.

Brecht, Bertolt. *Mother Courage and Her Children* [*MC*], ed. John Willett and Ralph Mannheim, trans. John Willett. New York: Penguin, 2007.

Brecht, Bertolt. "Texts by Brecht," *Mother Courage* 85–138.

Brecht, Bertolt. *The Collected Poems* [*CP*], ed. and trans. Tom Kuhn, David Constantine, and Charlotte Ryland. New York: Liveright/Norton, 2019.

Breton, André, and Diego Rivera. *Manifesto for an Independent Revolutionary Art,* 1938. https://www.marxists.org/subject/art/lit_crit/works/rivera/manifesto.htm

Brooke, Rupert. "Peace," *Poetry,* April 1915. https://www.poetryfoundation.org/poetrymagazine/poems/13074/peace

Brooke, Rupert. "The Soldier," *Poetry,* April 1915. https://www.poetryfoundation.org/poetrymagazine/browse?contentId=13076

Bruccoli, Matthew J. *The Only Thing that Counts: The Ernest Hemingway/Maxwell Perkins Correspondence, 1925–1947.* New York: Scribner's, 1996.

Byron, Lord. *Childe Harold's Pilgrimage,* in *Byron,* ed. Jerome J. McGann. New York: Oxford University Press, 1986: 21–206.

Carrdus, Anna. "The Uses of Rhetoric in Brecht's *Svendborg Poems*." Speirs 135–52.

Castle, Terry. "Stockhausen, Karlheinz," *New York,* August 27, 2011. https://nymag.com/news/9-11/10th-anniversary/karlheinz-stockhausen/

Caton, P. E. *1939–40: Une guerre perdue en 4 jours,* Tome II: *Contre-Témoignages sur une catastrophe.* Paris: L'Amitié par le livre, 1974.

Cenedese, Marta Laura. "The Rhythm of Unity: Irène Némirovsky's Suite française and Leo Tolstoy's War and Peace," *Comparative Literature* 71.1 (2019): 64–85.

Chamberlain, Neville. Speech to the House of Commons, September 28, 1938. https://api.parliament.uk/historic-hansard/commons/1938/sep/28/prime-ministers-statement#S5CV0339P0_19380928_HOC_13

Channon, Henry. *Chips: The Diaries of Sir Henry Channon*, ed. Robert Rhodes James. London: Weidenfeld & Nicolson, 1967.

Chasar, Mike. "Field Notes: Writers at War," *Los Angeles Review of Books*, July 22, 2016. https://lareviewofbooks.org/article/field-notes-writers-war/

Churchill, Winston. *While England Slept*. London: George G. Harrap, 1938.

Churchill, Winston. "The Munich Agreement." House of Commons, October 5, 1938. *International Churchill Society*. https://winstonchurchill.org/resources/speeches/1930-1938-the-wilderness/the-munich-agreement/

Churchill, Winston. "We Shall Fight on the Beaches." House of Commons, June 4, 1940. *International Churchill Society*. https://winstonchurchill.org/resources/speeches/1940-the-finest-hour/we-shall-never-surrender/

Churchill, Winston. *The Gathering Storm*, 2 vols. Boston, MA: Houghton Mifflin, 1948.

Churchill, Winston. *Memoirs of the Second World War*. Boston, MA: Houghton Mifflin, 1991.

Ciano, Galeazzo. *The Ciano Diaries, 1939–1943*, trans. and ed. Hugh Gibson. Garden City, NY: Doubleday, 1945.

Cohen, Milton A. "Robert Jordan's (and Ernest Hemingway's) 'True Book': Myths and Moral Quandaries in *For Whom the Bell Tolls*." *Hemingway Review* 36.2 (Spring 2017): 42–64.

Collingwood, R. G. *The Idea of History* (1946), ed. Jan van der Dussen. Oxford: Clarendon Press, 1993.

Collins, Michael, and Matthew Price. *The Story of Christianity*. London: Dorling Kindersley, 1999.

Conrad, Joseph. *Heart of Darkness*, in *9 Short Novels*, ed. Richard Ludwig and Marvin B. Perry, 2nd ed. Boston, MA: D.C. Heath, 1964: 396–463.

Costello, Bonnie, and Rachel Galvin, eds. *Auden at Work.* New York: Palgrave Macmillan, 2015.

Crick, Joyce. "The Fourth Door: Difficulties with the Truth in the *Svendborg Poems*." Speirs 114–34.

Cuddy-Keane, Melba. Introduction. Woolf, *Between the Acts* xxxv–xlvi.

Danto, Arthur C. "Narrative Sentences," *History and Theory* 2.2 (1962): 146–79.

Darnton, Robert. "Writing News and Telling Stories." *Daedalus* 104.2 (1975): 174–95.

Davies, Tony. "Strength and Clarity: Brecht, Auden, and the 'True Democratic Style.'" Speirs 86–99.

Deer, Patrick. "Two Cities: Berlin and New York," in *W.H. Auden in Context*, ed. Tony Sharpe. Cambridge: Cambridge University Press, 2013: 24–34.

Diamond, Hanna, *Fleeing Hitler: France 1940.* Oxford: Oxford University Press, 2007.

Donne, John. "The Canonization." *Poetry Foundation*. https://www.poetryfoundation.org/poems/44097/the-canonization

Eliot, T. S. "The Metaphysical Poets" (1921), in *The Norton Anthology of Literature*, ed. M. H. Abrams and S. Greenblatt, 7th ed., vol. 2. New York: Norton, 2000: 2401–8.

Ellis, Steve. *British Writers and the Approach of World War II.* Cambridge: Cambridge University Press, 2014.

Ellmann, Richard. *James Joyce.* Revised edition. Oxford: Oxford University Press, 1982.

Fenimore, Edward. "English and Spanish in *For Whom the Bell Tolls*," *English Literary History* 10.1 (March 1943): 73–86.

Fink, Carol, "Marc Bloch and the *drôle de guerre*: Prelude to the 'Strange Defeat,'" *Historical Reflections / Réflexions Historiques* 22.1 (Winter 1996): 33–46.

Fisher, Max. "Putin's Case for War, Annotated," *The New York Times*, February 24, 2022. https://www.nytimes.com/2022/02/24/world/europe/putin-ukraine-speech.html

Frankl, Michal. "Prejudiced Asylum: Czechoslovak Refugee Policy, 1918–60," *Journal of Contemporary History* 49.3 (July 2014): 537–55.

Franklin, Ruth. "Scandale Française: The Nasty Truth about a Literary Heroine," *The New Republic*, January 30, 2008. https://newrepublic.com/article/61151/scandale-francaise

Fraser, Ronald. *Napoleon's Cursed War: Spanish Popular Resistance in the Peninsular War, 1808–1814*. London: Verso, 2008.

Fuller, John. *W.H. Auden: A Commentary*. Princeton, NJ: Princeton University Press, 1998.

Fussell, Paul, *The Great War and Modern Memory*. New York: Oxford University Press, 1975.

Galvin, Rachel, "Auden's 1939 Journal: A Wartime Writer at Work," Costello and Galvin 24–48.

Gardiner, Juliet. *The Blitz: The British Under Attack*. London: HarperCollins, 2011.

Gedye, G. E. B., "Refugee Problem Disturbs Czechs," *The New York Times*, October 11, 1938: 16.

Gellhorn, Martha. "Obituary of a Democracy," *Collier's*, December 10, 1938: 12–13, 28, 32–33, 36.

Gellhorn, Martha. *A Stricken Field* [*StF*] (1940). Foreword by Caroline Morehead. Chicago, IL: University of Chicago Press, 2011.

Gellhorn, Martha. "Afterword" (1985). Gellhorn 303–14.

Ginsburgs, George. "A Case Study in the Soviet Use of International Law: Eastern Poland in 1939," *American Journal of International Law* 52.1 (January 1958): 69–84.

Goldhagen, Daniel. *Hitler's Willing Executioners: Ordinary Germans and the Holocaust.* New York: Vintage Books/Random House, 1996.

Goodman, Adam. *The Deportation Machine: America's Long History of Expelling Immigrants*. Princeton, NJ: Princeton University Press, 2020.

Gordon, John. "Joyce's Hitler," in *Joyce through the Ages: A Nonlinear View*, ed. Michael Patrick Gillespie. Gainesville, FL: University Press of Florida, 1999: 179–98.

Gordon, Robert. "Brecht, Interruptions, and Epic Theatre," *British Library Discovering Literature: 20th Century*, September 7, 2017. https://www.bl.uk/20th-century-literature/articles/brecht-interruptions-and-epic-theatre

Grant, Linda. "In the Zone of the Living," *The Guardian*, January 30, 2004. https://www.theguardian.com/books/2004/jan/31/israelandthepalestinians.society

Green, Henry. *Surviving: The Uncollected Writings of Henry Green*, ed. Matthew Yorke. London: Chatto & Windus, 1992.

Green, Henry. *Pack My Bag: A Self-Portrait* (1940), Introduction by Sebastian Yorke. New York: New Directions, 2004.

Green, Henry. *Caught* (1943), Introduction by James Wood. New York: New York Review of Books, 2016.

Grenaudier-Klijn, F. N. "Street Names in Patrick Modiano's Work: La Place de L'étoile and the Case of Rue Lauriston," *Neohelicon. Acta Comparationis Litterarum Universarum* 44.1 (2017): 217–27.

Hamilton, Patrick. *Hangover Square: A Story of Darkest Earl's Court*. Introduction by J. B. Priestley. London: Constable, 1982.

Harari, Yuval Noah. *Sapiens: A Brief History of Humankind*. New York: Harper, 2015.

Heaney, Seamus. *The Redress of Poetry*. New York: Farrar, Straus & Giroux, 1995.

Heffernan, James A. W. "'Cruel Persuasion': Seduction, Temptation, and Agency in Hardy's Tess," *Thomas Hardy Year Book* 35 (2005): 5–18. See also https://victorianweb.org/authors/hardy/heffernan.html

Heffernan, James A. W. "History and Autobiography: The French Revolution in Wordsworth's *Prelude*," in *Representing the French Revolution: Literature, Historiography, and Art*, ed. J. A. W. Heffernan. Hanover, NH: Dartmouth College Press, 1993: 41–62.

Heffernan, James A. W. "Text and Design in Blake's *Songs of Innocence and Experience*," in *Cultivating Picturacy: Visual Art and Verbal Interventions*. Waco, TX: Baylor University Press, 2006: 83–99.

Hemingway, Ernest. *Green Hills of Africa*. New York: Scribner's, 1935.

Hemingway, Ernest. "Fascism is a Lie," Speech to the American Writers Congress, Carnegie Hall, June 4, 1937. *For Whom the Bell Tolls*, Appendix 1: 479–81.

Hemingway, Ernest. *Men at War* [*MW*]. New York: Crown Books, 1942.

Hemingway, Ernest. *A Farewell to Arms* [*FA*]. New York: Scribner's, 1957.

Hemingway, Ernest. *Selected Letters, 1917–1961* [*SL*], ed. Carlos Baker. New York: Scribner's, 1971.

Hemingway, Ernest. *For Whom the Bell Tolls* [*FWBT*], ed. Seán Hemingway. New York: Scribner's, 2019.

Hemingway, Seán. Introduction. Hemingway, *For Whom the Bell Tolls*, xiii–xxiii.

Herbert, George. "The 23rd Psalme," from *The Temple* (1633). https://www.georgeherbert.org.uk/archives/selected_work_09.html

Hitler, Adolf. "Speech of May 1, 1933." https://der-fuehrer.org/reden/english/33-05-01.htm

Hitler, Adolf. "Speech at Nuremburg on September 12, 1938," *Bulletin of International News* 15.19 (September 24, 1938): 8–11.

Hitler, Adolf. "Speech in the Sportpalast, September 26, 1938." *The British War Bluebook*, No. 7 / Yale Avalon Project. https://avalon.law.yale.edu/wwii/blbk07.asp

Hitler, Adolf. "Speech by Herr Hitler at Wilhelmshaven on April 1, 1939." *The British War Bluebook*, No. 20 / Yale Avalon Project. https://avalon.law.yale.edu/wwii/blbk20.asp

Hodgson, Katharine, "Exile in 'Danish Siberia': The Soviet Union in the *Svendborg Poems*." Speirs 66–85.

Hynes, Samuel. *The Soldiers' Tale: Bearing Witness to Modern War*. New York: Allen Lane/Penguin, 1997.

International Organization for Migration [*IOM*]. "Almost 6.5 Million People Internally Displaced in Ukraine," *IOM: UN Migration*, March 21, 2022. https://www.iom.int/news/almost-65-million-people-internally-displaced-ukraine-iom. Accessed March 22, 2022.

Ironside, Sir Edmund, *The Ironside Diaries 1937–1940*, ed. Roderick Macleod and Denis Kelly. London: Constable, 1962.

Isherwood, Christopher. *Goodbye to Berlin*. New York: Random House, 1939.

Jackson, Dana. "From History to the Stage: An Account of Shakespeare's Adaptation of Julius Caesar." *Shakespeare Online*. http://www.shakespeareonline.com/essays/fromhistorytostage.html

Jackson, Julian. *The Fall of France: The Nazi Invasion of 1940*. Oxford: Oxford University Press, 2003.

James, Henry. *Portrait of a Lady* (1880–81, 1908), ed. Robert D. Bamberg. A Norton Critical Edition. New York: Norton, 1995.

Joyce, James. *Portrait of the Artist as a Young Man* (1916), ed. Chester G. Anderson. New York: Penguin, 1977.

Joyce, James. *Ulysses* [*U*], ed. Hans Gabler. New York: Random House, 1984. Cited by chapter number and line number(s), e,g. 2: 377.

Joyce, James. *Finnegans Wake* [*FW*], ed. Robert Jan Henkes, Erik Bindervoet, and Finn Fordham. World Classics Paperback. Oxford: Oxford University Press, 2012.

Karski, Jan. *Story of a Secret State* [*SS*]. Boston: Houghton Mifflin, 1944.

Karski, Jan. *The Great Powers & Poland 1919–1945: From Versailles to Yalta* [*GPP*]. New York: University Press of America, 1985.

Kershaw, Ian. *The "Hitler Myth": Image and Reality in the Third Reich.* New York: Oxford University Press, 1987.

Kershaw, Ian. *Hitler 1936–45: Nemesis* [*H*]. London: Allen Lane, 2000.

Klay, Phil. "After War: A Failure of Imagination," *The New York Times*, February 8, 2014. https://www.nytimes.com/2014/02/09/opinion/sunday/after-war-a-failure-of-the-imagination.html

Klemperer, Klemens von. *German Resistance against Hitler: The Search for Allies Abroad, 1938–1945.* Oxford: Clarendon Press, 1992.

Klemperer, Victor. *I Will Bear Witness: A Diary of the Nazi Years, 1933–1941*, trans. Martin Chalmers. New York: Random House, 1998.

Knickmeyer, Ellen. "Costs of the Afghanistan War, in Lives and Dollars," *AP News*, August 17, 2021. https://apnews.com/article/middle-east-business-afghanistan-43d8f53b35e80 ec18c130cd683e1a38f

Kochanski, Halik. *The Eagle Unbowed: Poland and the Poles in the Second World War.* Cambridge, MA: Harvard University Press, 2012.

Kuhn, Tom, "'Visit to a Banished Poet': Brecht's *Svendborg Poems* and the Voices of Exile." Speirs 47–65.

Laqueur, Walter, "The Artist in Politics," *The New York Times*, May 15, 1983, Section 7: 11.

Lattimore, Steven. "Introduction." Thucydides xii–xxi.

Laughlin, James. "A Letter to Hitler," *Partisan Review* 6.4 (Summer 1939): 69.

Lee, Laurie. *A Moment of War.* London: Viking, 1991.

Leeder, Karen. "Those Born Later Read Brecht: The Reception of 'An die Nachtborenen.'" Speirs 211–40.

Lefebvre, Michel. "La Memoire des Brigades internationales: le cas André Marty," in *La Guerre d'Espagne*, ed. Roger Bourderon. Paris: Tallandier, 2007: 389–403.

Little, Douglas. *Malevolent Neutrality.* Ithaca, NY: Cornell University Press, 1985.

Lochner, Louis Paul. *What About Germany?* New York: Dodd, Mead, 1942.

London, Louise, *Whitehall and the Jews, 1933–1948: British Immigration Policy, Jewish Refugees, and the Holocaust.* Cambridge: Cambridge University Press, 2000.

Los Angeles Times [*LAT*]. "Bomber Fall Kills Pilot: Test Flight Ends in Fiery Plunge," January 24, 1939.

Lukes, Igor. *Czechoslovakia between Stalin and Hitler: The Diplomacy of Edvard Beneš in the 1930s.* New York: Oxford University Press, 1996.

Lukes, Igor. "The Czechoslovak Partial Mobilization in May 1938: A Mystery (almost) Solved," *Journal of Contemporary History* 31.4 (October 1996): 699–720.

Lyon, James K. *Bertolt Brecht in America.* Princeton, NJ: Princeton University Press, 2014.

MacLeish, Archibald. "Public Speech and Private Speech in Poetry," *The Yale Review* 27 (Spring 1938): 536–47.

Maddox, Brenda. *Yeats's Ghosts: The Secret Life of W.B. Yeats*. New York: HarperCollins, 2000.

Mann, Thomas. *The Coming Victory of Democracy*, trans. Agnes E. Mayer. New York: Alfred A. Knopf, 1938.

Mann, Thomas. *This War*, trans. Eric Sutton. New York: Knopf, 1940.

Mann, Thomas. *Reflections of a Nonpolitical Man*, trans. Walter D. Morris. New York: Frederick Ungar, 1983.

Manning, Olivia. *The Great Fortune* [*GF*] (1960), vol. I of *The Fortunes of War: The Balkan Trilogy*. New York: New York Review of Books, 2010.

Margalit, Ruth. "Trains to Nowhere." Review of Ulrich Alexander Boschwitz, *The Passenger*, trans. Philip Boehm (New York: Metropolitan Books, 2021). *New York Review of Books* 68.18 (November 18, 2021): 15–16.

McDonald, Dwight. "This Quarter: War and the Intellectuals: Act II," *Partisan Review* 6:3 (Spring 1939): 3–20.

McDowell, Edwin. "Publishing: Pulitzer Controversies," *The New York Times*, May 11, 1984: C26.

McGrath, Charles, and Others. "The Real Story: Literary Fact and Fiction," Transcript of Conversation at Lincoln Center, *Pen America* 1.1 (Winter 2000): 115–29. https://pen. org/the-real-story-literary-fact-and-fiction/

McMenamin, Michael. "Regime Change, 1938: Did Chamberlain 'Miss the Bus'?," *Finest Hour* 162 (Spring 2014): 22. http://www.winstonchurchill.org/publications/finest-hour/ finest-hour-162/regime-change-1938-did-chamberlain-miss-the-bus

McSmith, Andy. *Fear and the Muse Kept Watch.* New York: The New Press, 2015.

Mendelson, Edward. "The Auden-Isherwood Collaboration" [*A-I*], *Twentieth Century Literature* 22.3 (October, 1976): 276–85.

Mendelson, Edward. *Early Auden* [*EA*]. New York: Viking, 1981.

Mendelson, Edward. *Later Auden* [*LA*]. New York: Farrar, Straus & Giroux, 1999.

Meyers, Jeffrey. *Hemingway: A Biography* [*H:B*]. London: Macmillan, 1985.

Meyers, Jeffrey. "*For Whom the Bell Tolls* as Contemporary History" [*FWBT-CH*], *The Spanish Civil War in Literature* (1990): 85–107.

Meyers, Jeffrey. *Orwell: Wintry Conscience of a Generation.* New York: Norton, 2000.

Meyers, Jeffrey. "Hemingway and the Peninsular War" [*HPW*], *Notes on Contemporary Literature* 40.2 (2010). https://www.thefreelibrary.com/Hemingway+and+the+ Peninsular+War.-a0231714519

Midgley, David, "Svendborg 1938: A Historical Sketch." Speirs 16–28.

Miller, Kristine. *British Literature of the Blitz: Fighting the People's War.* London: Palgrave Macmillan, 2009.

Milthorpe, Naomi. "The Rake's Progress: Evelyn Waugh's Return to Satire in *Basil Seal Rides Again*," *Papers on Language and Literature: A Journal for Scholars and Critics of Language and Literature* 47.4 (Fall 2011): 439–42.

Mitford, Nancy. *The Pursuit of Love.* London: Hamish Hamilton, 1945.

Nasaw, David. "America's Immigration Paradox," *The New York Times* (*Book Review*), May 19, 2020: 16.

Naudeau, Ludovic. "Adoptons-Nous aux Circonstances Extérieurs," *L'Illustration*, April 4, 1936 (94th year, no. 4857): 388–89.

Nelson, John S. "Review Essay: *Metahistory. The Historical Imagination in Nineteenth-Century Europe.* By Hayden V. White," *History and Theory* 13.1 (February 1975): 74–91.

Némirovsky, Irène. *Suite Française* [*SF*]. Paris: Éditions Denoël, 2004.

Némirovsky, Irène. *Suite Française* [*SF_T*], trans. Sandra Smith. New York: Knopf/Random House, 2006.

Nijinsky, Vaslav. *The Diary of Vaslav Nijinsky*, ed. Romola Nijinsky. New York: Simon & Schuster, 1936.

Nilsson, Anton. "Ernest Hemingway and the Politics of the Spanish Civil War," *The Hemingway Review* 36.1 (Fall 2016): 81–93.

Olschowsky, Heinrich. "'Where Southeast Poland Once Was': Bertolt Brecht and the Hitler-Stalin Pact," *Osteuropa* 61.4 (April 2011): 71–81. Trans Marcus A. Mamourian.

Olson, Lynne. *Citizens of London: The Americans Who Stood with Britain in its Darkest, Finest Hour.* New York: Random House, 2010.

Olson, Lynne, and Stanley Cloud. *A Question of Honor. The Kosciuszko Squadron: Forgotten Heroes of World War II.* New York: Vintage Books, 2004.

Österling, Anders. Award Ceremony Speech for the Nobel Prize for Literature 1962. https://www.nobelprize.org/prizes/literature/1962/ceremony-speech/

O'Toole, Fintan. "The Lie of Nation Building," *New York Review of Books* 65.15 (October 7, 2021): 16–19.

Ousby, Ian. *Occupation: The Ordeal of France, 1940–1944.* London: John Murray, 1997.

Owen, Wilfred. "Dulce et Decorum Est," in *Poems.* New York: Viking, 1921: 15.

Paillat, Claude. *Dossiers Secrets de la France Contemporaine, vol. 1: La Répétition Générale* [*RG*]. Paris: Robert Laffont, 1983.

Paillat, Claude. *Dossiers Secrets de la France Contemporaine, vol. 2: La Guerre Immobile* (avril 1939–10 mai 1940) [*GI*]. Paris: Robert Laffont, 1984.

Paillat, Claude. *Dossiers Secrets de la France Contemporaine, vol. 4: Le Désastre de 1940.* Paris: Robert Laffont, 1984.

Parker, Stephen. *Bertolt Brecht: A Literary Life.* New York: Bloomsbury, 2014.

Parssinen, Terry. *The Oster Conspiracy of 1938: The Unknown Story of the Military Plot to Kill Hitler and Avert World War II.* New York: Harper Collins, 2003.

Payne, Stanley G. *The Spanish Civil War, the Soviet Union, and Communism.* New Haven, CT: Yale University Press, 2003.

Philipponnat, Olivier, and Patrick Lienhardt. *Le Vie d'Irène Némirovsky, 1903–1942.* Paris: Éditions Grasset et Fasquelle, 2007.

Phillips, Dave, Peter Baker, Maggie Haberman and Helene Cooper. "Trump's Intervention in SEALs Case Tests Pentagon's Tolerance," *The New York Times*, December 1, 2019: 1, 25.

Podhorodecki, Leszek. *Rapier i Koncerz.* Warsaw: Ksiazka i Wiedza, 1985.

Polizzotti, Mark. *Revolution of the Mind: The Life of André Breton.* New York: Farrar, Straus & Giroux, 1995.

Prazmowska, A. J. "Poland's Foreign Policy September 1938–September 1939," *The Historical Journal* 29.4 (1986): 853–73.

Presner, Samuel Todd. "What a Synoptic and Artificial View Reveals: Extreme History and the Modernism of W. G. Sebald's Realism," *Criticism* 46.3 (Summer 2004): 341–60.

Proust, Marcel. *In Search of Lost Time, vol. III: The Guermantes Way* [*GW*], trans. C. K. Scott-Moncrieff and Terence Kilmartin. London: Chatto & Windus, 1992.

Rahv, Philip. "A Variety of Fiction," *Partisan Review* 6.3 (Spring 1939): 106–13.

Rahv, Philip. "This Quarter: Twilight of the Thirties," *Partisan Review* 6.4 (Summer 1939): 3–14.

Rigney, Ann. "When the Monograph is No Longer the Medium: Historical Narrative in the Online Age," *History and Theory, Theme Issue* 49 (December 2010): 100–17.

Roosevelt, Franklin Delano. "State of the Union 1939," January 4, 1939. http://www.let.rug.nl/usa/presidents/franklin-delano-roosevelt/state-of-the-union-1939.php

Roosevelt, Franklin Delano. Press Conference #521, January 27, 1939. http://www.fdrlibrary.marist.edu/archives/collections/franklin/?p=collections/findingaid&id=508

Roosevelt, Franklin Delano. *The Public Papers and Addresses of Franklin D. Roosevelt. 1939 volume, War and Neutrality: With a special introduction and explanatory notes by President Roosevelt* [Book 1]. New York: Macmillan, 1941.

Rossi, John. "Evelyn Waugh's Neglected Masterpiece" [*EW:NM*], *Contemporary Review* 281 (November 2002): 296–300.

Rossi, John. "Evelyn Waugh: From Savage to Sober" [*EW:SS*], *The American Conservative*, May 3, 2018. https://www.theamericanconservative.com/articles/evelyn-waugh-from-savage-to-sober/

Russell, John. *Henry Green: Nine Novels and an Unpacked Bag.* New Brunswick, NJ: Rutgers University Press, 1960.

Samet, Elizabeth D. *Looking for the Good War: American Amnesia and the Violent Pursuit of Happiness.* New York: Farrar, Straus & Giroux, 2021.

Sansom, Ian. *September 1, 1939: A Biography of a Poem.* New York: Harper Collins, 2019.

Santiáñez, Nil. *The Literature of Absolute War: Transnationalism and World War II.* Cambridge: Cambridge University Press, 2020.

Santora, Marc, Michael Schwartz, and Micheal Levenson. "Zelensky Attacks Mayor's Arrest as 'Terror,'" *The New York Times*, March 13, 2022: 1.

Sassoon, Siegfriend. *Counter-Attack and Other Poems.* London: Heinemann, 1918.

Self, Robert. *The Neville Chamberlain Diary Letters, vol. 1: The Making of a Politician, 1915–20* [*NCDL* 1]. London: Routledge, 2000.

Self, Robert. *The Neville Chamberlain Diary Letters, vol. 4: The Downing Street Years, 1934–40* [*NCDL* 4]. London: Routledge, 2005.

Self, Robert. *Neville Chamberlain.* Burlington, VT: Ashgate, 2006.

Shachtman, Tom. *The Phony War: 1939–1940.* New York: Harper & Row, 1982.

Shelley, Percy Bysshe. Preface to *Prometheus Unbound* (1820), in *Shelley's Poetry and Prose*, ed. Donald Reiman and Sharon Powers. New York: Norton, 1977: 132–36.

Shirer, William F. *Berlin Diary: [BD] The Journal of a Foreign Correspondent, 1934–1941.* Baltimore, MD: Johns Hopkins University Press, 2002.

Shirer, William F. *The Collapse of the Third Republic: An Inquiry into the Fall of France in 1940.* Boston, MA: Da Capo Press, 1969.

Shirer, William F. *The Rise and Fall of the Third Reich: A History of Nazi Germany.* New York: Simon & Schuster, 1990.

Shirer, William F. *This is Berlin: Reporting from Nazi Germany 1938–40.* London: Hutchinson, 1999.

"Situation in American Writing, The: Seven Questions," *Partisan Review* 6.4 (Summer 1939), 25–51.

Speirs, Ronald, ed. *Brecht's Poetry of Political Exile.* Cambridge: Cambridge University Press, 2000.

Speirs, Ronald. Introduction. Speirs 1–15.

Speirs, Ronald. "The Poet in Time." Speirs 190–210.

Steinbeck, John. *The Grapes of Wrath.* New York: Viking, 1939.

Stern, Fritz, ed. *The Varieties of History: From Voltaire to the Present*, 2nd ed. New York: Vintage, 1973.

Stiazhkina, Olena. "In the First Days of War: A Dispatch from Kyiv," trans. Ali Kinsella. *Guernica Magazine*, March 7, 2022. https://www.guernicamag.com/in-the-first-days-of-war/

Suleiman, Susan Rubin. "Irène Némirovsky and the 'Jewish Question' in Interwar France," *Yale French Studies* 121 (2012): 8–33.

Suleiman, Susan Rubin. *The Némirovsky Question: The Life, Death, and Legacy of a Jewish Writer in Twentieth-Century France* [*TNQ*]. New Haven, CT: Yale University Press, 2016.

Sullivan, Hannah. "'Still Doing It By Hand': Auden and the Typewriter." Costello and Galvin 5–23.

Takayoshi, Ichiro. "The Wages of War: Liberal Gullibility, Soviet Intervention, and the End of the Popular Front." *Representations* 115 (Summer 2011): 102–29.

Tatlow, Antony. *Mask of Evil: Brecht's Response to the Poetry, Theatre, and Thoughts of China and Japan*. Bern: Peter Lang, 1977.

Tennyson, Alfred Lord. "Charge of the Light Brigade." *Poetry Foundation*. https://www.poetryfoundation.org/poems/45319/the-charge-of-the-light-brigade

The New York Times. "1939 Book Awards Given by Critics," *The New York Times*, February 14, 1940: 25.

The New York Times. "Evelyn Waugh, Satirical Novelist, Is Dead at 62," *The New York Times* (*Books*), April 11, 1966. https://movies2.nytimes.com/books/97/05/04/reviews/waugh-obit.html

Thomas, Fontaine, "Chronology of Repression and Persecution in Occupied France, 1940–44," *Mass Violence and Resistance*, November 19, 2007. https://www.sciencespo.fr/mass-violence-war-massacre-resistance/en/document/chronology-repression-and-persecution-occupied-france-1940-44.html

Thomas, Hugh. *The Spanish Civil War*. New York: Harper & Row, 2001.

Thucydides. *The Peloponnesian War*, trans. Steven Lattimore. Indianapolis, IN: Hackett, 1998.

Tolstoy, Leo. *War and Peace*, trans. Louise and Aylmer Maude. The Project Gutenberg eBook of War and Peace, April 2001. https://www.gutenberg.org/cache/epub/2600/pg2600-images.html

Tolstoy, Leo. *The Death of Ivan Ilyich* (1886), trans. Louise and Aylmer Maude. Bulgaria: Demetra Publishing, 2019.

Trilling, Lionel. "An American in Spain" [Review of Ernest Hemingway, *For Whom the Bell Tolls*], *Partisan Review* 8:1 (January 1941): 63–67.

Troianovski, Anton. "Putin Announces a 'Military Operation' in Ukraine," *The New York Times*, February 23, 2022. https://www.nytimes.com/2022/02/23/world/europe/putin-announces-a-military-operation-in-ukraine-as-the-un-security-council-pleads-with-him-to-pull-back.html

Trotsky, Leon. *Literature and Revolution*, trans. Rose Strunsky. New York: International Publishers, 1925.

Trotsky, Leon. "Art and Politics in Our Epoch," *Partisan Review* 5:3 (August–September 1938): 7–10.

Turner, Henry Ashby. *Hitler's Thirty Days to Power: January 1933*. Reading, MA: Addison-Wesley, 1996.

UNHCR. "Ukraine Refugee Situation," *Operational Data Portal*. https://data2.unhcr.org/en/situations/ukraine. Accessed March 22, 2022.

Updike, John. "Saint of the Mundane" [on Henry Green], *New York Review of Books*, May 18, 1978.

US State Department. *Foreign Relations of the United States* [*FRUS*]. Washington, DC: US Printing Office.

Vidal, Gore. "The Satiric World of Evelyn Waugh," *The New York Times* (*Books*), January 7, 1962. https://movies2.nytimes.com/books/97/05/04/reviews/waugh-battle.html

Vergil. *P. Vergili Maronis Aeneidos*, in *Opera.* Oxford: Clarendon Press, 1955 [I cite the Latin text by book and line number].

Virgil. *The Aeneid*, trans. Robert Fagles. Introduction by Bernard Knox. New York: Viking Penguin, 2006.

Wall, Stephen. "Admiring" [review of several books by Henry Green], *London Review of Books* 14.6 (March 26, 1992). https://www.lrb.co.uk/the-paper/v14/n06/stephen-wall/admiring

Warriner, Doreen, "Winter in Prague," *Slavonic and East European Review* 62.2 (1984): 209–39.

Watt, Donald Cameron. *How War Came: The Immediate Origins of the Second World War, 1938–1939.* New York: Pantheon, 1989.

Waugh, Evelyn. "Basil Seal Rides Again; or The Rake's Regress" (1963), in *The Complete Short Stories of Evelyn Waugh*, ed. Ann Pasternak Slater. London: Everyman, 1998: 485–518.

Waugh, Evelyn. *Men at Arms.* London: Chapman & Hall, 1952.

Waugh, Evelyn. *Put Out More Flags* [*POMF*]. New York: Back Bay Books/Little, Brown, 2012.

Waugh, Evelyn. *The Diaries of Evelyn Waugh* [*D*], ed. Michael Davie. London: Weidenfeld & Nicolson, 1976.

Waugh, Evelyn. *The Letters of Evelyn Waugh* [*L*], ed. Mark Amory. New York: Ticknor & Fields, 1980.

Wedgewood, C. V. *William the Silent, William of Nassau, Prince of Orange, 1533–1584* (1944). New York: Norton, 1968.

Weiss, Jonathan. *Irène Némirovsky: Biographie.* Paris: Éditions du Félin, 2005.

Wells, H. G. *Travels of a Republican Radical in Search of Hot Water.* Harmondsworth: Penguin, 1939.

Werckmeister, O. K. "Hitler the Artist," *Critical Inquiry* 23.2 (Winter, 1997): 270–97.

Wexler, Joyce. "The New Heroism," *War, Literature and the Arts: An International Journal of the Humanities* 27 (2015): 1–12.

White, Haydon V. "The Burden of History," *History and Theory* 5.2 (1966): 111–34.

White, Haydon V. *Metahistory:* [*M*] *The Historical Imagination in Nineteenth-Century Europe.* Baltimore, MD: The Johns Hopkins University Press, 1973.

Williams, Katherine J. *Translating Brecht: Versions of* Mutter Courage Und Ihre Kinder *for* The British Stage. PhD thesis, University of St. Andrews, 2009. https://research-repository.st-andrews.ac.uk/handle/10023/761

Wimsatt, W. K., and Monroe Beardsley. "The Intentional Fallacy," in *The Verbal Icon: Studies in the Meaning of Poetry.* Lexington, KY: University Press of Kentucky, 1954: 3–19.

Wizisla, Ermut. *Benjamin and Brecht: The Story of a Friendship*, trans. Christine Shuttleworth. New Haven, CT: Yale University Press, 2009.

Wood, E. Thomas, and Stanisław M. Jankowski. *Karski: How One Man Tried to Stop the Holocaust* (1994). Revised edition with Introduction by Michael Berenbaum. Lubbock, TX: Texas Tech University Press/East Stroudsburg, PA: Gihon River Press, 2014.

Woolf, Virginia. *Between the Acts*, ed. Melba Cuddy-Keane. New York: Houghton Mifflin Harcourt, 2008.

Wordsworth, William. *The Prelude 1799, 1805, 1850*, ed. Jonathan Wordsworth, M. H. Abrams, and Stephen Gill. New York: Norton, 1979.

World Future Fund. "The French and British Betrayal of Poland in 1939." *World Future Fund*. http://www.worldfuturefund.org/wffmaster/Reading/History/polandbetrayal. htm

Wykes, David. *Evelyn Waugh: A Literary Life.* New York: St. Martins Press, 1999.

Young, Jin Lynn. *One Mighty and Irresistible Tide: The Epic Struggle Over American Immigration, 1924–1965.* New York: Norton, 2020.

Index